MASTERING AMERICAN ENGLISH

Mastering

AMERICAN ENGLISH

A Handbook - Workbook of Essentials

Rebecca E.	**HAYDEN**
Dorothy W.	**PILGRIM**
Aurora Quiros	**HAGGARD**

Englewood Cliffs, New Jersey

PRENTICE - HALL, INC.

© Copyright, 1956, by
PRENTICE-HALL, INC.
Englewood Cliffs, N. J.

All rights reserved. No part of this book may be reproduced in any form, by mimeograph or any other means, without permission in writing from the publishers.

Library of Congress
Catalog Card No.: 56-11335
ISBN: 0-13-560045-6

Current printing (last digit):
45 44 43 42 41 40 39 38 37

Printed in the United States of America

56004-C

PREFACE

A handbook and a workbook as well, *Mastering American English* covers the basic sentence patterns and major grammatical structures, and provides drill and review through diversified exercises. It is intended primarily for adults who are at an intermediate or advanced level in the study of English as a foreign language, but need further review and drill in order to develop fluency and accuracy in its use.

Convenience of reference and review has dictated the arrangement of the material into large Units (Word Order, Verbs, and so on). Some of the Units with a large amount of material, such as Word Order, have been divided into two or more Parts; the Parts in turn are divided into sections numbered consecutively throughout the book. Presented in this way, the material provides flexibility in adapting the text to various learning situations. We have tried to focus attention throughout on the learning of grammatical structures rather than on memorization of rules, and the numerous details represent our attempt to answer some of the questions put to us by students. About half of the book consists of exercises designed for aural, oral, and written drill to aid the student in mastering the structures described in the text.

This handbook-workbook is the latest of a series that has resulted from our experience in teaching in a program of language instruction, orientation, and counseling activities for foreign students initiated over a decade ago at the University of California at Berkeley. The program was organized and the original materials prepared by Aurora M. Quiros (now Aurora Quiros Haggard). In the preparation of *Mastering American English,* therefore, it has been possible to draw on a background of teaching more than two thousand students—whose countries range the alphabet from Afghanistan to Yugoslavia.

TO THE TEACHER

We do not necessarily intend that the parts should be studied in the exact order in which they appear in the book. The unit approach makes it possible for each teacher to determine the order of presentation of material best suited to the particular needs of a class. For those teachers who may be interested we include the following outline of our use of the material:

It has been our experience that the students first need intensive practice, particularly oral drill, in the basic word order patterns (Parts I and II). However, before we get very far, we find it necessary to introduce a review of the formation of verb tenses and verb tense phrases, presented in Part VI. At this time, we may also introduce some of the uses of the various tenses in Parts VII, VIII, and IX in preparation for intensive work at a later time. While we are studying these parts we may also discuss articles, prepositions, etc. as they come up. In this way, the students are constantly mastering, sometimes indirectly, material which will be reviewed in detail later.

Once the basic patterns are well established, we continue with the word order material in Parts III, IV, and V and follow that by an intensive review of the uses of the various verb tenses and verb tense phrases in Parts VII, VIII, and IX. We have found that the diagrams in these parts prove helpful to the student if the instructor refers to them in explaining the uses of the tenses in various situations. Following uses of the tenses, we take up sequence of tenses, passive constructions, and auxiliary verbs (Parts X and XI).

From here on the order is largely determined by the level and needs of the group. For example, we might turn our attention to articles (Part XV) and basic prepositions (Part XVI), or we might continue with the verb structures in Parts XII and XIII and with verbals in Part XIV.

Special mention should be made of the phrasal combinations in Part XVII. If the material is to be covered in detail, we suggest that a few combinations be introduced at regular intervals during the course.

We want to stress the fact that the exercises may be used in various ways. Although we have not always specifically said so in the directions, almost every exercise can be used for aural, oral, and written practice. For example, in addition to the instructions given for Exercise 1, the exercise might be used as follows: First, the instructor might ask the students to repeat affirmative and negative questions after him, either individually or as a group. Then, for further aural practice, he might dictate the statements or questions. Also, the class might be divided into groups of three or four students for further oral drill under the supervision of a native speaker.

We also mention that most of the exercises for articles and prepositions can be used for aural work (the instructor reads and the student fills in or checks what he hears), for oral work (the student reads and gives the forms as directed), and for written work (the student writes the forms as directed).

Our general procedure in presenting new material is to give a brief explanation or demonstration followed by a period of intensive aural, oral, and written practice. The student is then asked to study the text at home and assigned written exercises at the end of the part.

Finally, we believe constant review and diversified practice of the material presented is essential. We try to use every opportunity to carry over the major principles and structures as we progress from one lesson to another throughout the course of study.

We hope that you and your students will find much of value in this book. We are interested in any questions, comments, or suggestions you may have as a result of your experience in using this book.

ACKNOWLEDGEMENTS

As with most texts, this one could not have been written without the work previously done by others in the field. We have undoubtedly been influenced in our thinking by the works of scholars such as Curme, Fries, Hornby, and Jespersen. In addition, we found Paul Roberts' *Understanding Grammar* and L. M. Myers' *A Guide to American English* delightful and useful references.

This book has been a long time growing, and many more persons than we can give credit to here have given freely of their time, energy, and suggestions during its development. The teachers who have used the syllabus material during the past seven years, our colleagues in the English language program at the University of California at Berkeley, and the students whom we have had in our classes have contributed in many ways to the present book.

Among the persons to whom we wish to express our special appreciation for guidance on this book are Professor David P. Harris of the University of Florida, who read a good part of the manuscript and gave us many ideas on content and format, and Professor Lois M. Wilson of San Francisco State College for the reading of the manuscript and for her valuable comments and encouragement. Above all, are we deeply indebted to Professor David W. Reed of the University of California, whose expert and tactful criticism encouraged us to work even harder in our attempt to produce a good book. We, of course, accept the responsibility for any weaknesses which may remain. We also extend thanks to Mrs. Alida Dixon and Mrs. Celia Wakefield for typing the manuscript.

REBECCA E. HAYDEN
DOROTHY W. PILGRIM
AURORA Q. HAGGARD

CONTENTS

UNIT 1 WORD ORDER

PART I Basic Word Order

1. Introduction   1
2. Affirmative Statements   1
3. Negative Statements   3
4. Affirmative Questions   4
5. Long and Short Responses to Questions   5
6. Negative Questions   6

Exercises for Part I   9

PART II Basic Word Order (continued)

7. Questions Introduced by Interrogatives   13
8. Responses to Questions Introduced by Interrogatives   14
9. Short Questions Attached to Statements   14
10. Responses to Short Questions Attached to Statements   15
11. Requests and Commands   16

Exercises for Part II   19

PART III Position of Modifiers of Nouns

12. Introduction   25
13. Single Words and Word Groups That Modify Nouns   25
14. Phrases and Clauses That Modify Nouns   28

Exercises for Part III   31

PART IV Position of Modifiers of Verbs, Adverbs, and Adjectives

15. Introduction   35
16. Single Words and Expressions   35
17. Clauses   41

Exercises for Part IV   45

PART V — Patterns of Connected Statements

- **18** Introduction 51
- **19** Connected Affirmative Statements 51
- **20** Connected Negative Statements 52
- **21** Connected Affirmative and Negative Statements 52
- **22** Summary of Connected Statements 53

Exercises for Part V 55

UNIT 2 VERBS

PART VI — Principal Parts and Tense Forms

- **23** Introduction 59
- **24** The Simple Present Tense 59
- **25** The Simple Past Tense 61
- **26** The Future Tense 62
- **27** The Perfect Tenses 62
- **28** The Progressive Tenses 63
- **29** Irregular Verb Forms 64

Exercises for Part VI 67

PART VII — Usage of Tenses

- **30** Introduction 71
- **31** Uses of the Simple Present Tense 71
- **32** Uses of the Present Progressive Tense 75

Exercises for Part VII 77

PART VIII — Usage of Tenses (continued)

- **33** Uses of the Simple Past Tense 81
- **34** Uses of the Past Progressive Tense 83
- **35** Uses of the Future Tense 84
- **36** Uses of the Future Progressive Tense 85

Exercises for Part VIII 87

CONTENTS

PART IX   Usage of Tenses (continued)

     37   Uses of the Present Perfect Tense   91
     38   Uses of the Present Perfect Progressive Tense   93
     39   Uses of the Past Perfect Tense   94
     40   Uses of the Past Perfect Progressive, the Future Perfect, and the Future Perfect Progressive Tenses   95

Exercises for Part IX   97

PART X   Sequence of Tenses

     41   Introduction   101
     42   Sequence in Clauses That Modify Verbs   101
     43   Sequence in Clauses That Modify Nouns   103
     44   Sequence in Clauses That Function as Nouns   103

Exercises for Part X   105

PART XI   The Passive Construction and Auxiliary Verbs

     45   The Passive Construction   109
     46   Introduction to Auxiliary Verbs   110
     47   Auxiliaries or Equivalent Phrases That Express Ability to Do Something   110
     48   Auxiliaries Used in Requesting and Giving Permission to Do Something   111
     49   Auxiliaries or Equivalent Phrases That Express Obligation and Necessity   112
     50   Auxiliaries or Equivalent Phrases That Express Possibility and Probability   113
     51   Auxiliaries or Equivalent Phrases Used in Expressing Preferences and Wants   114

Exercises for Part XI   117

PART XII   Verb Forms in Clauses Involving Wishes, Demands, and Conditions

     52   Introduction   121
     53   **Wish (that)** + Noun Clause   121
     54   Expressions such as **demand that** and **it is necessary that** + Noun Clause   122
     55   Clauses of Condition   123

Exercises for Part XII   125

PART XIII Troublesome Verbs

56   SAY and TELL   129
57   TALK and SPEAK   130
58   DO and MAKE   130
59   LIE-LAY; RISE-RAISE; SIT-SET   131

Exercises for Part XIII   133
REVIEW EXERCISES FOR VERBS (Unit 2)   135

UNIT 3   VERBALS

PART XIV   Verbals

60   Introduction   143
61   Infinitives and Gerunds as Objects of Verbs   143
62   Infinitives as Complements   146
63   The Gerund as Object of a Preposition   146
64   The Infinitive and Gerund in Expressions of Purpose   147
65   The Present and Past Participles as Adjectives   147
66   Infinitives and Participles Following Complements or Objects   148
67   Perfect and Passive Forms of Infinitives, Gerunds, and Participles   149

Exercises for Part XIV   151

UNIT 4   ARTICLES

PART XV   Definite and Indefinite Articles

68   Introduction   155
69   Articles with Singular Countable Nouns   155
70   Articles with Plural Countable Nouns   156
71   Articles with Non-Countable Nouns   157
72   Summary of Articles with Countable and Non-Countable Nouns   159
73   Articles with Proper Names   160
74   Articles with Nouns Modified by Proper Names and Possessives   162
75   Some Specific Uses of the Definite Article   163

Exercises for Part XV   165

CONTENTS

UNIT 5   PREPOSITIONS

PART XVI   Basic Uses of Prepositions

    76   Introduction   171
    77   Prepositions of Place or Position   171
    78   Prepositions of Direction   173
    79   Prepositions of Time   174
    80   Prepositions of Manner   176
    81   Some Other Types of Prepositions   176
    Exercises for Part XVI   177

PART XVII   Prepositions in Phrasal Combinations

    82   Introduction   183
    83   Verb and Preposition-Adverb Combinations   183
    84   Verb and Preposition Combinations   187
    85   Combinations with **be** and **have**   188
    86   Other Prepositional Combinations   190
    Exercises for Part XVII   191

UNIT 6   NOUNS AND PRONOUNS

PART XVIII   Noun and Pronoun Forms

    87   Noun Forms   197
    88   Pronoun Forms   201
    89   A Note on Gender   202
    Exercises for Part XVIII   205

PART XIX   Agreement

    90   Introduction   209
    91   Agreement of Subject and Verb   209
    92   Agreement of Pronoun with the Noun or Pronoun to Which It Refers   212
    Exercises for Part XIX   215

UNIT 7   ADJECTIVES AND ADVERBS

PART XX   Comparison of Adjectives and Adverbs

    93   Introduction   217
    94   Comparative and Superlative Forms of Adjectives and Adverbs   217
    95   Constructions of Comparison   220

Exercises for Part XX   223

UNIT 8   PUNCTUATION

PART XXI   A Guide to Punctuation

    96   Introduction   225
    97   Capitalization   225
    98   The Period (.)   226
    99   The Question Mark (?)   226
   100   The Exclamation Point (!)   226
   101   The Comma (,)   227
   102   The Semicolon (;)   228
   103   The Colon (:)   229
   104   Quotation Marks (" ...... ")   229
   105   Underlining   230
   106   The Apostrophe (')   231
   107   Parentheses (())   231
   108   Brackets ([ ])   231
   109   Triple Dots (...)   231
   110   The Dash (—)   232

Exercises for Part XXI   233

GENERAL REVIEW EXERCISES FOR PARTS I–XXI   239

Appendix

   A   Verb Conjugations   245
   B   Letter Forms   247
   C   List of American-English Speech Sounds   250

Subject Index   253

Word Index   257

UNIT 1 | WORD ORDER

PART 1 | Basic Word Order

1. INTRODUCTION

Mastering *basic word order patterns* is an essential step in learning English. Native speakers frequently vary these patterns, but the student learning English would do well to concentrate on basic word order until he is able to use the patterns of *statements, questions, requests,* and *commands* automatically.

2. AFFIRMATIVE STATEMENTS

The regular order of words in affirmative statements is SUBJECT + VERB + COMPLEMENT or OBJECT.

SUBJECT + VERB — George smokes.
SUBJECT + VERB + COMPLEMENT — They are students.
SUBJECT + VERB + OBJECT — John likes Mary.

2a. The verb **be** is frequently followed by a *complement*. The complement may be an adjective, a noun, or a pronoun.

SUBJECT	VERB	COMPLEMENT
Jack	is	ill.
They	are	friends.
It	was	mine.

When the following verbs are similar in meaning to **be,** they may be followed by an adjective: **appear, become, feel, look, seem, smell, sound, taste.**

I **feel** tired.
She **looks** happy.
He **became** ill.

Become may also be followed by a noun or pronoun.

The brothers **became** engineers.
The fortune **will become** his.

2b. Verbs other than **be** are frequently followed by an *object*. The object may be a noun, a pronoun, or a noun-equivalent. (A noun-equivalent is a word, phrase, or clause that is a substitute for a noun.)

SUBJECT	VERB	OBJECT
Alfred	collects	stamps.
I	saw	them.
He	likes	swimming.

2c. Certain verbs are frequently followed by two objects: an *indirect object* and a *direct object*. Some examples are the verbs **bring, get, give, hand, leave, offer, pass, send, take, tell, read, write, teach, buy, sell, fix, make.**

The indirect object is the person *to* whom, or occasionally *for* whom, something (the direct object) is given, sent, told, and so forth. When a verb is followed by two objects, the order after the verb is INDIRECT OBJECT + DIRECT OBJECT.

		INDIRECT OBJECT	DIRECT OBJECT
He	gave	me	the book.
Jim	bought	Mary	a present.

Frequently a phrase introduced by **to** or **for** is used instead of the indirect object. The **to**-phrase may follow all of the verbs listed above except **buy, fix,** and **make.** The **for**-phrase follows **buy, fix,** and **make.**[1] When the **to-** or **for**-phrase is used, the word order after the verb is DIRECT OBJECT + PHRASE. Compare:

		INDIRECT OBJECT	DIRECT OBJECT	PHRASE
He	gave	me	the book.	
He	gave		the book	to me.
Jim	bought	Mary	a present.	
Jim	bought		a present	for Mary.

The **to-** or **for**-phrase is generally used when the direct object is a pronoun. Compare:

        He gave me the book.
        He gave the book **to me.**
BUT: He gave it **to me.**   (NOT: He gave me it.)

A few verbs, including **deliver, describe, explain, return, say,** are regularly followed by DIRECT OBJECT + PHRASE.

        She **described** her house **to us.**
        He **explained** the theory **to us.**
        He **returned** it **to me.**

2d. Single-word modifiers of the *subject, object,* or *complement* are ordinarily placed before the word modified.

Modifiers	SUBJECT	VERB	Modifiers	COMPLEMENT or OBJECT
	Richard	is	very[2]	ill.
	He	bought	three	shirts.
The tall	man	wants	that	suitcase.
His older	brother	is	a very brilliant[3]	lawyer.

---

[1] Many verbs followed by a **to**-phrase may also be followed by a **for**-phrase, but there is an obvious change in meaning. Compare:
        I wrote several letters **to** her.   I wrote several letters **for** her.

[2] Modifiers of adjectives usually indicate intensity or degree. Examples:
        too hot   **extremely** tired
        very long   **more** difficult

Enough follows the adjective it modifies.
        The coffee is **hot enough.**

BASIC WORD ORDER

2e. Most modifiers of *verbs* are regularly placed *after* the verb and *after* the complement or object, if any.

SUBJECT	VERB	COMPLEMENT or OBJECT	Modifiers of Verb
They	went		home.
The paper	is		here.
He	was	ill	yesterday.
Joe	saw	Bob	on Tuesday.
I	like	music	very [4] much.

2f. An important exception to the regular order of *subject + verb* occurs in statements beginning with **there is, there are,** etc. In sentences of this kind, **there** appears in the subject position. The real subject follows the verb.

> **There is** a lecture today.
> **There are** many people here.
> **There was** a fire this morning.

3   NEGATIVE STATEMENTS

A statement may be made negative by using **not** with the verb. Three basic principles operate in making statements negative.

(1) With simple present and past tense forms of **be:**

Not is placed after **am, is, are, was, were.**

He	is		a student.
He	is	**not**	a student.
He	isn't		a student.

Contractions of **is, are, was** and **were + not** are generally used in conversational English.

 isn't = is not   **aren't** = are not
 wasn't = was not   **weren't** = were not

> He **isn't** (is not) here.
> They **aren't** (are not) students.
> It **wasn't** (was not) mine.
> Those **weren't** (were not) yours.
> I **am not** ready.

(2) With simple present and past tense forms of verbs other than **be:**

The original verb is first changed to a verb phrase composed of **do (does)** or **did** + the simple form of the verb.[5] Then **not** is placed after **do (does)** or **did.**

---

[3] The intensifier **very** modifies the adjective **brilliant;** in turn, the adjective **brilliant** modifies **lawyer.**

[4] The intensifier **very** modifies the adverb **much.** Modifiers of adverbs are ordinarily placed before the word modified.

[5] The simple form of the verb is the same as the infinitive without **to.**
   to walk = infinitive   **walk** = simple form

WORD ORDER

He			likes	coffee.
He	does	**not**	like	coffee.
He	does**n't**		like	coffee.
He			liked	coffee.
He	did	**not**	like	coffee.
He	did**n't**		like	coffee.

Contractions of **do, does** and **did** + **not** are generally used in conversational English.

don't = do not   **doesn't** = does not   **didn't** = did not

I **don't** (do not) want that book.
She **doesn't** (does not) speak French.
They **didn't** (did not) arrive yesterday.

(3) With constructions of auxiliary + principal verb: [6]
Not is placed after the auxiliary.

He	will		be	a student.
He	will	not	be	a student.
He	wo**n't**		be	a student.
He	is		working	here.
He	is	not	working	here.
He	is**n't**		working	here.

Contractions of the auxiliaries + **not** are generally used in conversational English.

haven't = have not   **won't** = will not   **wouldn't** = would not
hasn't = has not   **can't** = cannot   **shouldn't** = should not
hadn't = had not   **couldn't** = could not

He **hasn't** (has not) arrived yet.
Jack **can't** (can not) come.
You **shouldn't** (should not) go home yet.

4 | AFFIRMATIVE QUESTIONS

Three basic principles operate in changing statements to questions.

(1) With the simple present and past tense forms of **be:**
The verb is placed before the subject. Compare:

---

[6] Combinations of auxiliary verbs and principal verbs are called verb phrases. The verb that expresses the main meaning is called the *principal* verb; the other verb (or verbs) is called an *auxiliary* (or *helping*) verb. **Go, going, gone** are the principal verbs in the following examples: will **go**, is **going**, has **gone**, can **go.**

BASIC WORD ORDER

	He	is	a student.
Is	he		a student?
	He	was	a student.
Was	he		a student?

(2) With simple present and past tense forms of verbs other than **be:**
The original verb is first changed to **do (does)** or **did** + the simple form of the verb. Then **do (does)** or **did** is placed before the subject. Compare:

	He	likes	coffee.
Does	he	like	coffee?
	He	studied	English.
Did	he	study	English?

(3) With constructions of auxiliary + principal verb:
The auxiliary is placed before the subject. Compare:

	He	will	be	a doctor.
Will	he		be	a doctor?
	He	can	drive	a car.
Can	he		drive	a car?

5 LONG AND SHORT RESPONSES TO QUESTIONS

Questions like those in Section 4 normally receive a **yes** or **no** type of response. The response may be either *long* (a full statement) or *short*. Short responses are very frequently used in conversational English.

QUESTION	TYPICAL LONG RESPONSES	TYPICAL SHORT RESPONSES
Is Bob in his room?	Yes, he's there. No, he isn't there now.	Yes, he is. No, he isn't.
Were you there?	Yes, I was there. No, I wasn't there.	Yes, I was. No, I wasn't.
Do you like beer?	Yes, I like it very much. No, I don't like it.	Yes, I do. No, I don't.
Did he fail the course?	Yes, he failed it all right. No, he passed it.	Yes, he did. No, he didn't.
Has he left already?	Yes, he left at noon. No, he hasn't gone yet.	Yes, he has. No, he hasn't.
Are you going with us?	Yes, I'm going with you. No, I'm sorry, but I can't.	Yes, I am. No, I'm not.

WORD ORDER

The following contractions of subject and verb are frequently used in conversational English:

I'm	= I am	**he's**	= he is	**you're**	= you are
I've	= I have	**he'll**	= he will	**you've**	= you have
I'll	= I will	**she's**	= she is	**you'll**	= you will
we're	= we are	**she'll**	= she will	**they're**	= they are
we've	= we have	**it's**	= it is	**they've**	= they have
we'll	= we will			**they'll**	= they will

6 | NEGATIVE QUESTIONS

In the negative forms of questions, **not** may be *contracted* with the *verb form before* the subject or may be placed after the subject.

Is	he			a student?
Is	he	**not**		a student?
Isn't	he			a student?
Does	he		like	coffee?
Does	he	**not**	like	coffee?
Doesn't	he		like	coffee?
Will	he		give	a speech?
Will	he	**not**	give	a speech?
Won't	he		give	a speech?

A negative question does not express simple negation in the same way that a negative statement does. Three general types of meaning may be expressed by negative questions.

(1) A negative question may suggest an emotional tone or bias on the part of the speaker.

      Haven't you cleaned your room yet?
      Won't you help me?

The person to whom such questions are directed usually senses the emotional tone or bias and responds accordingly.

    For example, in the first question, he may detect ridicule or the implication that he *should* have already cleaned the room, and he would probably qualify his answer to defend himself. He might give one of the following responses:

      Of course I have. I cleaned it yesterday.
      No, I've been too busy studying.

In the second question, he may detect in the tone of the speaker an uncertainty or doubt about his willingness to help. To assure the speaker, he might give the following response:

      Certainly I'll help you. Have I ever refused?

(2) A negative question may also suggest that the speaker expects a certain response, usually agreement.

      Isn't she pretty?
      Shouldn't we leave now?

Although the speaker may *expect* affirmative responses to these questions, the response may be either affirmative or negative.

For example, the responses to the first question might be as follows:

>Yes, she is.
>You may think so, but I don't.

(3) In some situations, negative and affirmative questions may express practically the same meaning, although the negative form seems to suggest greater interest or concern on the part of the speaker. Compare:

>Will you have some coffee?
>Won't you have some coffee?

The responses to either question might be as follows:

>Yes, thank you.
>No, thank you.

EXERCISES FOR PART I

The following exercises may be used for both oral and written practice:

EXERCISE 1

(a) Change the following affirmative statements to negative statements.
(b) Make questions out of the statements.

    Example: It is late.
             (a) It isn't late.
             (b) Is it late?

1. It is a nice day.

2. He was at home all day.

3. There were many people at the meeting.

4. They enjoy good movies.

5. Mary plays the violin.

6. They arrived last night.

7. She will come to see you tomorrow.

8. He is going to telephone you tonight.

9. They are listening to the radio.

10. John is studying English this semester.

11. There will be a lecture on Thursday.

12. He can drive a car.

13. Ernest Ross is an architect.

14. You were late to class this morning.

15. George was absent last Monday.

16. He likes hamburgers for lunch.

17. They usually go home for lunch.

18. Jim brought her many souvenirs.

19. Mr. Hall will take his vacation in June.

Exercises for Part I

Exercise 1 (continued)

20. We made a good impression on them.

21. He is working on his thesis.

22. They were here last night.

23. Joe handed in his assignment.

24. Mrs. Bell is going to leave tomorrow.

25. They are going to the opera tonight.

26. She went to the concert last night.

27. She is ready.

28. They play golf every Sunday.

29. The truck driver wanted to pass the car.

30. We have a quiz tomorrow.

31. It is too late to go to the movies.

32. Mr. Sloan has offered him a job.

33. He is going to call on you this afternoon.

34. He has paid his registration fee.

35. He heard the news broadcast at noon.

36. John told us the truth.

37. There is a pen in my briefcase.

38. I left my hat in this room.

39. Mr. Stripp is going to sell his house to Mr. Tabler.

40. There are many people in the park today.

EXERCISE 2

Complete the answers to the following questions. Give <u>long</u> responses.

    Examples: Were you late today?   Did you find your book?
                    No, I was on time.   Yes, I found it in the classroom.

1. Are you tired?

   Yes,

2. Is Betty a senior?

   No,

3. Was the bus on time this morning?

   No,

4. Do you live in a dormitory?

   Yes,

5. Does he visit you often?

   No,

6. Did Mr. Jones telephone me today?

   Yes,

7. Have you ever been to South America?

   No,

8. Has he finished the test already?

   No,

9. Shall we leave now?

   No,

10. Is there a telephone in the lobby?

    Yes,

11. Were there any tickets available?

    No,

12. Does she ever write to you?

    Yes,

13. Can you answer the question?

    No,

14. Isn't the professor going to give a lecture today?

    No,

15. Don't you ever watch television?

    Yes,

EXERCISE 3

Complete the answers to the following questions. Give _short_ responses:

    Example: Are you a student?
              Yes, I am.

1. Are you interested in mathematics?

    Yes,

2. Was he late?

    No,

3. Were they on time?

    Yes,

4. Do you know John Smith?

    No,

5. Does he take cream in his coffee?

    No,

6. Did you send her a present?

    Yes,

7. Have you read the paper yet?

    Yes,

8. Will they be here tomorrow?

    No,

9. Is she waiting for you?

    Yes,

10. Can you read German?

    No,

11. Is there any coffee left?

    No,

12. Do you have a ticket?

    No,

13. Have you heard from John this week?

    No,

14. Aren't you taking English this semester?

    Yes,

15. Can't you solve that problem?

    No,

PART II Basic Word Order (continued)

7 QUESTIONS INTRODUCED by INTERROGATIVES

7a. When **who, what, which,** or **whose** is the subject or the modifier of the subject of the question, the word order is like that of a regular statement. **What, which,** and **whose** may appear alone or with a noun. Compare:

John	arrived	late.
Who	arrived	late?
What person	made	this rule?
What	happened	yesterday?
Which answer	is	correct?
Which	is	correct?
Whose grade	was	the highest?
Whose	was	the highest?

Who refers to persons; **what,** to things; **which** and **whose,** to persons or things. **What** may appear before a noun that refers to either persons or things.

7b. When **whom, what, which,** or **whose** is the object of a verb or a preposition or modifies the object, the word order is like that of a regular question. Compare:

	Did you see	them?
Whom[1]	did you see?	
What plan	do you suggest?	
What	do you suggest?	
Which movie	are you going to see?	
Which	are you going to see?	
Whose book	did she borrow?	
Whose	did she borrow?	
	Did you go with	them?
Whom[2]	did you go with?	
What	did you go for?	
Which class	did he go to?	
Which	did he go to?	

7c. After **when, where, how,** and **why,** the word order of regular questions is also used. Compare:

	Did you go?
When	did you go?
Where	are you going?
How	have you been?
Why	is he angry?

---

[1] **Who,** instead of **whom,** is frequently heard in spoken English, although some people consider this substitution unacceptable.

[2] A more formal pattern for this sentence is "With whom did you go?" A more informal pattern is "Who did you go with?" (Also see Footnote 1.)

How is often used with words like **much, many,** and **far.**

> **How much** does this cost?
> **How many** times have you gone there?
> **How far** is it to the post office?

8 | RESPONSES to QUESTIONS INTRODUCED by INTERROGATIVES

Questions introduced by interrogatives may be answered by both long and short responses. Short responses may be one word or a group of words.

QUESTION	TYPICAL LONG RESPONSES	TYPICAL SHORT RESPONSES
Who telephoned this afternoon?	John telephoned this afternoon.	John. John did.
When did he telephone?	He telephoned at 2:30. He telephoned this morning.	At 2:30. This morning.
Where was he?	He was at the office. He was downtown.	At the office. Downtown.
What are you doing?	I'm studying. I'm combing my hair.	Studying. Combing my hair.
Why are you studying so hard?	I'm studying because I have a quiz tomorrow. I'm trying to finish my term paper.	Because I have a quiz. To finish my term paper.
Whose course is it for?	It's for Mr. Smith's course in modern European history	Mr. Smith's. For Mr. Smith's history course.
How long will it take you to finish?	I hope I can finish by midnight. It may take me another day or two.	Till about midnight. About two days.

9 | SHORT QUESTIONS ATTACHED to STATEMENTS

9a. A question may be formed by attaching a short question to a statement. If the statement is affirmative, the attached question is negative; if the statement is negative, the attached question is affirmative. Three basic principles operate in attaching questions to statements.

(1) With simple present and past tense forms of **be**:
An affirmative statement is followed by a short negative question: *verb* + **not** (usually contracted) + *subject*. A negative statement is followed by a short affirmative question: *verb* + *subject*. Compare:

John **is** here,	**isn't** he?	John **isn't** here,	**is** he?
We **are** late,	**aren't** we?	We **aren't** late,	**are** we?

(2) With simple present and past tense forms of verbs other than **be**:
An affirmative statement is followed by a short negative question: **do (does)** or **did** + **not** (usually contracted) + *subject*. A negative statement is followed by a short affirmative question: **do (does)** or **did** + *subject*. Compare:

BASIC WORD ORDER

He **plays** golf,	**doesn't** he?	He **doesn't play** golf,	**does** he?
They **went** home,	**didn't** they?	They **didn't go** home,	**did** they?

(3) With constructions of auxiliary + principal verb:
An affirmative statement is followed by a short negative question: *auxiliary* + **not** (usually contracted) + *subject*. A negative statement is followed by a short affirmative question: *auxiliary* + *subject*. Compare:

You **can drive** a car,	**can't** you?	You **can't drive** a car,	**can** you?
They **are coming,**	**aren't** they?	They **aren't coming,**	**are** they?

The person asking a question that begins with an affirmative statement usually expects the other person to agree with him. For example, if he says, "It's a nice day, isn't it?" he expects as a response, "Yes, it is." [3] On the other hand, if he says, "It isn't a nice day, is it?" he expects, "No, it isn't." However, the person responding may either agree or disagree. (See Section 10.)

9b. A short question that is ordinarily *separated* from the statement it follows is similar to, but should not be confused with, the *attached* question. The subject in the statement does not refer to the same person or thing as the subject in the separated question. Compare:

John is here, isn't **he?**
John is here. Is **Bill?**

You didn't telephone, did **you?**
I didn't telephone her. Did **you?**

You can be there by six o'clock, can't **you?**
I can't be there by six o'clock. Can **you?** [4]

10 | RESPONSES to SHORT QUESTIONS ATTACHED to STATEMENTS

Short questions attached to statements are usually followed by the **yes** or **no** type of response. The responses may be either long or short.

QUESTION	TYPICAL LONG RESPONSES	TYPICAL SHORT RESPONSES
He's here, isn't he?	Yes, he's here. / No, he isn't here.	Yes, he is. / No, he isn't.
He owns a car, doesn't he?	Yes, he has a convertible. / No, he doesn't own a car.	Yes, he does. / No, he doesn't.
He went home, didn't he?	Yes, he went home almost an hour ago. / No, he hasn't gone yet.	Yes, he did. / No, he didn't.
They'll come, won't they?	Yes, they're planning to come. / No, they won't be able to come.	Yes, they will. / No, they won't.

---

[3] Short negative questions attached to affirmative statements have the effect of regular negative questions. (See Section 6.) Compare:
        It is a nice day, **isn't it?**   **Isn't** it a nice day?

[4] The short questions separated from the preceding statement are actually shortened forms of regular questions described in Section 4.

WORD ORDER

QUESTION	TYPICAL LONG RESPONSES	TYPICAL SHORT RESPONSES
It wasn't difficult, was it?	Yes, it was very difficult. No, it wasn't difficult at all.	Yes, it was. No, it wasn't.
We don't have time, do we?	Yes, we have plenty of time. No, we don't have enough time.	Yes, we do. No, we don't.
He can't go, can he?	Yes, he can go with us. No, he can't go this time.	Yes, he can. No, he can't.

11 | REQUESTS and COMMANDS

The subject is not usually stated in a request or command. Requests and commands are not necessarily followed by oral or written responses. The response is often in the form of an action that carries out the request or command. For example, if you see a sign that says STOP, you stop; an oral response is not called for. The following are examples of requests and commands and typical responses.

ORAL REQUEST OR COMMAND	TYPICAL RESPONSES
Come here.	Wait a minute.
You come here right now.	Oh, all right.
Please sit down.[5]	Thank you. I prefer to stand, thank you.
Hand in your paper, please.	I haven't finished yet. Yes, Mr. Wilson.
Close the door, please.	Yes, certainly. Why? Sorry, I'm busy.
Let's go now.[6]	All right. That's fine with me.

11a. **Do not** or the contraction **don't** is placed before the verb to indicate a negative request or command.

ORAL COMMAND OR REQUEST	TYPICAL RESPONSES
Don't smoke in here.	Why not?
Please **don't** smoke in here.	Sorry, I didn't see the sign.
Don't hurry.	All right, I won't. Don't worry. I'll take my time.
Do not forget to pay your income tax.	Don't worry. I won't.

11b. Other constructions, such as those in boldface type in the following examples, are also used in making polite requests and commands.

ORAL REQUEST OR COMMAND	TYPICAL RESPONSES
Do you mind opening the door?[7]	Not at all. Certainly not. Of course not.
Would you mind sitting here?	No, I wouldn't mind. Thank you.
Will (Won't) you please be quiet?[8]	Oh, I'm sorry. I beg your pardon.
Would you please come on time?	I'll certainly try to. I'm sorry, but I may not be able to.

BASIC WORD ORDER

11c. The constructions in boldface type in the following examples are used in requesting permission to do something.

ORAL REQUEST	TYPICAL RESPONSES
Do you mind if I turn on the radio?	No, go right ahead. Of course not. I'm sorry. I'd rather you wouldn't.
May I have some coffee?	Certainly. Help yourself. Yes, I'll bring it right away.
Would you mind if I didn't come?	Oh, I wish you would. No, that'll be all right. Well, everyone will miss you.

11d. The following are some examples of written requests and commands, often seen in the form of signs:

POST NO BILLS.   DO NOT ENTER.   DO NOT CROSS THE TRACKS.
KEEP OUT.   STOP. LOOK. LISTEN.   Please pay your bill immediately.
KEEP OFF THE GRASS.

---

[5] The addition of **please** makes a request or command more polite.
[6] **Let's** is a contraction of **let us**. **Let's** is used to introduce requests that include the speaker.
[7] The expressions **do you mind** and **would you mind** are followed by gerunds (**ing-**form), not infinitives. See Section 61b for further details.
[8] Using **would** instead of **will** softens the request.
    Would you please be quiet?

EXERCISES FOR PART II

The following exercises may be used for both oral and written practice:

EXERCISE 4

Answer the following questions:

    <u>Example</u>: Where is my book?
                It's on your desk.

1. Who is your teacher?

2. Who is going with you to the baseball game?

3. Whose sweater is this?

4. What happened to Sally?

5. What time is it?

6. Which bus goes to the railroad station?

7. Which newspaper do you want?

8. Whom shall I give this book to?

9. When did you get here?

10. Why are you laughing?

11. Where does your friend live?

12. How are you getting along?

13. How far is it to your house?

14. How many feet are there in a mile?

15. It's cold today, isn't it?

16. You usually have lunch at one o'clock, don't you?

17. He didn't see you, did he?

18. They are going with you, aren't they?

19. You weren't at the meeting, were you?

20. There was a message for me, wasn't there?

EXERCISE 5

Make questions based on the statements below. Begin the questions with the interrogatives given.

    Example: Mary went to town yesterday.
             When did Mary go to town?
             She went yesterday.

1. Mr. McCoy began his new job last week.

    When

2. Stanley is going to India for six months.

    Where

3. She goes to work by bus.

    How

4. Mrs. Berg has gone to Baltimore because of her mother's illness.

    Why

5. They are playing bridge.

    What

6. He wants the blue tie.

    Which

7. Margaret told her the news.

    Who

8. John's grade was the highest.

    Whose

9. Phyllis went to the dance with Jeff.

    Whom

10. It takes twenty minutes to get from here to their house.

    How long

11. It's four blocks to the post office.

    How far

12. He paid $30 for his radio.

    How much

Exercises for Part II

EXERCISE 6

Attach a short question to each of the statements below; then give responses to the questions.

Example: She bought a new hat, <u>didn't she</u>?
<u>Yes</u>, <u>she did</u>.

1. He arrived at 11:30,

2. You are from Indonesia,

3. This answer isn't correct,

4. The postman didn't bring any mail today,

5. The bus stops at every other block,

6. They won't return before Saturday,

7. He is going with you,

8. Alfred told you the news,

9. They have lived here for five years,

10. We should go soon,

11. You don't want cream in your coffee,

12. He doesn't work here,

13. It is almost time for dinner,

14. This is a nice day,

15. You have read that book,

16. Mr. Loomis prefers to travel by air,

17. It will take about two more hours to get to the city,

18. You are going to the meeting,

19. There's no class today,

20. There are several people waiting in the office,

EXERCISE 7

Give oral responses to the following commands and requests:

> Example: May I come in?
> Yes, of course.

1. Please close the door.

2. Sit down over there, please.

3. Help me take off my coat, please.

4. Please hand in your paper now.

5. Let's go out for dinner tonight.

6. Let's go for a walk.

7. Please don't interrupt me.

8. Don't be so slow.

9. Do you mind closing the window?

10. Do you mind helping me for a few minutes?

11. Would you mind showing me the new books?

12. Would you mind getting me a newspaper?

13. Won't you please answer the doorbell?

14. Will you please turn off the radio?

15. Would you bring your book to class tomorrow?

16. Do you mind if I stay here awhile?

17. Would you mind if I borrowed your pen?

18. May I borrow your pencil for a second?

19. Would you please hand me that package?

20. May I go with you to the lecture?

EXERCISE 8

Use the verbs below in the constructions illustrated in Examples A and B. After your exercises have been corrected, use them for oral practice. For example, read your commands and requests aloud and have another student answer you; then reverse the process.

    Example A: mail (1) Please mail this letter.
                           (2) Do you mind mailing this letter?
                           (3) Would you mind mailing this letter?
                           (4) Would you please mail this letter?

help (1)

      (2)

      (3)

      (4)

give (1)

      (2)

      (3)

      (4)

get (1)

     (2)

     (3)

     (4)

    Example B: borrow (1) May I borrow this book?
                             (2) Do you mind if I borrow this book?
                             (3) Would you mind if I borrowed this book?

ask (1)

     (2)

     (3)

show (1)

      (2)

      (3)

take (1)

      (2)

      (3)

EXERCISE 9

Write groups of questions and responses using interrogatives (<u>how</u>, <u>why</u>, <u>when</u>, <u>where</u>, <u>what</u>, <u>which</u>, <u>whose</u>, <u>whom</u>, <u>who</u>). Use the model below as a guide. After your exercise has been corrected, use the questions for oral practice. Work with another student, if possible.

Question	Long Response	Short Response
(a) What is your name?	My name is Helen Kelly.	Helen Kelly.
(b) Where are you from?	I'm from Dublin, Ireland.	Dublin, Ireland.
(c) When did you arrive in the U. S.?	I arrived on March 10, 1955.	In March, 1955.
(d) Why have you come to the U. S.?	I've come to get a Master's degree in physics.	To get a Master's degree in physics.
(e) How do you like it here?	I like it very much.	Fine!
(f) Who is your faculty adviser?	My adviser is Professor Walsh.	Professor Walsh.
(g) Which courses are you taking this semester?	I'm taking three courses in physics and one course in mathematics.	Three physics courses and one math course.

(a)

(b)

(c)

(d)

(e)

(f)

(g)

(h)

PART III — Position of Modifiers of Nouns

12 INTRODUCTION

Modifiers of nouns may be single words, phrases, or clauses. Compare:

The tall man is Mr. Stewart.
The tall man **in the brown suit** is Mr. Stewart.
The tall man **who has on the brown suit** is Mr. Stewart.

13 SINGLE WORDS and WORD GROUPS THAT MODIFY NOUNS

13a. Single-word modifiers of nouns ordinarily precede the noun modified.

the	books
my	books
some	books
good	books

13b. When a series of modifiers precedes a noun, the modifiers may be placed in the order illustrated in the following chart.

Articles, Demonstratives, Possessives, Indefinite Adjectives	Numerals	Descriptive (a) Quality or Characteristic	Descriptive (b) Size or Shape	Descriptive (c) Color	Other Nouns	NOUN
the	third				algebra	problem
the	first three [1]					chapters
these	four			brown		rocks
her	first					job
John's		surprising				attitude
the actor's [2]		classic				profile
my brother's [3]		new British				car
many		modern			redwood	houses
several			narrow	black	picture	frames

There is more flexibility in the position of descriptive adjectives than is shown by the chart. For example, we may say, "the dirty, narrow street" or "the narrow, dirty street." The order seems to depend upon whether we have in mind a dirty street that is narrow or a narrow street that is dirty.

---

[1] Numerals like **first** precede numerals like **three**.
[2] When an article and a possessive noun are both used, the article comes first.
[3] The possessive pronoun **my** modifies the possessive noun **brother's**.

Some notes on the types of modifiers in the chart are as follows:

(1) *Articles:* **a, an, the**

A (**an** before a vowel sound) or **the** is used before a singular countable noun (a noun that can be counted as a single unit). **A (an)** refers to an indefinite person or thing; **the** refers to or points out a definite person or thing. Compare:

> Please give me **a** pencil.
> Please give me **an** apple.
> Please give me **the** pencil on **the** table.

The is also used before plural nouns to point out specific persons or things.

> Please give me **the** pencils on the table.[4]

(2) *Demonstratives:* **this, that, these, those**

This and **that** are used before singular nouns; **these** and **those**, before plural nouns. **This** and **these** refer to objects that are close at hand from the point of view of the observer; **that** and **those**, to objects at a distance.

> **This** book belongs to me.
> **Those** books belong to my brother.

(3) *Possessives:* **my, his, their, John's,** etc.

The possessive does not change in form to agree with the noun modified: **his** sister, **his** sisters, **their** sister, **their** sisters.[5]

> **Mary's** coat is in **my** office.
> I met **her** cousin at the **mayor's** reception.
> We discussed **their** plans to establish **boys'** clubs here.

(4) *Indefinite adjectives:* **some, many, much,** etc.

Some indefinite adjectives are used with plural countable nouns and non-countable nouns to indicate *indefinite quantity.* (A non-countable noun refers to something which cannot be counted as a single unit or item, such as **sugar, music, information.**)

The indefinite adjectives in the following example are used with *plural countable nouns.*

> I have { **several** / **many** / **few** / **a few** } books on that subject.

Few means *not many;* **a few** means *some but not many.*

> He has **few** books.   (*not very many*)
> He has **a few** books.   (*some but not many*)

The indefinite adjectives in the following example are used with *non-countable nouns.*

> I have { **much** / **a great deal of** / **little** / **a little** } information on that subject.

Little means *not much;* **a little** means *some but not much.*

> He has **little** time.   (*not much*)
> He has **a little** time.   (*some but not much*)

---

[4] See Part XV for a detailed description of articles.

[5] A possessive does not always indicate actual ownership; it may show such relationships as measure, origin, source, or association.

> a **month's** salary   **life's** joys and sorrows

(Also see Section 87 for noun forms and Section 88 for pronoun forms.)

POSITION OF MODIFIERS OF NOUNS

The indefinite adjectives in the following examples are used with *both* plural countable nouns and non-countable nouns.

He has { **some** / **a lot of** / **enough** } pennies.   He has { **some** / **a lot of** / **enough** } money.

Some is used in affirmative statements only, but is used in both affirmative and negative questions.

> He wants **some** crackers.
> Do (Don't) you want **some** crackers?

Any and **no** are used with both plural countable nouns and non-countable nouns to express *absence of quantity*.

Any is used in negative statements.

> There aren't **any** sandwiches left.[6]
> There isn't **any** coffee left.

Any is used in both affirmative and negative questions.

> Are (Aren't) there **any** sandwiches left?
> Is (Isn't) there **any** coffee left?

No before a noun expresses negation. (**No** is not used before a noun in a statement or question which is already negative.)

> There are **no** sandwiches left.
> There is **no** coffee left.
> Are there **no** sandwiches left?
> Is there **no** coffee left?

The indefinite adjectives **much, many, little,** and **few** may be modified by **too** and **very.** (Also see Section 16j.)

> You are making **too much** noise.
> There are **too many** people here.
> We have **very little** time left.
> There were **very few** people here.

Other indefinite adjectives are listed in the chart below according to the types of nouns they may modify.

COUNTABLE NOUNS (singular)	COUNTABLE NOUNS (plural)	NON-COUNTABLE NOUNS
. . . . . .	**all** books	**all** ink *
. . . . . .	**more** books	**more** ink
. . . . . .	**most** books	**most** ink
. . . . . .	**fewer** books [7]	**less** ink
. . . . . .	**enough** books	**enough** ink
the **other** book [8]	**other** books	the **other** ink *
another book	. . . . . .	**another** ink *
each book	. . . . . .	**each** ink *
every book	. . . . . .	**every** ink *
either book	. . . . . .	**either** ink *
neither book	. . . . . .	**neither** ink *

All ink means **all kinds** (*types, brands, varieties*) **of ink; the other ink** means **the other kind** (*type, brand, variety*) **of ink.** The other constructions marked with an asterisk (*) convey similar meanings.

---

[6] In a construction of this kind, the indefinite article is ordinarily used with a singular countable noun.
> I don't want **a** sandwich.

When **any** is used before a singular countable noun, the meaning is *any at all*.
> I don't have **any** book (at all) on that subject.

[7] **Less,** instead of **fewer,** is frequently heard in spoken English, although some people consider this substitution unacceptable.

[8] When **other** is used with a singular countable noun, it is preceded by **the.**

(5) *Numerals:* **one, two,** etc.; **first, second,** etc.
One is used only with a singular countable noun; **two, three,** etc., with plural nouns.

He gave me **one** book and **two** magazines.

Numerals like **first, second,** etc., do not change in form to agree with the noun modified. The article **the** precedes the numeral.

We were **the first** people to arrive.
We will discuss **the third** chapter tomorrow.

(6) *Descriptive adjectives:* **new, tall, blue,** etc.

Descriptive adjectives do not agree with the noun modified; that is, the adjective is the same whether the noun is singular or plural, masculine or feminine.

She bought a **brown** hat to match her **brown** gloves.
He is a **tall** man, and she is a **tall** woman.

Descriptive adjectives modifying a *singular countable* noun *are preceded by* an article (**a, an, the**), a demonstrative (**this, that**), a possessive, an indefinite adjective, or the numeral **one.**

That charming woman is our hostess.
There is **one large room** for rent.
Their rich uncle gave them **a new car.**
Each new student must see an adviser.

Descriptive adjectives modifying a *plural* noun *may be preceded by* the article **the,** a demonstrative (**these, those**), a possessive, an indefinite adjective, or a numeral (except **one**).

These old buildings have narrow halls.
John's brown shoes cost ten dollars.
Our assignment consists of **several difficult problems.**

A descriptive adjective may be modified by **very.** (Also see Section 16j.)

Eric is a **very good** student.

(7) *Nouns that modify nouns:* **oak, paper,** etc.

Nouns that modify nouns, like descriptive adjectives, do not change to agree with the noun modified.

May I borrow your **history** book?
He collects **jazz** records.

Nouns that modify a *singular countable* noun *are preceded by* an article, a demonstrative, a possessive, an indefinite adjective, or the numeral **one.**

This oak door has **an iron key.**

Plural nouns modified by other nouns *may be preceded by* the article **the,** a demonstrative, a possessive, an indefinite adjective, or a numeral.

Here are **four paper napkins.**

14 | PHRASES and CLAUSES THAT MODIFY NOUNS

Phrases ordinarily follow the noun modified; clauses always follow the noun modified.

the lamp	on the table
the lamp	which is on the table

14a. Two types of phrases that function as modifiers of nouns are as follows:

(1) Phrases composed of a preposition (**on, in, to, of,** etc.) + noun, pronoun, or noun-equivalent:

POSITION OF MODIFIERS OF NOUNS

the box **on the desk**
the man **in the office**
the key **to the house**
the door **of the car** [9]

the work **before us**
the girl **with that woman**
the money **for the tickets**
a book **on mountain climbing**

(2) Phrases composed of a present participle (**ing-**form) + a noun or pronoun:

the man **driving the truck**
the person **buying books**

the professor **giving the lecture**
the child **watching television**

14b. A clause modifying a noun is usually introduced by a *relative pronoun:* **that, which, who, whom, whose.** (Most phrases in Section 14a can be expanded into clauses that modify nouns.)

(1) The relative pronouns **that, which, who**—as subject of the clause:

the box **that is on the desk**
the money **which is for the tickets**
the man **who is driving the truck**

That refers to either persons or things; **which** refers only to things; **who** refers only to persons.

(2) The relative pronouns **that, which, whom**—as object of the clause:

the vase **(that) you put on the table** [10]
the man **(that) you see in the office**
the money **(which) you gave me for the tickets**
the man **(whom) you saw driving the truck**

That refers to either persons or things; **which** refers only to things; **whom** refers only to persons.

(3) The relative pronoun **whose**—as modifier of the subject or the object of the clause:

the student **whose cousin is here**
the man **whose car you bought**
the newspaper **whose editor was fired**

Whose usually refers to persons, but may also refer to things.

14c. A phrase modifier may sometimes come between a clause modifier and the noun that the clause modifies.

The boy *in the blue sweater* **who is talking to the professor** is John's cousin.

(Assuming that more than one person is talking to the professor, the phrase **in the blue sweater** helps to identify the person. If the phrase were placed after the clause, it would then seem to identify the professor instead of the boy.)

---

[9] This phrase may also be expressed as **the car door.** (See Section 87b.)

[10] **That** is often omitted when it introduces a noun clause or is the object in a clause. **Which** and **whom**, functioning as objects in a clause, are also frequently omitted. We have included **that, which,** and **whom** in many sentences in this book to make it easier for students to see the structural relationships. However, in this section, the use of parentheses indicates that a **(that), (which),** or **(whom)** may be omitted.

EXERCISES FOR PART III

EXERCISE 10

Give responses to the following questions and requests.

    Example: What color is his new car?
                   His new car is dark green.

1. How many people are there in the room?

2. Is this morning's newspaper on the front steps?

3. Are you the one who knows my cousin?

4. Do you have a few minutes to talk to me?

5. Did the students who were here last night make a lot of noise?

6. Do you want a little sugar in your coffee?

7. Is the attractive woman sitting on the bench your aunt?

8. Do you live on the third or the fourth floor of the building?

9. Was there enough chocolate cake for everyone?

10. Is that distinguished, white-haired man talking to Dr. Kelly your mathematics professor?

11. Have you read the third chapter of your textbook?

12. Would you please carry these two heavy packages?

13. Do you mind if I select another book on the same subject?

14. Would you mind if I took a dozen copies of the conference report?

15. May I see some colored sport shirts, please?

16. Does she have an oval face or a round face?

17. Do those magazines on the table in the hall belong to you?

18. Do you have much money in your savings account?

Exercise 10 (continued)

19. Did you notice the well-dressed man who was here this morning?

20. Will the election take place on the first Tuesday in November?

21. Do most people who live in this area want lower taxes?

22. Are more foreign students enrolled in English classes this semester?

23. Was the door of the car badly damaged?

24. When does the opera season begin?

25. Where can you get tickets for the football game?

26. Where are the paper napkins that I bought this morning?

27. What do you think about the present world situation?

28. Why was the professor's lecture on modern art cancelled?

29. Mary's father is a famous architect, isn't he?

30. You are the man whose car was stolen, aren't you?

31. This is the second time that you have been here, isn't it?

32. I'd like some coffee. Wouldn't you?

33. I like the red dress in the window. Don't you?

34. I don't like historical novels. Do you?

35. That was an interesting picture that we saw last night, wasn't it?

36. Did you read every book that the professor assigned?

37. How do you get to the street that the post office is on?

38. When did you receive the telephone call from your friend in Miami?

39. Will you please bring me some stamps the next time that you go to the post office?

40. Is the woman in the green dress who is talking to the man in the brown suit the director of the museum?

Exercises for Part III

EXERCISE 11

Rewrite the following sentences, placing the adjective modifiers in parentheses in correct positions.

    Example: That book is mine. (on the table, French)
               That <u>French</u> book <u>on the table</u> is mine.

1. The table is on sale. (marble)

2. The man is a professor. (history, with the gray hair)

3. The lecture was very interesting. (evening, on life in Tibet)

4. The salesman sold a car to John. (used, who waited on you)

5. The girl is from Turkey. (who has on the green dress)

6. Jim has read books. (many, on photography)

7. The question was difficult. (examination, third)

8. The people enjoyed the concert. (few, who came)

9. Two knives are sharp. (steel, those, that are in the drawer)

10. There were clouds in the sky. (many, rain)

11. There isn't ink in my pen. (much, fountain)

12. Mr. Beck bought a suit yesterday. (gray, flannel)

13. The women wore evening dresses to the opera. (new, their)

14. Yesterday I met interesting people. (several, who work in television)

15. The men are army officers. (wearing the uniforms, Australian)

EXERCISE 12

Write sentences using the following words, phrases, and clauses as modifiers of nouns.

    Example: several
                Several people are here.

1. few

2. a few

3. little

4. a little

5. much

6. many

7. another

8. the other

9. on the blackboard

10. of my friend

11. talking to the professor

12. that we made

13. which you want

14. who left early

15. whom you saw

PART IV | Position of Modifiers of Verbs, Adverbs, and Adjectives

15 INTRODUCTION

As pointed out in Part I, modifiers of *adjectives* and *adverbs* are regularly placed *before* the word modified; modifiers of *verbs* are regularly placed *after* the verb and *after* the object, if any.[1] (There is some flexibility in the placement of modifiers of verbs. Variations, such as placement before the verb and at the beginning of the sentence, are mentioned in footnotes. It is suggested, however, that the student concentrate on the regular positions given in the main text before he tries to use the variations.)

16 SINGLE WORDS and EXPRESSIONS[2]

16a. Modifiers indicating *place* or *position* are regularly placed after the verb and after the object, if any.

He is { here. / there. / upstairs. / downstairs. / downtown. } He is { at home. / in the park. / up the street. / on the porch. / by the window. }

He went { out. / away. / in. / outside. } He walked { across the bridge. / towards the postoffice. / into the house. }

He moved { left. / right. / forward. / backward. } Hang your coat { over there. / up there. / on the hook.[3] }

16b. Modifiers indicating *manner* are regularly placed after the verb and after the object, if any.

He spoke { quietly. / loudly. / clearly. / hesitantly. / slowly. / rapidly. / poorly. } He worked { hard. / fast. / well. }

---

[1] It is important to remember that a modifier of a verb seldom separates the verb and object.
    He shut the door **quickly.** (NOT: He shut quickly the door.)

[2] The word "expressions" refers both to prepositional phrases, such as **to the store,** and to word groups, such as **over there.**

[3] Adverbs indicating place or direction are *not* placed before the verb. They are occasionally placed at the beginning of a sentence. In this position the word-order patterns are as follows:

  (a) *Adverb + (pro)noun + verb*   (b) *Adverb + verb + noun*
  There John stood.   **There** stood John.
  Away he went.   **Away** went John and Mary.
  Down we went.   **Down** went the people.
  Up we climbed.   **Over the door** was a sign.

He spoke { in a low voice.
with an accent. }

He walks { with effort.
like an actor. }

He went { by train.
by bus.
by car.
by ship.
on foot.[4] }

Adverbs with **-ly** endings (with a few exceptions such as **nicely, badly, poorly**) may also be placed *before* the verb. The adverb appears in this position particularly when there are other modifiers of the verb in the sentence or when the object has modifiers. Compare:

He walked **slowly.**
He **slowly** walked down the street with his son.
He answered the letter **promptly.**
He **promptly** answered the letter that I forwarded to him.

16c. Many single-word modifiers indicating *frequency* are regularly placed either after the verb and *after* the object, if any, or before the verb. Compare:

I write to her { often.
frequently.
rarely.
sometimes.
occasionally.
regularly.
daily.
weekly. }

I { often
frequently
rarely
sometimes
occasionally
regularly
daily
weekly } write to her.

He complained { continually.
repeatedly. }

He { continually
repeatedly } complained.[5]

The following adverbs are regularly placed *before* the principal verb: **always, usually, seldom, never, ever.**

He { always
usually
seldom
never } comes on time.

Ever is used only in negative statements, but is used in both affirmative and negative questions.

---

[4] Most of the modifiers indicating manner also appear at the beginning of a sentence, usually for emphasis.

Slowly he walked down the street.
Suddenly the door opened.
With effort he lifted the heavy box.

Hard, fast, well, nicely, badly, poorly are not placed before the subject, except in exclamations introduced by **how.**

How well she sang!
How nicely the child behaves!

[5] With constructions of auxiliary + principal verb, the adverb is usually placed before the principal verb, not before the auxiliary.

He has { often
rarely
never } asked me about you.

POSITION OF MODIFIERS OF VERBS, ADVERBS, AND ADJECTIVES

He doesn't **ever** come on time.
Does(n't) he **ever** come on time?

Single-word modifiers indicating frequency are regularly placed *after* the verb **be.**

He is { often / rarely / repeatedly / seldom / never } late to work.

Expressions indicating frequency are regularly placed *after* the verb and *after* the object, if any.

We see them { every day. / off and on. / now and then. / once in a while. / twice a day. / several times a month. / once a year.[6] }

16d. Single-word modifiers indicating *time*, such as **today, tonight, yesterday, tomorrow,** are regularly placed *after* the verb and *after* the object, if any.

He left { today. / tonight. / yesterday. }   He is going to leave { today. / tonight. / tomorrow. }

Expressions, such as **next week, a week ago, during the summer, for a month,** etc., are regularly placed *after* the verb and *after* the object, if any.

He left { this morning. / last week. / a week ago. / during the program. / at once. }   He is going to leave { this evening. / next week. / a week from now. / during the last act. / right away. }

The following single-word modifiers may be placed either *after* the verb and the object, if any, or *before* the principal verb: **soon, now, recently, immediately.** Compare:

---

[6] Modifiers indicating frequency sometimes appear at the beginning of a sentence, usually for emphasis.

Frequently
Sometimes } we write compositions in class.
Once in a while

When **seldom, never, rarely** are placed at the beginning of a sentence, the order of subject + verb is reversed.

Seldom is he in a bad mood.
Rarely does she give a bad performance.
Never have I heard of such a thing.

He will leave { now. / soon. / immediately. }   He will { now / soon / immediately } leave for the airport.[7]

I saw him **recently.**   I **recently** saw him at the club.

These modifiers are more likely to appear before the verb when the verb is followed by modifiers, as in "I **immediately** went **to the hospital.**"

Yet, lately, and **before** are regularly placed after the verb, but may occasionally appear before the principal verb. Compare:

I haven't seen him { yet. / lately. / before. }

He hasn't { yet / lately / before } realized the seriousness of the situation.

These modifiers are more likely to appear before the verb when there are other modifiers of the verb or when the object is followed by a modifier.

Already and **finally** are regularly placed before the principal verb, but may also be placed after the verb. Compare:

I have { finally / already } finished the book.   I have finished the book { finally. / already. }

The adverb **yet** is used only in negative statements; **already** and **finally,** only in affirmative statements.

I haven't seen him **yet.**
I have **already (finally)** seen him.

Yet and **already** are used in both affirmative and negative questions; **finally,** only in affirmative questions.

Have(n't) you seen him **yet (already)?**
Have you **finally** seen him?

Still is regularly placed before the principal verb.

He **still** works here.
He is **still** working here.

In negative statements **still** regularly precedes the auxiliary.

He **still** doesn't like it here.
He **still** hasn't finished the book.

All modifiers indicating time are regularly placed *after* the verb **be.**

---

[7] Modifiers that appear before the principal verb are sometimes placed before the auxiliary, usually for emphasis.

He **recently** has been doing better work.
You **immediately** will report to the director.

Many modifiers are also placed at the beginning of a sentence for emphasis.

Yesterday I went downtown to meet Mr. Harper.
Next week we plan to start a new project.
Recently we have been working hard.

In answering a question, the adverb is not ordinarily placed at the beginning of the sentence, although the adverb itself may constitute the answer.

When did you receive the telegram?
I received it **yesterday.**   *or*   **Yesterday.**
(NOT: Yesterday I received it.)

POSITION OF MODIFIERS OF VERBS, ADVERBS, AND ADJECTIVES

The meeting is **tonight.**
The party was **last week.**
That meeting will be **soon.**
She is **still** here.

Modifiers indicating time should agree logically with the time expressed by the verb. This means that certain modifiers are used with certain tenses only.

He **went** to town **yesterday.**   (past)
He **will go** to town **tomorrow.**   (future)
He **hasn't gone** to town **yet.**   (up to the present moment)

In some cases, the modifier is more important than the verb tense in establishing the time of an activity. In the following example, the tense form is the same, but the time expressed by the modifiers is different.

He is leaving { **now.**   (at the present time)
                tomorrow.   (in the future)

16e. When more than one modifier indicating *place, manner, frequency,* or *time* occurs in a sentence, the regular order *after* the verb and *after* the object, if any, is PLACE + MANNER + FREQUENCY + TIME.

	PLACE	MANNER	FREQUENCY	TIME
He is going	to Japan	by ship.		
The postman comes			twice a day	during December.
I saw them	at the game			last Saturday.
John went	to the library		every night	last week.
The King left	here	secretly		on Sunday.

However, when there is more than one modifier of the verb or when there is an object with modifiers, a single-word modifier indicating manner, frequency, or time is frequently placed *before* the principal verb.

He	secretly	burned the letters in the fireplace last night.
The Smiths	often	go to Florida in the winter.
John	recently	took a trip around the world.
Mr. Dall	quickly	opened the telegram on his desk.

16f. Modifiers indicating *agent* or *instrument* are regularly placed *after* the verb and *after* the object, if any.

This book was written { by a friend of mine.
                        by my history professor.
                        by Shakespeare.

He opened the can { with a knife.
                    with a can opener.

16g. Modifiers indicating *accompaniment* are regularly placed after the verb and the object, if any.

He went { with his uncle.
          with Maxine.
          with me.

16h. Expressions of *purpose* are regularly placed after the verb and the object, if any.

He came { for his book.
to get his book.
in order to get his book. }

He took a walk { for some exercise.
to get some exercise.
in order to get some exercise.[8] }

16i. Modifiers that express *affirmation, denial, possibility, doubt,* and so forth are regularly placed in the positions indicated in the following examples:

(1) At the beginning of a sentence:

Yes,
Perhaps
Maybe
Possibly } he will be here this afternoon.
Certainly
Surely
Indeed

No, he won't be here this afternoon.

(2) Before the principal verb or the auxiliary:

He will { surely / certainly / probably / possibly } be here today.   He { surely / certainly / probably / possibly } will be here today.

16j. The modifiers **very, too,** and **much too,** indicating *degree* or *intensity,* are regularly placed *before* the descriptive adjective (or adverb) modified.

The coffee is **very** hot.
He drives **too** fast.
He drives **much too** fast.

These modifiers are also used with the indefinite adjectives **much, many, little,** and **few** to indicate greater or lesser amount.

I don't have **very** much money.
You spend **much too** much time on small details
and **too** little time on important matters.

The modifier **enough** is regularly placed *after* the adjective or adverb modified.

This coffee is hot **enough** for me.
He doesn't work fast **enough.**

Too indicates more of a quality or quantity than is needed or desired for a certain purpose. The purpose is usually stated, but it may be implied.

This house is **too** small **for us.**
I don't think that is **too** small (for you).
That car is **too** old **to make the trip.**

---

[8] When the verb is followed by an object or modifiers, the expression **in order to . . .** is sometimes placed at the beginning of the sentence.

In order to get the information, I went to the library last night.

POSITION OF MODIFIERS OF VERBS, ADVERBS, AND ADJECTIVES

Very indicates a large amount or a high degree of a quality or quantity.

> She is **very** tired.
> It is raining **very** hard.

Enough indicates a sufficient amount of a quality or quantity for a certain purpose, either stated or implied.

> The day is warm **enough to go without a coat.**
> He works hard **enough** already.

The modifiers **very much, very little, too much,** and **enough** may modify verbs. The regular position is *after* the verb and *after* the object, if any.

> I like that hat **very much.**
> He laughs **very little.**
> She talks **too much.**
> You don't relax **enough.**

The following modifiers are regularly placed *before* the adjective, adverb, or principal verb modified: **almost, nearly, partly, simply, merely, scarcely, hardly.**

They are { almost / nearly } ready.   We are { almost / nearly } there.

He { almost / nearly / partly / simply / merely } finished his work.   He can { scarcely / hardly } walk.[9]

17 | CLAUSES

17a. Clauses that modify *verbs* regularly follow the main clause.

MAIN CLAUSE	MODIFYING CLAUSE
He put the sign	where everyone could see it.
I sing	when I am happy.
He hurried	because he was late.

Such clauses are introduced by *conjunctions* (**where, when,** etc.). Examples are as follows:

(1) Clauses indicating *place:*

WHERE: Shall we stop **where the road ends?**

> (where = at the place that)

WHEREVER: He will go **wherever you want to go.**

> (wherever = anywhere)

---

[9] The modifiers **only, just,** and **almost** should logically be placed before the word modified, but in actual usage they often appear before the verb.

(a) *Logical Position*   (b) *Frequent Variation*
The room can hold **only** ten people.   This room can **only** hold ten people.
We heard from him **just** yesterday.   We **just** heard from him yesterday.
I was **almost** late to class.   I **almost** was late to class.

(2) Clauses indicating *time:*

WHEN:	He telephoned me **when he received the message.**
	(**when** = at the time that)
WHENEVER:	He will come **whenever he can.**
	(**whenever** = anytime)
WHILE:	I saw him **while I was waiting for Helen.**
	(**while** = during the time that)
UNTIL:	I waited **until he arrived.**
	(**until** = up to the time that)
SINCE:	I haven't seen him **since he arrived.**
	(**since** = from the time that)
BEFORE:	We got there **before they did.**
AFTER:	They arrived **after we did.**

Clauses indicating *time* are frequently placed at the beginning of the sentence.

When she heard the news, she was pleased.
While they have been here, we have been very busy.

(3) Clauses indicating *reason:*

BECAUSE:	We decided to go home **because it was very late.**
	(**because** = for the reason that)
SINCE:	We didn't say anything **since we weren't certain of your plans.**
	(**since** = because)

Clauses indicating reason are frequently placed at the beginning of the sentence.

Because it is getting late, we had better go home.
Since I didn't know the answer, I kept quiet.

(4) Clauses indicating *purpose:*

SO THAT:	He works on Sundays **so that he can earn enough to pay his tuition.**
	(**so that** = in order that)

17b. Clauses that modify an *adjective* or an *adverb* in the main clause are constructed in special ways.

(1) Clauses indicating *frequency:*

AS + adverb of frequency + AS

He comes **as often as he can.**
They will call you **as frequently as they can.**

(2) Clauses indicating *degree:*

AS + $\left\{ \begin{array}{c} \text{adjective} \\ \text{adverb} \end{array} \right\}$ + AS

John is **as old as I am.**
(the same age)

You sing **as well as she does.**

$\left. \begin{array}{c} \text{adjective} \\ \text{adverb} \end{array} \right\}$ + THAN

POSITION OF MODIFIERS OF VERBS, ADVERBS, AND ADJECTIVES

John is **older than I am.**

(not the same age)

He solved the problem **more quickly than I did.**[10]

(3) Clauses indicating *result:*

SO + { adjective / adverb } + THAT

It is **so hot that I cannot work.**
They went **so far that they got lost.**

SO + { MANY / FEW } + plural countable noun + THAT

The professor gave us **so many assignments that we couldn't go to the concert.**
I have **so few opportunities to speak French that I'll never learn it.**

SO + { MUCH / LITTLE } + mass noun + THAT

There is **so much sugar in this coffee that I can't drink it.**
There is **so little time that we can't finish the work today.**

SUCH A + adjective + singular countable noun + THAT

It is **such a beautiful day that I feel like taking a walk.**

SUCH + adjective + { mass noun / plural countable noun } + THAT

It is **such nice weather that I hate to stay indoors.**
They are **such friendly people that everyone likes them.**

---

[10] Adjectives and adverbs in this construction are in the comparative form; that is, they either end in **-er** or are preceded by **more.** (See Part XX for an explanation of comparative forms and usage.)

EXERCISE 13

In the following sentences, place in **regular** positions the modifiers listed in parentheses. (In this exercise, do **not** place modifiers at the beginning of a sentence.)

    Example: He answers his correspondence on time . . .   (always)
             He **always** answers his correspondence on time.

1. He has read that book . . .   (already)

2. This book is interesting . . .   (extremely)

3. I haven't been there . . .   (before)

4. He is on time . . .   (seldom)

5. The elevator operates . . .   (automatically)

6. Mr. Larson will announce the results of the contest . . .   (soon)

7. The secretary opens the mail . . .   (never, before eight o'clock)

8. He has a bad cold in his chest . . .   (today, very)

9. We read the magazine . . .   (eagerly, every week)

10. He telephones me . . .   (always, in the morning)

11. He has worked . . .   (three weeks, at this store)

12. He doesn't travel . . .   (ever, by plane)

Exercise 13 (continued)

13. He arrives . . .   (on time, never, at the meeting)

14. She will return the book . . .   (next week, to the library)

15. I saw John . . .   (at the lecture, last night)

16. She planted tulips . . .   (yesterday, in the garden)

17. He has been . . .   (three times, today, here)

18. Mr. Cary takes his vacation . . .   (usually, in the winter)

19. They sit on the lawn . . .   (often, in the afternoon)

20. She went . . .   (yesterday morning, downtown)

21. Lloyd went to Chicago . . .   (last year, several times)

22. Mr. Evans goes home . . .   (for lunch, seldom)

23. He makes a report . . .   (daily, by telephone)

24. I will be there . . .   (certainly, by two o'clock)

25. He left the office . . .   (this afternoon, early)

Exercises for Part IV

EXERCISE 14

Complete the following sentences by placing the modifiers in parentheses in correct positions:

1. The speaker will be glad to talk with you . . .   (after he has given his lecture)

2. Mr. Neeley came immediately . . .   (here, when he heard the news)

3. He is in a hurry . . .   (always, because he never starts on time)

4. They have been to the museum . . .   (never, since they have been here)

5. George will take you . . .   (downtown, whenever you are ready)

6. The secretary didn't answer your letter . . .   (right away, because she was ill)

7. I waited for you . . .   (at the postoffice, as long as I could)

8. I see Mrs. Perkins . . .   (occasionally, while I am waiting for the bus)

9. Please wait here . . .   (for a few minutes, until Dr. Jones returns)

10. They will leave tomorrow . . .   (probably, before you do)

Exercise 14 (continued)

11. He came home . . .   (early, because he was tired)

12. It was so hot that she fainted . . .   (in the room)

13. I'll feel better after I have rested . . .   (much, a little while)

14. There were so many people that we had to stand . . .   (there, when we arrived)

15. I have been there . . .   (never, before)

16. He travels by air . . .   (always, when he goes East on business)

17. We waited . . .   (there, until they arrived)

18. We saw them . . .   (twice, while we were in Cleveland)

19. He is working now . . .   (hard, so that he can take a vacation soon)

20. Would you please leave my ticket . . .   (at the box office, so that I can pick it up)

Exercises for Part IV

EXERCISE 15

Complete the following sentences:

    Example: I was studying when you <u>telephoned me last night</u>.

1. We will meet you wherever you _____.

2. I missed the lecture because I _____.

3. I listened to the radio while John _____.

4. The lecture will not begin until Professor Allen _____.

5. Peter was eating breakfast when his cousin _____.

6. She goes to the symphony as often as she _____.

7. This lesson is longer than the one that _____.

8. He was so old that he _____.

9. It was such an interesting lecture that we _____.

10. There was so much noise that we _____.

11. I believe that you are as excited as I _____.

12. Would you please lend me your pen so that I _____.

13. They were such stimulating speakers that the audience _____.

14. What did you do when you _____?

15. Have you talked to Lois since she _____?

EXERCISE 16

The instructor will read each of the statements below, adding a conjunction (<u>when</u>, <u>because</u>, etc.). The student will then complete the sentence.

    <u>Example</u>: We were studying ....
              (The instructor might add <u>when</u>; the student might say "you telephoned last night.")

1. We went home early ....

2. They stayed there ....

3. We haven't heard from them ....

4. I received your letter ....

5. Mr. Matson went to Alabama ....

6. I'll take you ....

7. He finished the assignment ....

8. I missed the bus ....

9. I'm afraid to ride with him ....

10. We will meet you ....

11. They have studied hard all week ....

12. I saw my cousin ....

13. He told us so many amusing stories ....

14. I haven't seen Steve ....

15. We listened to the radio ....

16. She will call you ....

17. I had such a nice time ....

18. We listened to the radio ....

19. They will return to their country ....

20. He spends a lot of time in the lab ....

PART V — Patterns of Connected Statements

18 — INTRODUCTION

It is sometimes convenient to use connected statements in order to avoid a needless repetition of words or an elementary-sounding pattern of speech. Compare:

> I like to discuss politics. My cousin likes to discuss politics too.
> I like to discuss politics, and my cousin does too.

Three basic principles operate in determining the verb form in connected statements.

(1) When a simple present or simple past tense form of the verb **be** is used in the first statement, **am, is, are, was,** or **were** is used in the connected statement. (The verb agrees with the subject.)

> Walter **is** a scientist, and his brother **is** too.
> She **was** tired, and we **were** too.

(2) When a simple present or simple past tense form of a verb other than **be** is used in the first statement, **do (does)** or **did** is used in the connected statement. (The auxiliary agrees with the subject.)

> I **want** to go to the game, and they **do** too.
> They **left** early, and we **did** too.

(3) When a verb consisting of an auxiliary + principal verb is used in the first statement, the *auxiliary* is used in the connected statement. (The auxiliary agrees with the subject.)

> He **is studying** medicine, and she **is** too.
> Susan **has been** to Mexico, and I **have** too.

19 — CONNECTED AFFIRMATIVE STATEMENTS

(1) Affirmative Statement + **and** + Subject + Verb + **too**

	and		
John is a senior,	and	Bill is	too.
She plays tennis,	and	he does	too.
Robert went to Yale,	and	George did	too.
Ben is studying Chinese,	and	I am	too.
He can go with us,	and	they can	too.

(2) Affirmative Statement + **and** + **so** + Verb + Subject

	and	**so**	
Mr. Russell was there,	and	so	was Mr. Barr.
Ray likes to travel,	and	so	do I.
Mrs. Rich gave ten dollars,	and	so	did Mrs. King.
David has been in Turkey,	and	so	has Mike.
I should study,	and	so	should you.

51

20 CONNECTED NEGATIVE STATEMENTS

(1) Negative Statement + **and** + Subject + Verb + **not** + **either**

Dick wasn't here today,	**and**	Tony was**n't**	**either.**
I don't like tea,	and	he doesn't	either.
She can't go,	and	he can't	either.
Laura won't be there,	and	Walter won't	either.

(2) Negative Statement + **and** + **neither** + Verb + Subject

My answer isn't correct,	**and**	**neither**	is yours.
I didn't see her,	and	neither	did he.
John won't sing,	and	neither	will Charles.
I do not have to go,	and	neither	do you.

21 CONNECTED AFFIRMATIVE and NEGATIVE STATEMENTS

(1) Affirmative Statement + **but** + Subject + Verb + **not**

Margaret was there,	**but**	Jane was**n't.**
They went home,	but	we didn't.
Wayne will help us,	but	Edmond won't.

(2) Negative Statement + **but** + Subject + Verb

Margaret wasn't there,	**but**	Jane was.
They didn't go home,	but	we did.
Wayne won't help us,	but	Edmond will.

22 SUMMARY of CONNECTED STATEMENTS

Section	FIRST STATEMENT	SECOND STATEMENT
19	*Affirmative*	*Affirmative*
(1)	Mary speaks Russian,	**and** John does **too**.
	He can swim,	**and** she can **too**.
		or
(2)	Mary speaks Russian,	**and so** does John.
	He can swim,	**and so** can she.
20	*Negative*	*Negative*
(1)	Mary does**n't** speak Russian.	**and** John does**n't either.**
	He ca**n't** swim,	**and** she ca**n't either.**
		or
(2)	Mary does**n't** speak Russian,	**and neither** does John.
	He ca**n't** swim,	**and neither** can she.
21	*Affirmative*	*Negative*
(1)	Mary speaks Russian,	**but** John does**n't**.
	He can swim,	**but** she ca**n't**.
	Negative	*Affirmative*
(2)	Mary does**n't** speak Russian,	**but** John does.
	He ca**n't** swim,	**but** she can.

EXERCISE 17

Make connected statements out of the following pairs of statements. (Refer to Section 19.)

　　Example: Jane is from Canada. Betty is from Canada too.
　　　　(a) Jane is from Canada, and Betty is too.
　　　　(b) Jane is from Canada, and so is Betty.

1. The train was late. The bus was late too.

   (a)

   (b)

2. Paul bought a new tie. Bob bought a new tie too.

   (a)

   (b)

3. I took chemistry last semester. Herbert took chemistry last semester too.

   (a)

   (b)

4. Janet will make a speech tomorrow. Joseph will make a speech tomorrow too.

   (a)

   (b)

5. Ralph has been to Pakistan. Sam has been to Pakistan too.

   (a)

   (b)

6. Leonard is studying engineering. Edward is studying engineering too.

   (a)

   (b)

EXERCISE 18

Make connected statements out of the following pairs of statements. (Refer to Section 20.)

    Example: Don doesn't swim. Jack doesn't swim either.
              (a) Don doesn't swim, and Jack doesn't either.
              (b) Don doesn't swim, and neither does Jack.

1. This necklace wasn't expensive. This bracelet wasn't expensive either.

   (a)

   (b)

2. I don't hear anything. Gerry doesn't hear anything either.

   (a)

   (b)

3. Carl didn't take the quiz on Friday. I didn't take the quiz on Friday either.

   (a)

   (b)

4. The Smiths won't be at the reception. The Bakers won't be at the reception either.

   (a)

   (b)

5. I can't drive a car. Celia can't drive a car either.

   (a)

   (b)

6. We aren't going to the meeting tonight. They aren't going to the meeting tonight either.

   (a)

   (b)

Exercises for Part V

EXERCISE 19

Make connected statements out of the following pairs of statements. (Refer to Section 21.)

> Example (a): Ann smokes. Margaret doesn't smoke.
> Ann smokes, but Margaret doesn't.

1. The train usually leaves on time. The bus doesn't usually leave on time.

2. Ingrid passed the examination. Pierre didn't pass the examination.

3. Beverly can sing well. Nancy can't sing well.

4. This problem is difficult. That problem isn't difficult.

5. Bill has a summer job. Roy doesn't have a summer job.

> Example (b): Ashley doesn't belong to a fraternity. Jim belongs to a fraternity.
> Ashley doesn't belong to a fraternity, but Jim does.

1. Mrs. Butterfield isn't a good cook. Her husband is a good cook.

2. Ricardo doesn't go to nightclubs often. Hugo goes to nightclubs often.

3. I haven't seen that movie. Ruth has seen that movie.

4. That book wasn't interesting. This book was interesting.

5. Fred didn't go to the conference. Guy went to the conference.

EXERCISE 20

Complete the following sentences:

> Example: I like ice cream, and so <u>does he</u>.

1. This milk tastes sour, but that milk _____.

2. I smell smoke, and so _____.

3. I don't understand the question, and neither _____.

4. Tony is looking at the map, and Miriam _____.

5. Mr. Geiger didn't call today, but Mr. Wolf _____.

6. Mrs. Lee won't tell her age, and Miss Young _____.

7. I should study much harder, and so _____.

8. I have never met Mrs. March, but Ben and Louise _____.

9. Professor Smart isn't teaching this semester, and neither _____.

10. My father doesn't have much money, but my uncle _____.

11. Dick likes pretty girls, and so _____.

12. We didn't get there on time, and neither _____.

13. This pen is broken, but that pen _____.

14. His jokes are always funny, and so _____.

15. This sweater isn't clean, but that sweater _____.

UNIT 2 | VERBS

PART VI | Principal Parts and Tense Forms[1]

23 INTRODUCTION

The principal parts of a verb used in the formation of the simple present and simple past tenses and of the future, progressive, and perfect tense phrases are the *simple form*, the *past form*, the *past participle*, and the *present participle*.

> walk = simple form (infinitive without **to**)
> walked = past form
> walked = past participle
> walking = present participle (**ing**-form)

24 THE SIMPLE PRESENT TENSE

The simple present tense of all verbs except **be** is based on the *simple form*. The present tense form of all verbs (except **be**) *is* the simple form for all persons except the third person singular.

SEE:	I see	we see
	you see	you see
	he, she, it **sees**	they see
PASS:	I pass	we pass
	you pass	you pass
	he, she, it **passes**	they pass
BE:	I am	we are
	you are	you are
	he, she, it is	they are

The third person singular of almost all verbs is made by adding **s** or **es** to the simple form.

(1) The ending **es** is added in the following cases:

(a) To a simple form ending in the letters **ch, s, sh, x,** or **z:**

> pass passes catch catches
> push pushes tax taxes

(b) To a simple form ending in **y**, preceded by a consonant (after changing **y** to **i**):

> study studies worry worries
> try tries cry cries

(c) To **do** and **go:**

> do does go goes

---

[1] The principal parts of verbs and tense forms are given in Part VI. The uses of the various tenses are explained in Parts VII, VIII, and IX. Part VI may be studied separately or in conjunction with Parts VII, VIII, and IX as the uses of the tenses are taken up.

(2) The ending **s** is added to the simple form of all other verbs (except **have**):

see	sees	like	likes
get	gets	buy	buys

BUT: have **has**

Some notes on the pronunciation of the third person singular of the simple present are as follows:

(1) The ending is pronounced as a separate syllable [ɪz] or [əz] when the simple form ends in a sibilant sound /s/, /z/, /ʃ/, /ʒ/, /tʃ/, or /dʒ/.[2]

pass	(final sound s)	passes
rise	(final sound z)	rises
push	(final sound ʃ)	pushes
rouge	(final sound ʒ)	rouges
catch	(final sound tʃ)	catches
pledge	(final sound dʒ)	pledges

} ending = [ɪz] or [əz]

(2) The ending is pronounced /s/ when the simple form ends in a voiceless consonant sound[3] (other than a sibilant sound).

ask	(final sound k)	asks
beat	(final sound t)	beats
hope	(final sound p)	hopes

} ending = /s/

(3) The ending is pronounced /z/ when the simple form ends in a vowel or a voiced consonant sound[4] (other than a sibilant sound).

lean	(final sound n)	leans
see	(final sound i)	sees
go	(final sound o)	goes

} ending = /z/

(4) The vowel sounds change in the third person singular of **do** and **say**. The vowel in **do** is the same as in **you**; the vowel in **does** is the same as in **buzz**. The vowel in **say** is the same as in **day**; the vowel in **says** is the same as in **sets**.

---

[2] The symbols representing *sounds* are from the International Phonetic Alphabet (IPA). Since English is not a phonetic language (that is, letters and sounds are not always the same), spelling should not be confused with pronunciation. (See the Appendix, page 250, for a list of symbols for American-English sounds. IPA symbols, as well as symbols from two standard dictionaries, are given.)

[3] The *voiceless consonant sounds* are as follows:

/ tʃ / as in catch	/ p / as in hope
/ f / as in laugh	/ s / as in pass
/ h / as in hat	/ ʃ / as in wish
/ hw / as in why	/ t / as in let
/ k / as in pick	/ θ / as in bath

English words do not end in the sounds / h / or / hw /.

[4] The *voiced consonant sounds* are as follows:

/ b / as in rob	/ r / as in wear
/ d / as in ride	/ ð / as in bathe
/ g / as in beg	/ v / as in give
/ dʒ / as in judge	/ w / as in we
/ l / as in sell	/ j / as in you
/ m / as in hum	/ z / as in rise
/ n / as in run	/ ʒ / as in rouge
/ ŋ / as in sing	

English words do not end in the sounds /w/ or /j/.

25 THE SIMPLE PAST TENSE

The simple past tense is the same as the *past form* of a verb. The form is the same for all persons, singular and plural. **Be** is an exception.

WANT:	I wanted		we wanted
		you wanted	
	he wanted		they wanted
SING:	I sang		we sang
		you sang	
	he sang		they sang
BE:	I was		we were
		you were	
	he was		they were

The past form of all regular verbs is made by adding **d** or **ed** (occasionally **t**) to the simple form of the verb.

(1) The ending **d** is added when the simple form ends in **e** or **ee**.

hope	hope**d**
free	free**d**
agree	agree**d**
raise	raise**d**

(2) The ending **ed** is added to all other verbs. The following changes in spelling occur:

(a) Final **y,** preceded by a consonant, is changed to **i** before adding **ed**.

study	stud**ied**
cry	cr**ied**
try	tr**ied**
empty	empt**ied**

(b) A final consonant letter (except **h, w, x, y**), preceded by a single vowel letter, is doubled in words of one syllable.

beg	beg**ged**
stop	stop**ped**
BUT: tax (ends in **x**)	tax**ed**

(c) A final consonant letter (except **h, w, x, y**), preceded by a single vowel letter, is doubled in words accented on the last syllable.

permit	permit**ted**
occur	occur**red**
BUT: attempt (*ends in three consonant letters*)	attempt**ed**
gather (*accent on first syllable*)	gather**ed**

(3) Occasionally **t** is added to the simple form. An example is **mean — meant.**

The past forms of *irregular* verbs are given in Section 29.

Some notes on the pronunciation of the past tense forms of *regular* verbs are as follows:

(1) The ending is pronounced as a separate syllable [ɪd] or [əd] when the simple form ends in a /t/ or /d/ sound.

heat, hate } (final sound **t**) heat**ed**, hat**ed** } ending = [ɪd] or [əd]
add, decide } (final sound **d**) add**ed**, decid**ed**

(2) The ending is pronounced /d/ when the simple form ends in a voiced sound (other than /d/).

show	(final sound **o**)	show**ed**
rob	(final sound **b**)	rob**bed**
lean	(final sound **n**)	lean**ed**
raise	(final sound **z**)	rais**ed**

ending = /d/

(3) The ending is pronounced /t/ when the simple form ends in a voiceless sound (other than /t/).

laugh	(final sound **f**)	laugh**ed**
talk	(final sound **k**)	talk**ed**
stop	(final sound **p**)	stop**ped**
push	(final sound ʃ)	push**ed**

ending = /t/

26 THE FUTURE TENSE

What is generally called the *future tense* is a verb phrase composed of the auxiliary **will** (sometimes **shall**)[5] + the *simple form.*

I will go   we will go
you will go
he will go   they will go

The verb phrase **be going to** + the *simple form* is an equally important construction and may be considered an equivalent to the future tense.

I am going to go   we are going to go
you are going to go
he is going to go   they are going to go

The verb phrase **be to** + the *simple form* may also be considered equivalent to the future tense.

I **am to see** her tomorrow.
He **is to leave** next week.
They **are to meet** on Friday.

27 THE PERFECT TENSES

What are generally called the *perfect tenses* are verb phrases composed of forms of the auxiliary **have** + the *past participle* of the principal verb.

I **have seen**
he **had worked**

The past participle of all regular verbs is the same as the *past form*; the past participles of irregular verbs are listed in Section 29.

The perfect tense phrases are as follows:

---

[5] **Will** is used today for all persons except in questions. (See Section 35b for the use of **shall** and **will** in questions.) It is traditionally correct, however, to use **shall** with the first person (**I, we**) and **will** with the second and third persons (**you, he, she, it, they**) to express simple futurity. In expressions showing determination, it is traditionally correct to use **will** with the first person and **shall** with the second and third persons.

(1) *The present perfect:* **have (has)** + past participle

    I have talked   we have talked
     you have talked
    he **has** talked   they have talked

(2) *The past perfect:* **had** + past participle

    I had worked   we had worked
     you had worked
    he had worked   they had worked

(3) *The future perfect:* **will have** + past participle

    I will have lived   we will have lived
     you will have lived
    he will have lived   they will have lived

28   THE PROGRESSIVE TENSES

What are generally called the *progressive tenses* are verb phrases composed of forms of the auxiliary **be** + the *present participle* (**ing-**form) of the principal verb.

  I **am** study**ing**
  he **was** study**ing**

The present participle of both regular and irregular verbs is formed by adding **ing** to the simple form of the verb.

    want want**ing**   see see**ing**
    ask   ask**ing**   buy buy**ing**

The following changes in spelling occur when adding **ing** to the simple form of the verb:

(1)   A final **e** that is not pronounced is dropped.

    write writ**ing**
    take   tak**ing**
    argue argu**ing**

    BUT: A final **ee** is retained.

      free free**ing**
      agree agree**ing**

(2)   A final consonant letter (except **h, w, x, y**), preceded by a single vowel letter, is doubled in words of one syllable.

    beg beg**ging**
    stop stop**ping**

    BUT: fix (*ends in* **x**) fix**ing**
      greet (*two vowel letters before consonant*) greet**ing**

(3)   A final consonant letter (except **h, w, x, y**), preceded by a single vowel letter, is doubled in words accented on the last syllable.

    begin begin**ning**
    permit permit**ting**

    BUT: suffer (accent on first syllable) suffer**ing**

(4)   A few verbs end in **ie**. The **ie** in some of these verbs changes to **y** when the **ing** ending is added.

    die dy**ing**   tie ty**ing** or tie**ing**
    lie ly**ing**   hie hy**ing** or hie**ing**

The **ing** ending of all present participles is pronounced as a separate syllable [ɪŋ]. The progressive tense phrases are as follows:

(1) *The present progressive:* **am (is, are)** + present participle

> I am waiting   we are waiting
> you are waiting
> he is waiting   they are waiting

(2) *The past progressive:* **was (were)** + present participle

> I was working   we were working
> you were working
> he was working   they were working

(3) *The future progressive:* **will be** + present participle

> I will be working
> he will be working
>   *etc.*

(4) *The present perfect progressive:* **have (has) been** + present participle

> I have been working
> he has been working
>   *etc.*

(5) *The past perfect progressive:* **had been** + present participle

> I had been working
> he had been working
>   *etc.*

(6) *The future perfect progressive:* **will have been** + present participle

> I will have been working
> he will have been working
>   *etc.*

29 | IRREGULAR VERB FORMS

29a. The following verbs have the same form for three parts:

SIMPLE FORM	PAST FORM	PAST PARTICIPLE
bet	bet	bet
broadcast	broadcast	broadcast
burst	burst	burst
cost	cost	cost
cut	cut	cut
hit	hit	hit
hurt	hurt	hurt
let	let	let
put	put	put
quit	quit	quit
set	set	set
shut	shut	shut

29b. The *simple form* and the *past form* of **beat** are the same, but the past participle is different:

beat	beat	**beaten** (sometimes **beat**)

29c. The *simple form* and the *past participle* of the following verbs are the same, but the past form is different:

SIMPLE FORM	PAST FORM	PAST PARTICIPLE
become	**became**	become
come	**came**	come
run	**ran**	run

PRINCIPAL PARTS AND TENSE FORMS

29d. The *past form* and the *past participle* of the following verbs are the same:

SIMPLE FORM	PAST FORM and PAST PARTICIPLE	SIMPLE FORM	PAST FORM and PAST PARTICIPLE
bring	brought	lose	lost
build	built	make	made
buy	bought	meet	met
catch	caught	pay	paid
dig	dug	read (pronounced [rid])	read (pronounced [rɛd])
feed	fed	say	said
feel	felt	sell	sold
fight	fought	send	sent
find	found	shoot	shot
get	got (also **gotten** for past participle)	sit	sat
hang	hung	sleep	slept
have	had	spend	spent
hear	heard	stand	stood
hold	held	teach	taught
keep	kept	tell	told
lay	laid	think	thought
lead	led	understand	understood
leave	left	win	won
lend	lent		

29e. The simple form, the past form, and the past participle of the following verbs are different:

SIMPLE FORM	PAST FORM	PAST PARTICIPLE	SIMPLE FORM	PAST FORM	PAST PARTICIPLE
arise	arose	arisen	know	knew	known
be	was	been	lie (to recline)	lay	lain
bear	bore	borne (born)[6]	ride	rode	ridden
begin	began	begun	ring	rang	rung
bite	bit	bitten (also **bit**)	rise	rose	risen
blow	blew	blown	see	saw	seen
break	broke	broken	shake	shook	shaken
choose	chose	chosen	show	showed	shown (also **showed**)
do	did	done	sing	sang	sung
draw	drew	drawn	sink	sank	sunk
drink	drank	drunk	speak	spoke	spoken
drive	drove	driven	steal	stole	stolen
eat	ate	eaten	strive	strove	striven
fall	fell	fallen	swear	swore	sworn
fly	flew	flown	swim	swam	swum
forget	forgot	forgotten	take	took	taken
forsake	forsook	forsaken	tear	tore	torn
freeze	froze	frozen	throw	threw	thrown
give	gave	given	wear	wore	worn
go	went	gone	weave	wove	woven (also **weaved**)
grow	grew	grown	write	wrote	written
hide	hid	hidden			

---

[6] **Borne** is the active form; **born**, the passive.
    She **has borne** seven children.
    He **was born** in Hong Kong.

EXERCISES FOR PART VI

EXERCISE 21

Read the following sentences. Change the verbs from the simple present to the simple past. (For practice in spelling, also write the forms in the spaces at the right.)

    Example: He <u>is</u> here.   was
             (Read: He <u>was</u> here.)

1. The child <u>wants</u> a drink of water.   _hoped_

2. We <u>hope</u> to see her again.   _____

3. Robert always <u>tries</u> hard.   _permitted_

4. He <u>permits</u> us to smoke in the classroom.   _came_

5. They <u>come</u> here often.   _brought_

6. He often <u>brings</u> flowers to her.   _____

7. Mr. Connor often <u>loses</u> his keys.   _____

8. You <u>pay</u> too much rent.   _____

9. He <u>makes</u> furniture as a hobby.   _____

10. They <u>sell</u> dictionaries.   _____

11. I <u>think</u> that <u>is</u> a good idea.   _____

12. I <u>am</u> surprised at you!   _____

13. He always <u>begins</u> his lectures with a joke.   _____

14. Walter <u>drives</u> much too fast.   _____

15. He <u>likes</u> botany.   _____

16. She <u>does</u> her shopping on Saturday.   _____

17. He always <u>knows</u> the right answers.   _____

18. We <u>see</u> them off and on.   _____

19. She <u>speaks</u> with an accent.   _____

20. He <u>writes</u> detective stories.   _____

EXERCISE 22

Read the following sentences, giving the past participle of the verb in parentheses. (For practice in spelling, also write the forms in the spaces at the right.)

    Example: I have always (like) opera.   liked
                 (Read: I have always <u>liked</u> opera.)

1. Mr. Weeks has (give) a large sum of money to the school.

2. They have (study) here for three years.

3. We have (beg) them to come here.

4. I have (bet) him that our team will win the game.

5. Marjorie has (become) quite interested in the idea.

6. They have recently (buy) a new house.

7. The train has always (leave) on time.

8. I have never (hear) that story before.

9. They have (make) some good suggestions.

10. He has never (pay) his rent on time.

11. Have you (send) the package yet?

12. How long had he (sit) there?

13. Had he (stand) there long?

14. Had anyone (tell) you that before?

15. Professor Clay has (teach) Greek for many years.

16. They have (be) here since 1954.

17. Have you (do) the assignment yet?

18. She hasn't (wear) her new dress yet.

19. I still haven't (see) Jim today.

20. Mr. Hall has (write) several books.

Exercises for Part VI

EXERCISE 23

Read the following sentences, giving the present participle of the verb in parentheses. (For practice in spelling, also write the forms in the spaces at the right.)

    Example: She is (wait) for you.   waiting
               (Read: She is <u>waiting</u> for you.)

1. He is (work) his way through college.   _____

2. I am (freeze).   _____

3. It is (begin) to rain.   _____

4. I am (take) zoology this semester.   _____

5. Richard is (write) his second novel.   _____

6. The students were (argue) with the professor.   _____

7. A car is (stop) in front of the house.   _____

8. Alfred was (fix) the broken chair.   _____

9. The plant is (die) from lack of water.   _____

10. I have been (try) to reach you all day.   _____

11. The paper is (lie) on my desk.   _____

12. The children were (play) in the yard.   _____

13. We have been (make) plans for the party.   _____

14. I'll be (see) you tomorrow.   _____

15. They have been (save) money for their vacation.   _____

16. Several people are (sit) in the lobby.   _____

17. I haven't been (sleep) well lately.   _____

18. He has been (put) the mail in this box.   _____

19. Mr. Allen has been (ride) to work with Mr. Jones.   _____

20. They are (eat) dinner now.   _____

EXERCISE 24

Read the following sentences, first giving the simple present tense of the verb in parentheses; second, the simple past; third, the future tense phrase <u>will</u> + simple form; fourth, the future tense phrase <u>be going to</u> + simple form.

    <u>Example</u>: Professor Ball (teach) French.
              Read: (1) Professor Ball <u>teaches</u> French.
                     (2) Professor Ball <u>taught</u> French.
                     (3) Professor Ball <u>will teach</u> French.
                     (4) Professor Ball <u>is going to teach</u> French.

1. Margaret (like) that book.

2. We (sing) that song frequently.

3. I (drive) to work.

4. They (live) here.

5. He (work) eight hours a day.

6. Robert (try) to make good grades.

7. George (play) the piano.

8. She (do) her homework in the afternoon.

9. He (say) nothing about his plans.

10. Jack (go) fishing often.

11. The employees (get) a raise every year.

12. He (leave) early every day.

13. The soldier (stand) in front of the building all day.

14. We (think) about you often.

15. He (write) a letter to his family every week.

PART VII | Usage of Tenses

30 | INTRODUCTION

Before studying the parts on verb tenses, the student should make certain that he does not confuse the terms *tense* and *time*. *Tense* refers to the form of the verb used; for example, he **goes** (simple present), he **went** (simple past), he **has gone** (present perfect), etc. *Time* is not a grammatical structure; time is a concept that exists in the mind of the speaker.

Tense (or verb form) and time do not necessarily correspond, as is shown by the uses of the simple present tense in the following sentences:

(1) I **feel** a draft.
(2) He **leaves** for Europe next Saturday.
(3) He **walks** to work every day.
(4) Water **boils** at 212° Fahrenheit at sea level.

In sentence (1) the verb **feel** indicates a perception in *immediate present time;* in (2) the verb **leaves,** with the help of the adverb **next Saturday,** indicates activity to take place in *future time;* in (3) the verb **walks,** with the help of the adverb **every day,** indicates activity that has occurred at intervals in *past time up to the present* and that will probably continue to occur at intervals in the future; in (4) the verb **boils** indicates a condition that might be said to exist for *all time,* past, present, and future.

Some of the uses of the various tenses are described in Parts VII, VIII, and IX. Since the time of the activity, condition, feeling, situation, and so forth, is established from the point of view of the person speaking, the *moment of speaking* is used as the focal point in the explanations and in the diagrams illustrating the uses of the tenses. (Some examples are given in the form of answers to questions, providing the opportunity for additional practice in mastering patterns of statements and questions.)

31 | USES of the SIMPLE PRESENT TENSE

31a. In the following examples, the simple present expresses perceptions, feelings, or states[1] that occur or exist *at the moment of speaking.* The perceptions, feelings, or states may, of course, extend somewhat beyond the moment of speaking, but the focal point is the immediate present.

QUESTION	ANSWER
How many planes do you see?	I **see** four.
Do you hear anything?	No, I **don't hear** anything.
What's the matter?	I **smell** something burning.

---

[1] The terms *feelings, perceptions, states, conditions, activities,* etc., are used only to suggest situations expressed by verbs. The terms do not describe all situations expressed by verbs, nor is an attempt made to describe each situation exactly.

72 VERBS

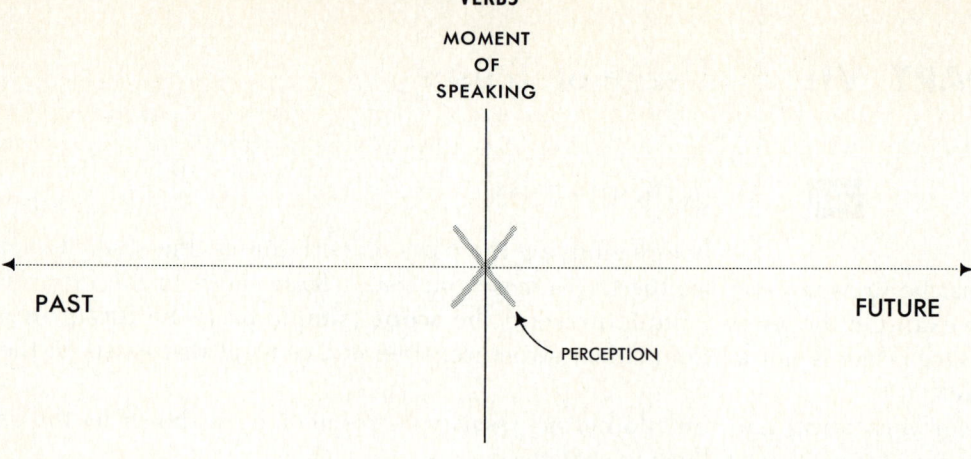

FIGURE 1

In this diagram and in the others that follow, the *moment of speaking,* indicated by the line drawn through the center of the time line, is roughly approximate to the *immediate present.* The extension of time into the past and into the future, indicated by dotted lines, includes what is called the *general present.* No attempt is made to put boundaries on periods of time: the line is intended to represent a continuum against which actions, conditions, and so forth may be indicated. The activity of the tense represented in each diagram is shown by the gray symbol.

Other examples:
This medicine **tastes** bitter to me.
Your hand **feels** cold.
This answer **seems** correct.
You **look** worried.
I'**m** hungry.
I **want** a cup of coffee.

31b. In the following examples, the simple present expresses activities (states, conditions, feelings, etc.) that *extend* for varying lengths of time beyond the moment of speaking. The activities have existed before, and will probably continue to exist after, the moment of speaking; but the beginning and the ending are unknown or unimportant.

QUESTION	ANSWER
Does your brother play the violin?	Yes, he **plays** very well.
Do you agree with me?	Yes, I **agree** with you completely.
What does Professor White teach?	He **teaches** zoology.

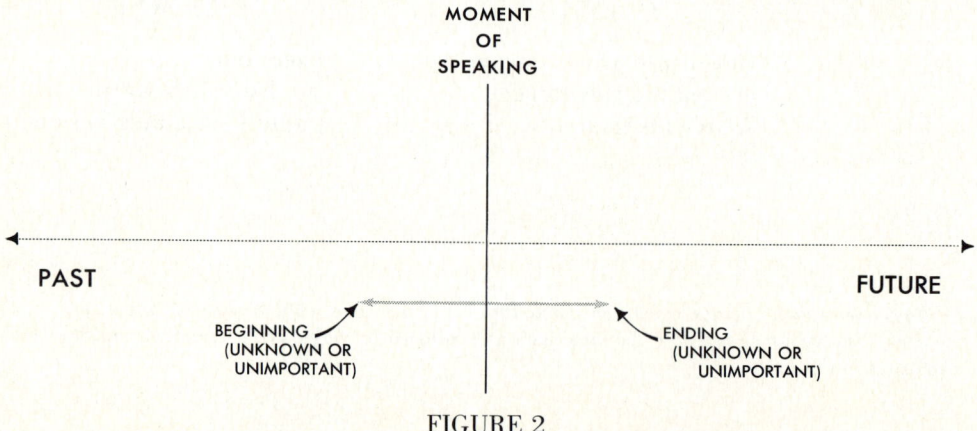

FIGURE 2

USAGE OF TENSES

Other examples:

Charles **prefers** classical music.
They **like** Japanese poetry.
People everywhere **want** peace.
He **dislikes** talkative women.
She **misses** her family very much.
She **is** an excellent secretary.

He **knows** many people in India.
We **have** many interests in common.
He **believes** that taxes are too high.
We **have** faith in you.
Few people **understand** the theory of relativity.

31c. In the following examples, the simple present expresses activities[2] which *have occurred* at intervals before, and will probably *continue* to occur at intervals after, the moment of speaking. Adverbs of frequency (**every day, usually,** etc.) often help the verb in expressing intervals of activity.

QUESTION	ANSWER
Does Steve go home often?	Yes, he **goes** home every week-end.
When do you play golf?	I **play** almost every Sunday morning.
Do you walk to school every day?	No, I **take** the bus.

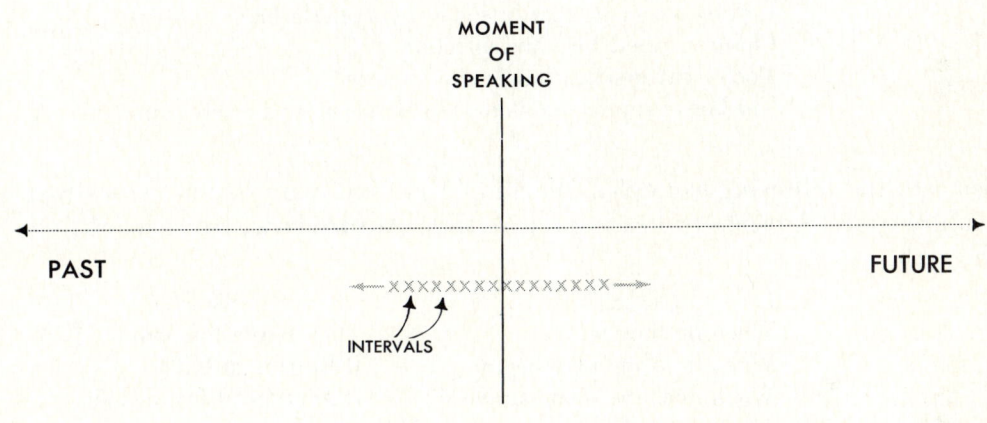

FIGURE 3

Other examples:

Maria **goes** to church every morning.
Mr. Smith **broadcasts** every Sunday.
Mrs. Rich usually **pays** her bills on time.
They seldom **go** to the movies.
I often **hear** my neighbors arguing.

31d. In the following examples, the simple present expresses activities that are relatively permanent. (Some of the statements are general truths.)

QUESTION	ANSWER
Where is Chicago?	It **is** in Illinois.
What is the freezing point of water?	Water **freezes** at 32° Fahrenheit.
What is the function of the liver?	It **secretes** bile and **performs** metabolic functions.

---

[2] In the explanations of the uses of the tenses that follow in this part and in Parts VIII and IX, the term *activities* will be used to stand for all situations (states, conditions, feelings, etc.) expressed by verbs.

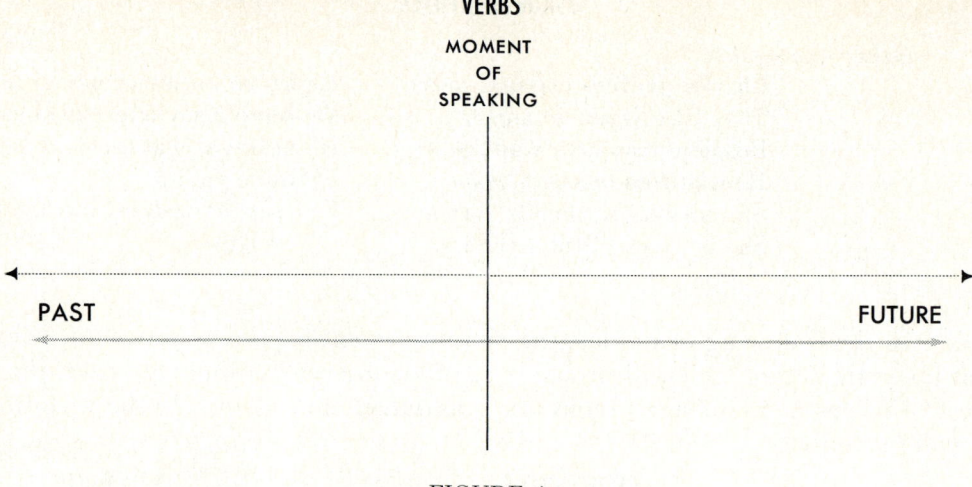

FIGURE 4

Other examples:
    The sun **rises** in the east.
    The earth **revolves** around the sun.
    It **snows** a great deal in some parts of Alaska.
    Children **need** love and affection.
    Poetry **intensifies** man's experiences.
    The law of supply and demand **sets** prices in a freely competitive market.

31e. In the following examples, the simple present expresses activities that will take place in future time. Adverbs indicating future time (**tomorrow, next week,** etc.) usually modify the verb.

QUESTION	ANSWER
When do they leave?	They **leave** tomorrow.
When does the play begin?	It **begins** at 8:30.
When does the plane arrive?	It **arrives** at five o'clock.

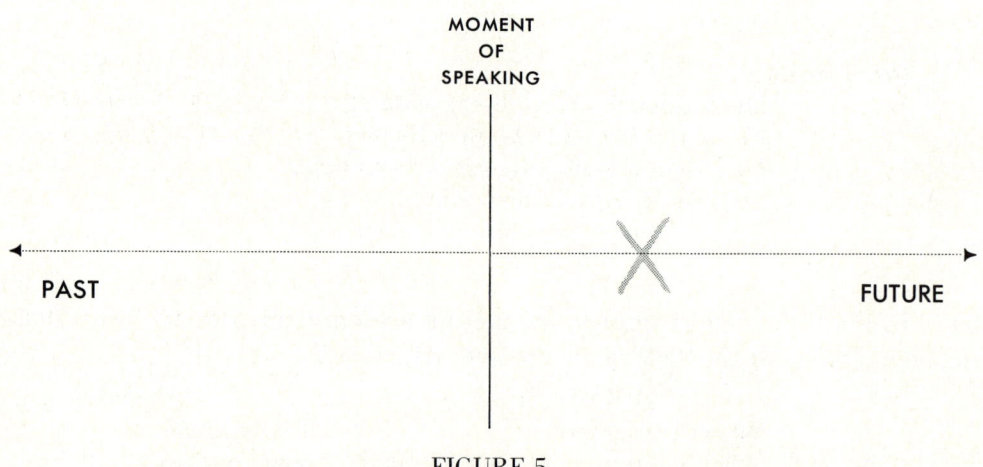

FIGURE 5

The symbol (X) indicating the future activity could be placed anywhere on the line extending from the moment of speaking into the future.

USAGE OF TENSES

Other examples:
> The Bonds **start** on their trip tomorrow.
> The next semester **begins** in three weeks.
> John **gets** back from the South tonight.
> I **go** to Hawaii next summer.

32 | USES of the PRESENT PROGRESSIVE TENSE

32a. In the following examples, the present progressive expresses activities that are in actual progress at the moment of speaking; the activities began a short time before, and are expected to end a short time after, the moment of speaking.

QUESTION	ANSWER
What are you doing?	**I'm washing** the dishes.
What is he doing?	**He's doing** his assignment.
What are they fixing?	**They're trying** to repair the radio.

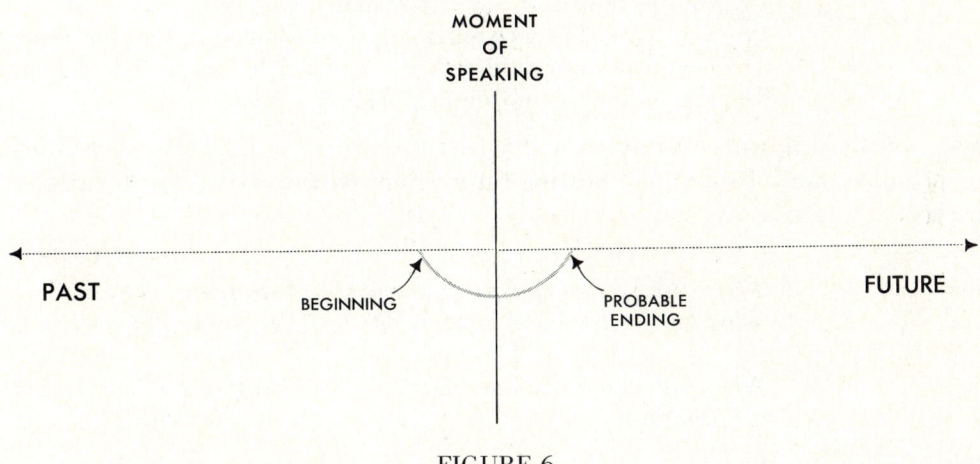

FIGURE 6

Other examples:
> John **is watching** television.
> They **are fixing** a flat tire.
> Martha **is practicing** the piano.
> The chairman **is speaking** now.[3]

32b. In the following examples, the present progressive expresses activities that began a relatively long time before, and that will probably end a relatively long time after, the moment of speaking. These activities, unlike the activities in Section 32a, are not necessarily taking place at the moment of speaking.

QUESTION	ANSWER
What's Don doing now?	**He's working** for a publishing firm.
Are you still having difficulty with math?	Yes, I **am having** a lot of trouble this semester.
Where are Mr. and Mrs. Jones?	They **are taking** a leisurely trip around the world this year.

---

[3] In some situations there is little difference in the meaning expressed by the simple present and the present progressive.

> I **am living** in Chicago now.
> (*or:* I **live** in Chicago now.)
> How **are** you **feeling** today? **I'm feeling** fine.
> (*or:* How **do** you **feel** today? I **feel** fine.)

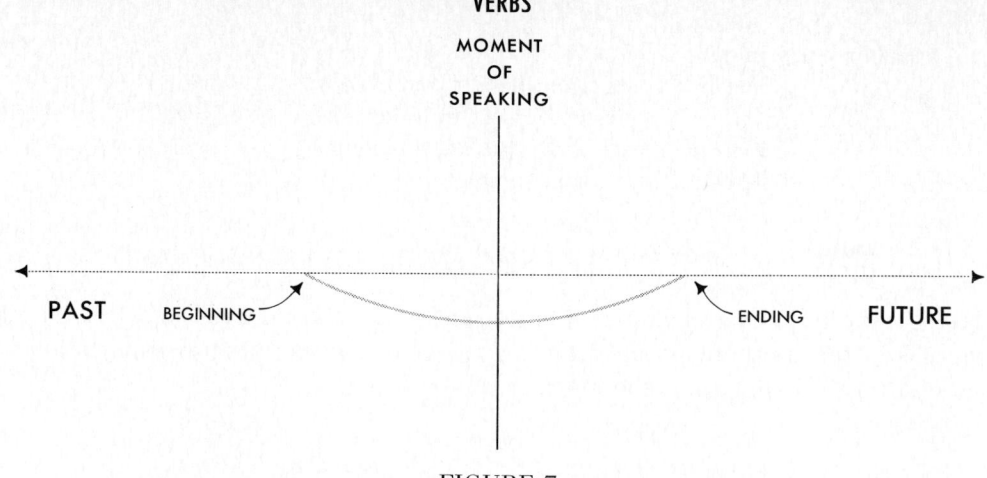

FIGURE 7

Other examples:

Dr. Phillips **is doing** cancer research.
Professor Chou **is teaching** a course in Chinese history this semester.
The newspaper **is running** a series of articles on juvenile delinquency.
The organization **is collecting** funds this month.

32c. In the following examples, the present progressive expresses activities that will take place in future time. Adverbs indicating future time (**tomorrow, next June,** etc.) often modify the verb.

QUESTION	ANSWER
Where are you going next summer?	**I'm going** to Peru.
What movie are you seeing tonight?	**I'm seeing** the Italian film at the Roxy.
When are you entertaining the Smiths?	**I'm having** them over for cocktails on Saturday.

FIGURE 8

The symbol (X) indicating the future activity could be placed anywhere on the line extending from the moment of speaking into the future.

Other examples:

Mr. Dill **is lecturing** on foreign policy next Wednesday.
Mrs. Astor **is giving** a party for foreign students next week.
We **are leaving** for London in two weeks.
I **am starting** on a diet tomorrow.

EXERCISE 25

Answer the following questions. Give long responses in order to have practice in using the simple present and the present progressive tenses.

<u>Example</u>: Where is Bill?
He's in the yard.

1. Do you hear a noise in the next room?

2. Does this milk taste sour to you?

3. Are you thirsty?

4. Does he work here?

5. Do you like sports?

6. Do you miss your friends?

7. Do you see him often?

8. Do you go to the library every night?

9. Does he usually walk to school?

10. What is the capital of your country?

11. What are you doing?

12. What's Dick doing?

13. Who is speaking now?

14. Is Charles studying electrical engineering?

15. Is she going on a trip this summer?

16. What are you doing tonight?

17. What are you having for dinner?

18. Who is that man?

19. What is he doing here?

20. Does he come here often?

EXERCISE 26

The instructor will read the following sentences.
(1) Change the statement into a negative statement.
(2) Change the statement into an affirmative question.

>   Example: They are listening to the radio now.
>   (1) They aren't listening to the radio now.
>   (2) Are they listening to the radio now?

1. It is raining very hard now.

2. Bill plays tennis on Saturday.

3. It rains a great deal in this part of the country.

4. He walks to school every day.

5. They are arriving tonight.

6. Henry is working in the post office now.

7. This milk tastes sour.

8. She wants some typing paper.

9. Mr. Brown understands the situation.

10. The bookkeeper goes to the bank every morning.

11. They are living in Boston now.

12. They like jazz music.

13. Mr. Borden is giving fencing lessons this year.

14. They are arriving on the six o'clock train.

15. He knows the answer.

Exercises for Part VII

EXERCISE 27

Read the following sentences. Give either the simple present or the progressive present of the verbs in parentheses to complete the sentences correctly. (Also write the forms in the spaces at the right.)

    Example: I (get) ready now.   am getting
                (Read: I am getting ready now.)

1. Professor Bailey usually (teach) graduate courses.   _____

2. The medical students (observe) an operation now.   _____

3. What is John doing? He (study) his French lesson.   _____

4. The students in this class (be) from many countries.   _____

5. The sun (rise) later in December than it does in June.   _____

6. George (live) in New York this year.   _____

7. It (rain) now.   _____

8. Do you see John? He (walk) across the lawn.   _____

9. I usually (hand) in my assignments on time.   _____

10. They seldom (see) their cousins.   _____

11. She rarely (get) home before six o'clock.   _____

12. The wind (blow) very hard in March.   _____

13. He sometimes (take) his sister to the soccer games.   _____

14. This soup (taste) good to me.   _____

15. I often (listen) to the five o'clock news broadcast.   _____

16. Water (freeze) at 32° Fahrenheit.   _____

17. She (talk) on the telephone right now.   _____

18. Lloyd (work) on his Ph.D. this year.   _____

19. The lungs (inhale) oxygen.   _____

20. We (watch) television once in a while.   _____

EXERCISE 28

(a) Write 8 questions using the simple present tense. (Refer to Section 31a-e.) After your questions have been corrected, use them for oral practice.

    Example: What do you want to do?
              I don't know. What do you want to do?

1.

2.

3.

4.

5.

6.

7.

8.

(b) Write 8 questions using the present progressive. (Refer to Section 32a-c.) After your questions have been corrected, use them for oral practice.

    Example: What are you doing now?
              I'm still going to school.

1.

2.

3.

4.

5.

6.

7.

8.

PART VIII Usage of Tenses (continued)

33 USES of the SIMPLE PAST TENSE

33a. In the following examples, the simple past expresses activities that existed or occurred in the past. Modifiers indicating time often specify a definite time in the past (**He went home yesterday**), but in some situations the time is not specified (**He went home**).

QUESTION	ANSWER
When did he leave?	He **left** yesterday.
Where were you last night?	I **was** at the movies.
Did you see the fire?	Yes, I **did.**

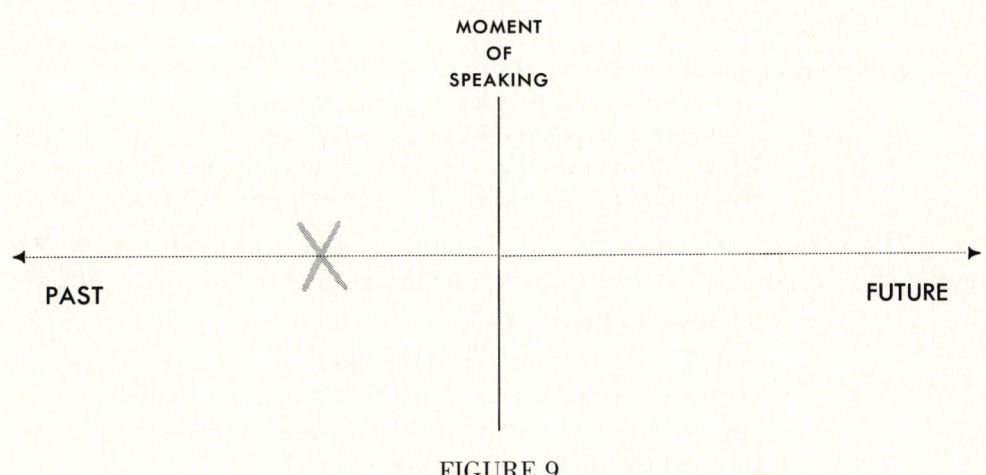

FIGURE 9

The symbol (X) indicating the past activity could be placed anywhere on the line extending from the moment of speaking into the past.

Other examples:
>They **left** an hour ago.
>I **received** two letters from home last Monday.
>They **were** very sorry to hear about the accident.
>They **had** two extra tickets for the show.
>I **recognized** his face, but I **didn't remember** his name.

33b. In the following examples, the simple past expresses activities that existed or occurred over a *period* of time in the past. In some situations, modifiers indicating time specify the period of the activity.

QUESTION	ANSWER
When were you in Cape Town?	I **was** there during the summer of 1954.
How many years did he sell insurance?	He **sold** insurance for ten years.
How long were you in the army?	I **was** in from 1943 to 1946.

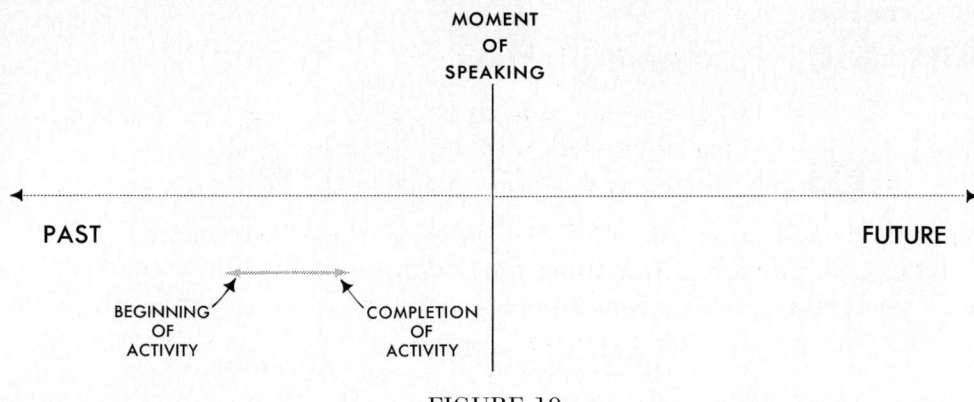

FIGURE 10

The length of time indicated by the symbol (◄——►) may vary, but the fact that the line does not extend to the moment of speaking indicates that the activity occurred during a period of time in the past.

Other examples:
    We **waited** for the telephone call all afternoon.
    I **heard** the carpenters working all day long.
    Mr. Hubbard **served** as chairman of the committee for two years.
    During the spring vacation, the students **went** on a camping trip.

The verb phrase **used to** + the simple form of the verb may also be used to indicate a state or condition that existed over a period of time in the past. Compare:

    Bill **used to be** very thin.
    Bill **was** very thin when he was a child.

    They **used to have** a lot of money, but they don't anymore.
    They **had** a lot of money once, but they don't anymore.

    He **used to work** in a bank years ago.
    He **worked** in a bank years ago.

33c. In the following examples, the simple past expresses activities that existed or occurred at *intervals* in past time. Modifiers indicating frequency often indicate the intervals of the activity.

QUESTION	ANSWER
Did he come to see you often?	Yes, he **came** every week.
Was the professor always on time for his lectures?	No, he **was** usually a few minutes late.
Did you hear many of the opera broadcasts last season?	Yes, I **heard** the broadcast almost every week.

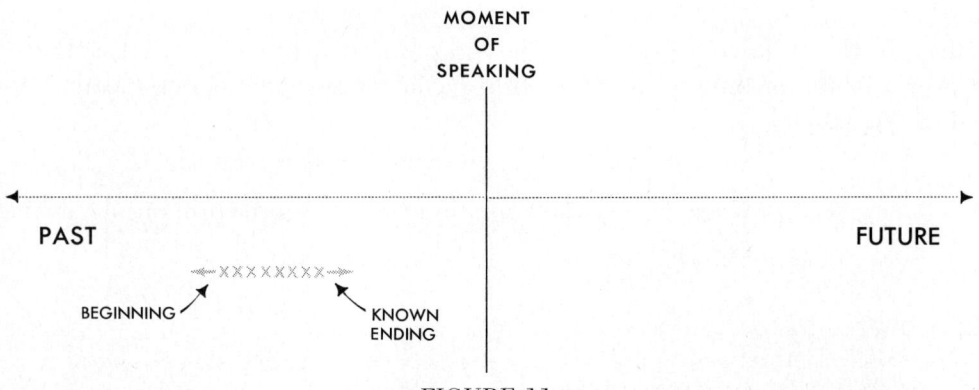

FIGURE 11

USAGE OF TENSES

Other examples:

We **saw** him from time to time.
He seldom **felt** lonesome while he was traveling.
My grandfather **rode** a horse to school every day when he was a child.
I **heard** the clock strike every hour last night.

The verb phrase **used to** + the simple form of the verb may also be used to indicate customary activity that occurred at intervals in the past. Compare:

Henry **used to play** tennis every Saturday.
Henry **played** tennis every Saturday.

We **used to spend** our vacations in the mountains.
We **spent** our vacations in the mountains.

I **used to read** a book every week.
I **read** a book every week.

34 | USES of the PAST PROGRESSIVE TENSE

34a. In the following examples, the past progressive expresses *temporary* activities which were in progress *at the time of another activity in the past*. The duration of the temporary activity may be relatively long or short. The other activity is usually expressed in another clause: for example, *I was studying* **when he telephoned.**

QUESTION	ANSWER
What were you doing when I telephoned you last night?	I **was doing** my chemistry assignment.[1]
Was it cloudy when you got up this morning?	No, it wasn't. As a matter of fact, the sun **was shining** brightly.
Was he feeling better when the doctor arrived?	Yes, he **was feeling** much better.

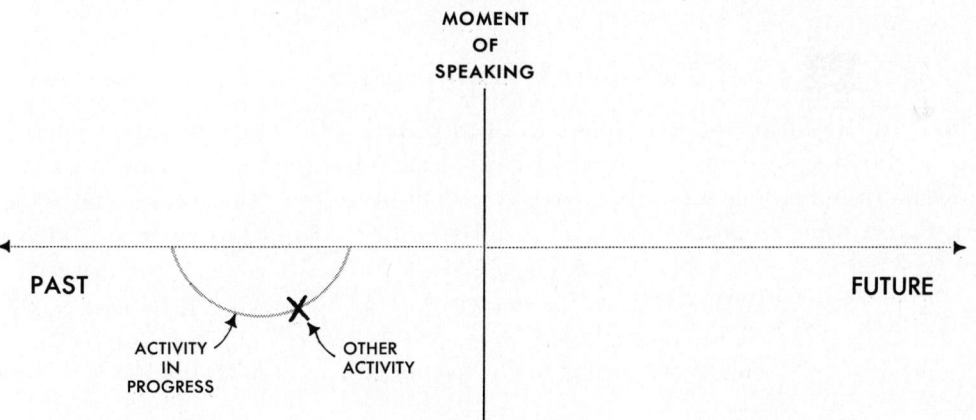

FIGURE 12

Other examples:

We had a flat tire while we **were crossing** the bridge.
He **was having** a good time when I saw him at the party.
Paul **was writing** a novel the last time that I saw him.
The idea came to me while I **was driving** to work.

---

[1] The other activity that occurred while the activity was in progress is not always stated; in this response, the implication is that the activity was going on *when I telephoned.*

34b. In the following examples, the past progressive expresses *temporary* activities that were in progress *at a point of time in the past.* The point of time is usually established by a modifier indicating time: for example, *He was sitting there* **a few minutes ago.**

QUESTION	ANSWER
Where was John last night?	He **was working** in the lab.[2]
Was he studying for his Ph.D. at that time?	No, he **was working** for his M.A.
Were you living here last year?	No, I **was living** in Washington.

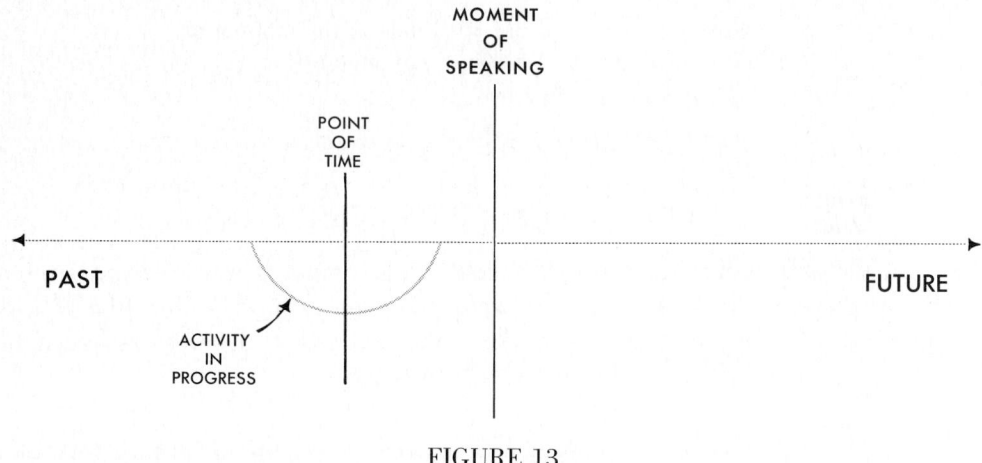

FIGURE 13

Other examples:

It **was raining** at seven o'clock this morning.
The car **was running** fine this afternoon.
He **was sitting** in the lobby an hour ago.
Professor Day **was doing** research at Cambridge last summer.[3]

35 USES of the FUTURE TENSE

35a. In the following examples, the future tense (or the equivalent verb phrase **be going to** + the simple form of the verb) expresses activities that will exist or occur in the future. Modifiers indicating time often specify a definite time in the future (**He will leave in an hour**), but in some situations the time is not specified (**He is going to go with me**).

QUESTION	ANSWER
Will he be here on time?	Yes, he**'ll be** here by five o'clock.[4]
Is he going to travel by train?	No, he**'s going to fly.**
When am I going to get my check?	You**'ll receive** it on Friday.

---

[2] The point of time is not always stated; in this response, the implication is that the activity was going on *last night.*

[3] In some situations, there is little difference in the meaning expressed by the simple past or the past progressive. Compare:

Where were you living at that time? I was living in London.
Where did you live at that time? I lived in London.
How was he feeling yesterday? He was feeling better.
How did he feel yesterday? He felt better.
Was it raining yesterday? Yes, it was raining very hard.
Did it rain yesterday? Yes, it rained very hard.

[4] The following contractions of pronouns and **will** are frequently used in conversational English:

I'll = I will   **we'll** = we will
he'll = he will   **they'll** = they will
she'll = she will   **you'll** = you will

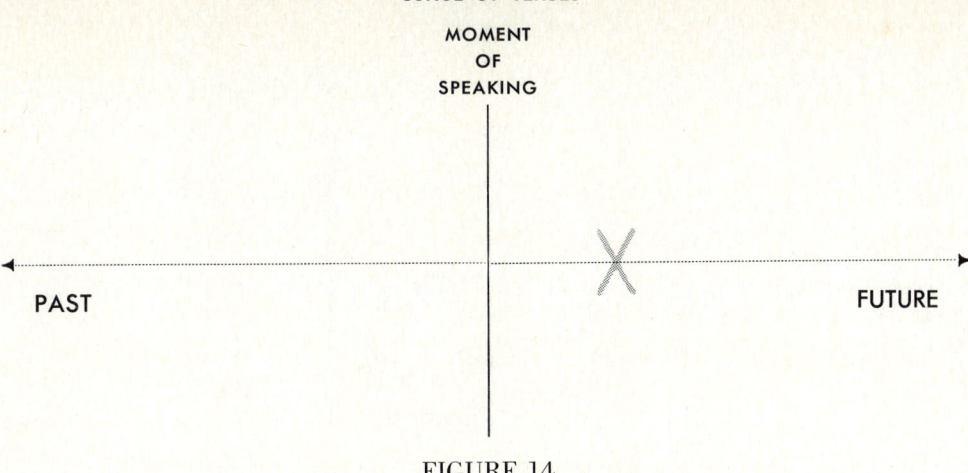

FIGURE 14

The symbol (X) indicating the future activity could be placed anywhere on the line extending from the moment of speaking into the future.

Other examples:
Mrs. Taylor **will spend** next year in Africa.
I'll telephone you in the morning.
I'm going to take an aspirin for my headache.
I'm going to write to you often.[5]

35b. In the following examples, the future tense is used in making *requests* or in asking for *permission* or *affirmation*. In requests of this type, the auxiliary **shall** is used with the first person, singular and plural; **will** is used with the second person.

REQUEST	TYPICAL RESPONSES
Will you **go** with me?	Yes, I'll be glad to.
Will you please **be** quiet?	Certainly. I'm sorry.
Shall I **begin** now?	Wait a minute, please.
Shall we **leave** now?	It's all right with me.

36 USES of the FUTURE PROGRESSIVE TENSE

In the following examples, the future progressive expresses temporary activities that will be *in progress* at a point of time, or that will extend over a limited period of time, in the future.[6]

QUESTION	ANSWER
What will you be doing at 7 o'clock?	I'll probably **be eating** dinner.
Will he be working on his thesis next semester?	No, he **will be studying** for his oral exams.
Will we be seeing you often?	Yes, I imagine that **I'll be seeing** you from time to time.[7]

---

[5] In this statement, the activity will occur at intervals in the future.

[6] The future progressive tense is not often used, but it is used regularly in a few situations such as those shown in the examples.

[7] In this statement, the activity will occur at intervals in the future.

VERBS

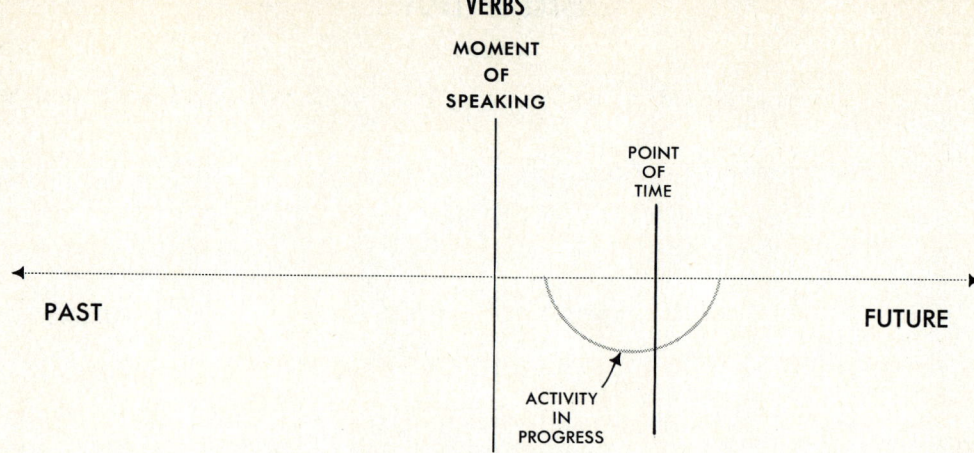

FIGURE 15

Other examples:
At this time next year, I hope that **I'll be earning** more money.
We'll be asking you for suggestions soon.
I'll be gambling in Monte Carlo by this time next week.

EXERCISES FOR PART VIII

EXERCISE 29

Answer the following questions. Give long responses in order to have practice in using the tenses.

    <u>Example</u>: Where were you last night?
             I was at the symphony.

1. Did you hear the fire engines last night?

2. Was he late to class?

3. Where did you go last Sunday?

4. Did she notice the package in the hall?

5. How long did you wait for him?

6. How many years did it take to build the bridge?

7. Were they always prompt?

8. Did he play soccer when he was in college?

9. Were you taking a nap when he called?

10. What were you doing a few minutes ago?

11. Was he studying medicine at that time?

12. Was the sun shining at 7 o'clock this morning?

13. Was Mrs. Brown living in that house when you met her?

14. Will Mr. Carlson be in town next week?

15. When is she going to get here?

16. Where are you going to hang that painting?

17. Are you going with us to the game on Saturday?

18. Shall we have lunch together tomorrow?

19. What will you be doing this evening?

20. Will we be seeing you soon?

EXERCISE 30

Read the following sentences. Give either the <u>simple past</u> or the <u>progressive past</u> tense of the verbs in parentheses to complete the sentences correctly. (Also write the forms in the spaces at the right.)

    Example: They (leave) a few minutes ago.   left
                (Read: They <u>left</u> a few minutes ago.)

1. Columbus (discover) America in 1492, didn't he?   _____

2. They (study) in the library when the fire alarm went off.   _____

3. It (snow) when I got up this morning.   _____

4. The man (drop) the heavy suitcase on my foot.   _____

5. Albert Einstein (die) on April 18, 1955.   _____

6. I (write) a letter to Janet when she telephoned.   _____

7. Tom (go) to the post office twice yesterday.   _____

8. Helen (wait) in the lobby, wasn't she?   _____

9. Professor Kittredge (teach) English at Harvard for almost fifty years.   _____

10. He (work) his way through college at that time.   _____

11. Mrs. Perkins was cooking dinner when we (arrive).   _____

12. The instructor (postpone) the quiz.   _____

13. The wind (blow) very hard when I went out this morning.   _____

14. He fell while he (go) down the stairs.   _____

15. She (try) to get into the movies when I last saw her.   _____

16. I (have) lunch with Jerry yesterday.   _____

17. My car (break) down this morning on the way to work.   _____

18. We saw John go by while we (wait) for you.   _____

19. She (buy) groceries when I saw her yesterday.   _____

20. He (go) to New York by train, didn't he?   _____

EXERCISE 31

Follow the directions below. (After your questions have been corrected, use them for practice. Work with another student, if possible.)

(a) Write 5 questions using the **simple past**. (Refer to Section 33.)

1.

2.

3.

4.

5.

(b) Write 5 questions using the **past progressive**. (Refer to Section 34.)

1.

2.

3.

4.

5.

(c) Write 5 questions using the **future** (or equivalent phrase). (Refer to Section 35.)

1.

2.

3.

4.

5.

EXERCISE 32

Read the following sentences. Give the <u>simple present</u>, the <u>simple past</u>, the <u>present progressive</u>, the <u>past progressive</u>, or the <u>future</u> tense of the verbs in parentheses to complete the sentences correctly. (Also write the forms in the spaces at the right.)

1. Ray (buy) several records last week. _____

2. It (take) a long time to do the last assignment. _____

3. They (arrive) some time tomorrow morning, won't they? _____

4. Henry (attend) Yale from 1950 to 1953. _____

5. The President (speak) over the radio next Tuesday evening, won't he? _____

6. We (go) to the symphony several times last winter. _____

7. It (rain) very hard now. _____

8. It (rain) very hard when I got up this morning. _____

9. Be quiet! I (want) to hear the news broadcast. _____

10. Egypt (produce) some of the finest cotton in the world. _____

11. Now he (realize) his mistake. _____

12. Where is Ernest? He (sit) on the front porch. _____

13. Martha (study) architecture at that time, wasn't she? _____

14. Mr. Martin (drive) to work every day, doesn't he? _____

15. My father (read) Shakespeare to me when I was a child. _____

16. I always (put) the key to my car in my pocket. _____

17. They (return) to their country in two years, aren't they? _____

18. We (start) on our vacation next week. _____

19. He always (keep) his promises when I knew him. _____

20. They (work) very hard when I saw them last night. _____

PART IX — Usage of Tenses (concluded)

37 USES of the PRESENT PERFECT TENSE

The present perfect expresses activities that began sometime in the past, but that are related in the mind of the speaker with the moment of speaking.

37a. In the following examples, the activities began in the past, have continued up to, and may extend beyond, the moment of speaking.

QUESTION	ANSWER
How long have you lived here?	I **have lived** here for ten years.[1]
Have you worked here for a long time?	Yes, I **have worked** here since 1945.
How many years has Mr. Reed been at the university?	He **has taught** here for about seven years.

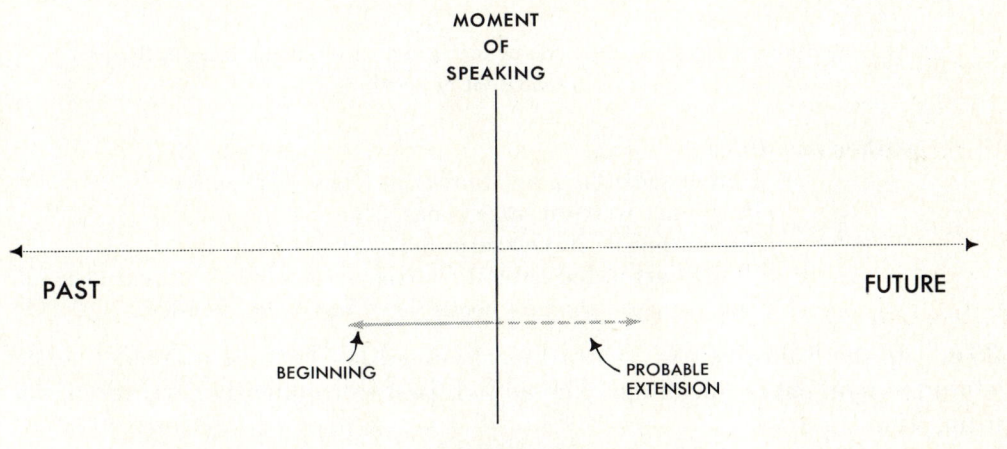

FIGURE 16

Other examples:
> I **have collected** coins for many years.
> Margaret **has studied** ballet since she was a child.
> George **has been** in business since he finished college.
> We **have known** the Bell family a long time.
> I **have** always **admired** her courage.

37b. In the following examples, the activities have existed or have occurred sometime in the past before the moment of speaking, but the exact time of the activity is either not known or not indicated.[2] Modifiers indicating frequency may indicate that the activity has occurred one or more times.

---

[1] The present progressive form is *not* used to express an activity of this kind.
> They **have lived** in Chicago for four years.
> (NOT: They are living in Chicago for four years now.)

[2] Compare the uses of the present perfect and the simple past in the following:
> Have you been there before?
> Yes, I **have been** there a few times. (*a few times* = unspecified past time)
> When did you go there?
> I **went** there last week. (*last week* = definite past time)

QUESTION	ANSWER
Have you met John?	No, I **have** never **met** him.[3]
Have they ever been to Miami before?[4]	Yes, they **have been** there several times.[5]
Have you ever traveled in Italy?	No, I **haven't**.

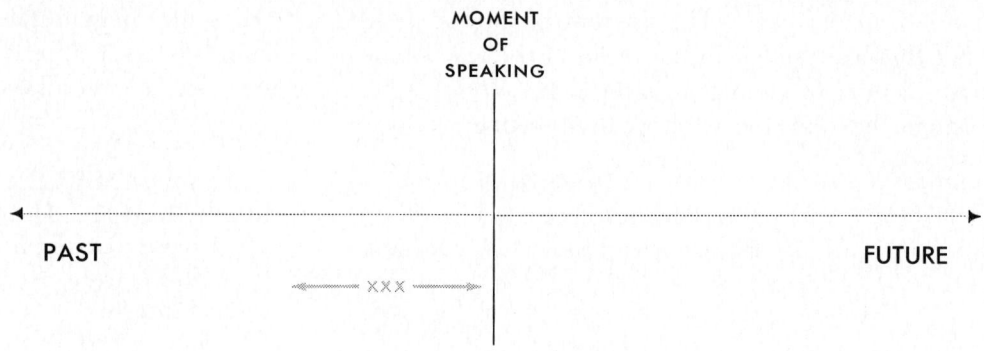

FIGURE 17

The activity may have occurred one or more times from some time in the past up to the moment of speaking.

Other examples:
I **have seen** the play *Macbeth* at least seven times.
Percy **has written** three books of poems.
Several people **have swum** the English Channel.
He **has attended** several sessions of the United Nations General Assembly.
This is one of the best books that I **have** ever **read.**

37c. In the following examples, the activities have been completed a relatively short time before the moment of speaking. The adverb **just** is frequently used to emphasize situations of this kind.

---

[3] The negative response indicates that the speaker has never met John at any time in the past up to the moment of speaking.

[4] Questions of this kind indicate that the speaker does not know whether the other person has been there at any time before the moment of speaking. The question may receive various responses, depending on the information given. Compare the following answers to the question:

Have they ever been there before?
- Yes, they **were** there yesterday.
  (The simple past with the adverb **yesterday** indicates the exact time of the activity.)
- Yes, they **go** there every summer.
  (The simple present indicates habitual activity at intervals before, up to, and probably after the moment of speaking.)
- Yes, they **have been** there twice.
  (The present perfect indicates activity that has occurred twice before, but the exact times are not stated.)
- No, this **is** their first trip there.
  (The simple present indicates either that they are there or that they are on their way there.)

[5] In an affirmative response, **ever** meaning "at any time" is not used. However, **ever** might be used in a negative response. Compare:
Yes, I have been there.
No, I haven't **ever** been there.

USAGE OF TENSES

QUESTION	ANSWER
Have they got back yet?	Yes, they **have** just **come in.**
Have you had lunch yet?	Yes, I **have** just **come** from the cafeteria.
Have you finished your assignment?	Yes, I **have** just **finished** the last problem.[6]

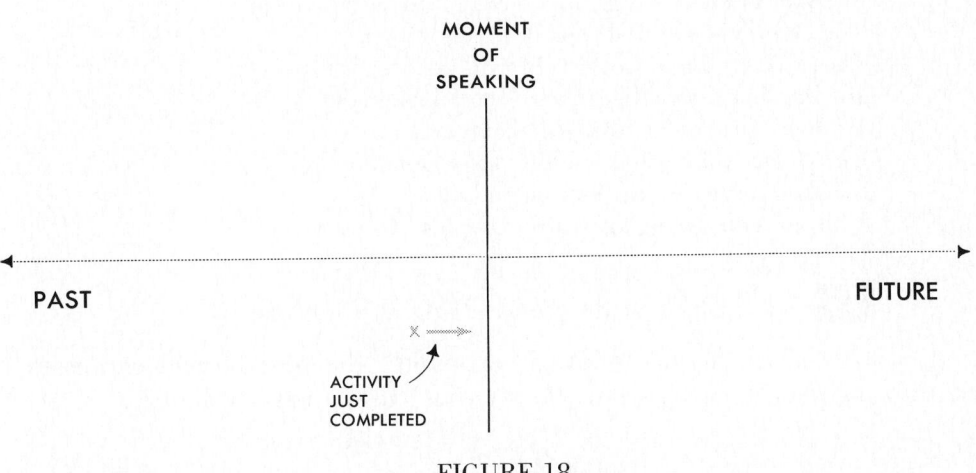

FIGURE 18

The lapse of time between the completion of the activity and the moment of speaking may vary, but in the mind of the speaker it is relatively close to the moment of speaking.

Other examples:
> I**'ve** just **had** a cup of coffee.
> You **have** already **turned in** your paper, haven't you?
> They **have** just **returned** from a trip to Mexico.
> We**'ve** just **heard** the news.
> I **haven't heard** from Suzanne recently.[7]

37d. In the following examples, the activities were completed in the past but are closely connected with other activities that extend into the present or future.

> Janet **has bought** a car so that she will have transportation to work.
> He **has studied** all day so that he can go to the dance tonight.
> I **have received** two tickets to the opera. Do you want to go with me?

38 | USES of the PRESENT PERFECT PROGRESSIVE TENSE

The present perfect progressive expresses activities similar to those described in Sections 37abc. The progressive form emphasizes the *continuous* nature of the activity. For this reason, verbs such as **be, know, believe, understand, like, prefer,**

---

[6] In an alternative response, such as "Yes, I **finished** a few minutes ago," **a few minutes ago** would indicate the time the activity was completed.

[7] **I haven't heard** indicates that the activity has not taken place recently.

94 VERBS

which do not convey the idea of continuous activity, are not ordinarily used in the progressive form.[8]

Some of the verbs that are regularly used in the progressive form are given in the examples below:

I **have been waiting** for you about twenty minutes.
He **has been sitting** in that chair all evening.
She **has been feeling** much better lately.
The child **has been sleeping** all afternoon.
These papers **have been lying** on his desk for a week.
Joe **has been working** on a farm all summer.
We **have** just **been talking** about you.
I **have been hearing** good things about your work.
She **has been seeing** him off and on.
I **have been going through** my files this week.

39 USES of the PAST PERFECT TENSE

In the following examples, the past perfect expresses activities that existed or occurred either *before* another activity in the past or *before* a point of time in the past.

QUESTION	ANSWER
Had you finished dinner when he telephoned?[9]	Yes, we **had** just **finished.**
Had you ever seen him before last night?[10]	No, I **had** never **seen** him before.

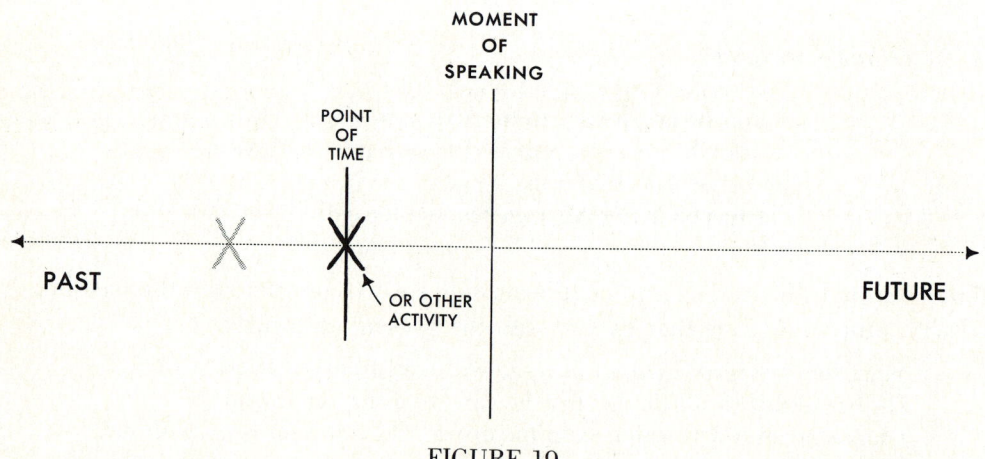

FIGURE 19

The gray symbol (X) indicates an activity which occurred before the point of time, indicated by the vertical line, or before another activity, indicated by the symbol (X) in black.

---

[8] Compare the following:

I've lived here for ten years.	I've been living here for ten years.
I have worked here since 1945.	I have been working here since 1945.
He has taught here for several years.	He has been teaching here for several years.
He has been a graduate student for two years.	. . . .
We have known him for a long time.	. . . .
We have liked all of the lectures.	. . . .

USAGE OF TENSES

Other examples:

I **had** just **finished** watering the lawn when it began to rain.
> (**Just** emphasizes that the activity occurred a relatively short time before the other activity.)

I **had** never **heard** that opera before.
> (**Before** implies either a point of time or another activity in the past.)

It was too late to do anything about it because he **had** already **mailed** the letter.
> (**Already** emphasizes that the activity expressed by the past perfect occurred before the other activity.)

He said that John **had told** him about our plans.[11]

40 | USES of the PAST PERFECT PROGRESSIVE, the FUTURE PERFECT, and the FUTURE PERFECT PROGRESSIVE TENSES [12]

40a. The past perfect progressive expresses activities similar to those described in Section 39. The progressive form emphasizes the continuous nature of the activity. Not all verbs are used in the progressive form. (See Section 38.)

> We **had been corresponding** regularly for many years before his death.
> He **had been living** in Oslo before he moved to Copenhagen.

40b. The future perfect expresses activities that exist or occur before another activity or point of time in the future.

> We'**ll have finished** the rehearsal by five o'clock. Why don't you come to the theatre at 5:30?
> That will be too late because we **will have gone** by then.

40c. The future perfect progressive expresses activities similar to those in Section 40b, but emphasizes their continuous nature. Not all verbs are used in the progressive form. (See Section 38.)

> We'**ll have been practicing** for two hours when the soloist arrives.
> He'**ll have been studying** for four months by the time he takes his examinations.

---

[9] The past perfect indicates an activity that occurred before another past activity, that is, **when he telephoned.**

[10] The past perfect indicates an activity that occurred before a point of time in the past, that is, **before last night.**

[11] There is a tendency, particularly in spoken English, to use the simple past in statements of this kind.
> He said that John **told** him about it.

[12] These tenses are not considered essential for the foreign student except perhaps on the recognition level; therefore, only brief mention is made of them here.

EXERCISES FOR PART IX

EXERCISE 33

Answer the following questions. Give long responses or a short response followed by an explanation in order to have practice in using the tenses.

Example: Have you heard from Joan recently?
Yes, I have. As a matter of fact, I got a letter from her yesterday.

1. How long have you known your roommate?

2. How many years has Boris taken piano lessons from Professor Gould?

3. How many times have you seen <u>Romeo and Juliet</u>?

4. Has he ever read <u>War and Peace</u>?

5. Have you turned in your paper?

6. Have you had breakfast yet?

7. How long have you been waiting for me?

8. Have you been studying English long?

9. Has the postman been here today?

10. Has he ever traveled in India?

11. Have you met the hostess yet?

12. Have you ever driven a car before?

13. Has that woman been sitting there all afternoon?

14. Have you been playing tennis all morning?

15. Did he say anything after he had read the letter?

16. Had she ever met him before your party?

17. Did Dave tell you that he had heard from Pete?

18. Had it begun to rain before you left the house this morning?

19. Had you been waiting long before he arrived?

20. How long have you known the Jones family?

Exercises for Part IX

EXERCISE 34

Read the following sentences. Give the present perfect, the present perfect progressive, or the past perfect tense of the verbs in parentheses to complete the sentences correctly. In some sentences an adverb is included in the parentheses; in these cases, use the adverb along with the verb. (Also write the forms in the spaces at the right.)

    Example: He (often be) here.   has often been
                (Read: He has often been here.)

1. We (see) her a few times recently. _____

2. Mr. Hart (try) to call you several times today. _____

3. We (wait) for you for two hours. _____

4. The author (write) novels for years before he wrote a book of poetry. _____

5. We (hear) many good programs on the radio this week. _____

6. Mr. Perkins (be) in the laundry business since he got out of the army. _____

7. She (just recover) from the measles when she came down with a bad cold. _____

8. You (just leave) home when he telephoned last night. _____

9. We (never meet) them before the reception yesterday. _____

10. Dr. Baer (practice) medicine here since 1948. _____

11. I (hear) a lot about him before I finally met him. _____

12. George (just arrive) when I got there. _____

13. Miss Welsh (already write) her report. _____

14. By the time we got there, they (go). _____

15. Mr. Taylor (make) several trips to Japan in the last ten years. _____

16. This is the best book that I (read) lately. _____

17. Charles said that he (received) a scholarship. _____

18. Not many people (climb) Mount Everest. _____

19. John (live) in Kansas City for about five years. _____

20. This is the nicest time that I (have) since I have been here. _____

Exercises for Part IX

EXERCISE 35

The following exercise is given for review of the tenses in Parts VII, VIII, and IX. Choose the verb form in the following sentences. Write the letter A or B in the space at the right.

Example: I (A) am living (B) have lived here since 1955.   B

1. They (A) listen (B) are listening to the radio now.   _____

2. George (A) went (B) has gone to the library last night.   _____

3. Miss Lang (A) makes (B) is making some coffee, isn't she?   _____

4. It (A) rained (B) has rained every day so far this week.   _____

5. We (A) drove (B) were driving downtown when we saw a terrible accident.   _____

6. I (A) have thought (B) am thinking about our last discussion many times.   _____

7. World War I (A) ended (B) had ended in 1918.   _____

8. The Johnsons (A) are living (B) have lived in that house for twenty years.   _____

9. We (A) traveled (B) were traveling all over the country during the summer.   _____

10. I (A) am (B) have been here only two months.   _____

11. My cousin (A) visits (B) is visiting us every summer.   _____

12. Robert (A) is going to wait (B) has been waiting for you since noon.   _____

13. I'll continue practicing until I (A) know (B) have known the lesson.   _____

14. I (A) slept (B) was sleeping soundly when I was suddenly awakened by a loud noise.   _____

15. Tropical plants (A) do not grow (B) are not growing well in cold climates.   _____

EXERCISE 36

Answer the following questions for oral practice. These are given for review of the tenses presented in Parts VII, VIII, and IX.

1. What are you reading?

2. Have you ever read anything by Mark Twain?

3. Did you read it in English or in your own language?

4. Have many of Mark Twain's books been translated into your language?

5. How is John feeling today?

6. When did he get out of the hospital?

7. Is he going to be able to return to classes next week?

8. Did many of his friends visit him in the hospital?

9. Has anyone been to see him today?

10. Have the Smiths ever been to Rome?

11. When did they go there?

12. Are they planning to go to Europe again this summer?

13. What are you watching on television?

14. Is the program interesting?

15. Do you see this program often?

16. Have you seen any of the programs on the new station?

17. Does your friend write to you every week?

18. Are you good about answering his letters?

19. You used to write to him more often, didn't you?

20. Have you been writing to each other very long?

PART X — Sequence of Tenses

41 INTRODUCTION

In the mind of the speaker, the time that an activity exists or occurs depends on its relationship to the moment of speaking. For example, if the speaker says, "I **bought** a new coat today," the time of the purchase is past in his mind. Here, the simple past **bought** expresses an activity completed in the past. The past progressive **was buying** also indicates past time, but this tense expresses activity of a continuous nature and would not be appropriate in this sentence.[1]

It is customary to use tenses that maintain a logical *sequence* in describing or relating activities. For example, it is *not* logical to say, " I **went** to town yesterday, and I *buy* a new coat"; the logical sequence is "I **went** to town yesterday, and I **bought** a new coat." However, in "I **went** to town yesterday, but I **am going to stay** home today," the change in tenses involves a logical shift from a past to a future activity.

When a clause functions as a modifier or a noun substitute,[2] the verb in the clause is controlled to a certain degree by the verb in the main clause. In some situations, the verb in each clause corresponds to the concept of time in the mind of the speaker, as in "I **bought** a newspaper when I *went* out for lunch." Here the sequence seems logical. In other situations, the verb in each clause does not correspond to the concept of time, as in "I'**ll wait** until he *comes*." Here the sequence may not seem logical, but this sequence is customary when a clause expressing time modifies a verb expressing future activity.

In the following sections, examples are given of the sequence of tenses in sentences containing clauses that function as modifiers and as noun substitutes. In the examples, the verb in the main clause is **in bold face;** the verb in the other clause, *in italics*.

42 SEQUENCE in CLAUSES that MODIFY VERBS[3]

The tense of the verb in the main clause ordinarily controls the tense of the verb in a clause modifying the verb.

(1) Sequence with the simple present in the main clause:

> The secretary always **leaves** as soon as her boss *goes* home.
>
> > (**Leaves** and *goes* both express customary activity in the present.)
>
> I usually **read** the newspaper while I *am waiting* for the bus.
>
> > (**Read** expresses customary activity in the present; *am waiting* emphasizes the continuous nature of the activity.)[4]

---

[1] The tense of a verb does not necessarily correspond with the concept of time. (See Section 30.) See Parts VII, VIII, and IX for explanation of the uses of tenses.

[2] Examples: I'll sit there **until you're ready.**
                (clause = modifier of the verb **sit**)
           The man **who is waiting in the lobby** is an insurance salesman.
                (clause = modifier of the noun **man**)
           He said **that he would be on time.**
                (clause = noun equivalent, object of the verb **said**)

[3] Also see Section 17 for a discussion of clauses that modify verbs.

[4] Also: I usually **read** the newspaper while I *wait* for the bus.
                (There is little difference in meaning: *wait* indicates customary activity.)

He never **goes** home before he *has finished* his work.

> (**Goes** expresses customary activity in the present; *has finished* emphasizes completion of the activity before the customary activity in the main clause.)[5]

(2) Sequence with the simple past in the main clause:

He **sat** there until the telephone *rang*.

> (**Sat** and *rang* both express completed activities in the past.)

The telephone **rang** while he *was sitting* there.

> (**Rang** expresses a completed activity in the past; *was sitting* emphasizes the continuous nature of the activity at the time of the past activity in the main clause.)

He **left** after he *had finished* the experiment.

> (**Left** expresses a completed activity in the past; *had finished* indicates an activity that was completed before the past activity in the main clause.)[6]

(3) Sequence with the past progressive in the main clause:

They **were** still **waiting** when I *got* there.

> (**Were waiting** expresses a continuous activity in the past at the time of the past activity expressed by *got*.)

John **was** still **going** to school while his brother *was becoming* a successful lawyer.

> (**Was going** and *was becoming* both express continuous activities at an implied point of time in the past.)

(4) Sequence with the future in the main clause:

We'**ll stay** here until the rain *lets up* a bit.[7]

> (**Will stay** expresses an activity that will continue until the future activity expressed by *lets up*.)

I'**ll think** it over while I'*m having* my lunch.

> (**Will think** expresses an activity that will continue during the future activity expressed by *am having*.)[8]

I'**m going to wait** until John *has finished* his coffee.

> (**Am going to wait** expresses an activity that will continue until completion of the future activity expressed by *has finished*.)[9]

(5) Sequence with the present perfect in the main clause:

Since the present perfect in the main clause expresses activity that began in the past and that may continue through the present and possibly into the future, the verb in the other clause may express an activity that exists or occurs in past, present, or future time.

I **have felt** much better since I *have been* here.

> (**Have felt** and *have been* both express activities that began in the past and may continue into the future.)

---

[5] Also: He never **goes** home before he *finishes* his work.
(There is little difference in meaning: *finishes* indicates customary activity.)

[6] Also: He **left** after he *finished* the experiment.
(There is little difference in meaning: *finished* indicates completed activity in the past.)

[7] The present tense is used in clauses that express time.
I'll be there when you *arrive*.
(NOT: I'll be there when you will arrive.)

[8] Also: I'**ll think** it over while I *have* my lunch.
(There is little difference in meaning: *have* indicates future activity.)

[9] Also: I'**m going to wait** until John *finishes* his coffee.
(There is little difference in meaning: *finishes* indicates future activity.)

SEQUENCE OF TENSES

I **have learned** a lot since I *have been attending* night school.

> (**Have learned** and *have been attending* both express activities that began in the past and may continue into the future; *have been attending* emphasizes the continuous nature of the activity.)

He **has played** the trumpet since he *was* a child.

> (**Has played** expresses an activity that began and has continued from the point of time in the past indicated by *since he was a child*.)

He **has worked** very hard so that he *will be able to finish* his thesis by June.

> (**Has worked** expresses an activity that began in the past for the purpose of achieving the future activity expressed by *will be able to finish*.)

(6) Sequence with the past perfect or the future perfect in the main clause:

The past perfect is ordinarily used only in relation to another past activity or point of time in the past; the future perfect, only in relation to another present or future activity or point of time.

We **had** just **come** in when you *called*.

> (**Had come** expresses an activity that occurred before the other activity in the past expressed by *called*.)

We**'ll have** already **gone** before you *get back*.

> (**Will have gone** expresses an activity that will be completed before the activity expressed by *get back*.)

43 | SEQUENCE in CLAUSES that MODIFY NOUNS [10]

Sequence in sentences with clauses that modify nouns may involve very different concepts of time in the mind of the speaker and still be logical. These clauses modify *nouns* and are not necessarily related to the activity expressed by the *verb* in the main clause.

The Carlo (that) I *know* **is** from Colombia.[11]
The letter (that) I *received* yesterday **is** on my desk.
Yesterday I **met** the man who *is going to speak* next.
He **puts** the letters (that) he *has answered* in this folder.
She **has** already **telephoned** the people who *are coming* tomorrow.
This **is** about the best book (that) I *have* ever *read*.

44 | SEQUENCE in CLAUSES that FUNCTION as NOUNS

Clauses often function as objects after such expressions as **says (that), believes (that),** and so forth.

(1) When the verb in the main clause is in the simple present, the present progressive, or the present perfect, the verb in the noun clause may be in tenses that express activities in the past, present, or future. The sequence of tenses seems logical in sentences of this type.

He **says** (that) he *comes* here often.
She **knows** (that) you *arrived* yesterday.

---

[10] See Section 14 for a discussion of clauses that modify nouns.

[11] Explanations are not given for the uses of the particular tenses in the examples here. (See preceding Sections 41 and 42 and Parts VII, VIII, and IX for explanations.)

The parentheses indicate that the (**that**) is often omitted in actual usage.

He **thinks** (that) Victor *will be* late.
In other words, you **are saying** (that) you *agree* with me.
You **have** already **told** me (that) you *are going to quit* your job.

(2) When the verb in the main clause is in the simple past, the past progressive, or the past perfect, the verb in the noun clause is ordinarily in a past tense. The sequence of tenses may not always seem logical.

He **knew** (that) you *were* in town.
He **said** (that) he *would be* here tomorrow.

(After **said,** *would be* expresses future activity.)

He **had thought** (that) he *might arrive* next week.

(After **had thought,** *might arrive* expresses possibility of future activity.)

He **believed** (that) his friend *had forgotten* him.
The doctor **was saying** just yesterday (that) she *would get* well.

When the verb in the noun clause expresses a fact or an activity that is relatively permanent, the simple present is ordinarily used.

The professor **said** (that) Persian *belongs* to the Indo-European group of languages.

EXERCISES FOR PART X   105

EXERCISE 37

Read the following sentences. Give the <u>simple present</u>, the <u>present progressive</u>, the <u>present perfect</u>, or a <u>future</u> tense form of the verb in parentheses in order to complete the sentences correctly. (Also write the forms in the spaces at the right.)

    Example: We'll wait until she (arrive).   <u>arrives</u>
               (Read: We'll wait until she <u>arrives</u>.)

1. Call Jack as soon as you (get) in town. _____

2. They say that they (arrive) by five o'clock. _____

3. I'll think about your suggestion while I (wait) for you. _____

4. Before Jack leaves New York he (see) several new plays. _____

5. They will be very happy when they (hear) the news. _____

6. I always (feel) better after I have rested a while. _____

7. This is the best performance of Hamlet that I (see) in years. _____

8. We'll have learned many new words before we (get) through this course. _____

9. It is two o'clock, and I (not finish) my homework yet. _____

10. We usually go out to dinner when we (work) late. _____

11. They (know) that you are going to be late. _____

12. I'll return the books to the library if I (have) time. _____

13. She will be ready when he (get) here. _____

14. The people that I (meet) here have been very friendly. _____

15. I believe that you (make) a wise decision. _____

16. The child always cries when his mother (go) out of the house. _____

17. They often listen to the radio while they (travel) in their car. _____

18. She says that she (pay) the bill next week. _____

19. That is the best book that I (read) on that subject. _____

20. Yesterday I met the woman who (help) us with the work next month. _____

EXERCISE 38

Read the following sentences. Give the <u>simple past</u>, the <u>past progressive</u>, or the <u>past perfect</u> tense (or an equivalent such as <u>would go</u>, <u>might go</u>, etc.) of the verb in parentheses to complete the sentences correctly. (Also <u>write the forms in the spaces at the right</u>.)

    Example: He said that he (arrive) on time.   <u>would arrive</u>
              (Read: He said that he <u>would arrive</u> on time.)

1. We saw several old friends while we (be) in Baltimore. _____

2. Raymond (buy) two new shirts when he was downtown today. _____

3. After we had breakfast, we (leave) the house. _____

4. I had heard the news before you (tell) me about it. _____

5. That (be) the best movie that I had seen in a long time. _____

6. It (rain) when I got up this morning. _____

7. He said that he (meet) me there at 4:30 this afternoon. _____

8. Mary was not feeling well when she (fall) down yesterday. _____

9. Maxwell (pay) three dollars for the tie he bought at Macy's. _____

10. I thought that you had forgotten me until I (get) your last letter. _____

11. He signed the contract after he (read) each statement carefully. _____

12. Jim had just turned out the lights when the doorbell (ring). _____

13. The salesman was telling me yesterday that he (sell) ten cars last week. _____

14. Did Bob say that he (graduate) from Princeton in 1951? _____

15. We bought a used car that had belonged to an old couple who used the car only when they (go) shopping. _____

16. We (look) at some photographs when the lights went out. _____

17. The man who will replace Mr. Stuart (arrive) yesterday. _____

18. I (feel) better after I had taken an aspirin. _____

19. We thought that they (move) to Arizona. _____

20. The doorbell rang while I (talk) on the telephone. _____

Exercises For Part X

EXERCISE 39

Complete the following sentences:

Example: The telegram arrived as we <u>were leaving the house.</u>

1. When they were in Boston, they _____

2. Here is the magazine that you _____

3. She said that she _____
   _____ tomorrow.

4. We went home after we _____

5. My uncle has often said that politics _____

6. Last night we saw several people whom we _____

7. I'm just killing time while I _____

8. He had just left the house when you _____

9. Joe has forgotten that he _____

10. That is without doubt the most uninteresting book that I _____

Exercise 39 (continued)

11. Is this the house where you _____

    _____ ?

12. Do you think that Chris _____

    _____ ?

13. Grace thought that her sister _____

    _____ next week.

14. Miriam always remembers the names of people that she _____

    _____

15. Max never says anything unless he _____

    _____

16. Had you been waiting long before we _____

    _____ ?

17. He has lived in Spain since he _____

    _____

18. Will you please ask her to call me as soon as she _____

    _____ ?

19. Did you know that they _____

    _____ ?

20. We didn't go to the concert because we _____

    _____

PART XI — The Passive Construction and Auxiliary Verbs

45. THE PASSIVE CONSTRUCTION

In the preceding parts, active verb constructions have been emphasized. This section introduces some patterns with passive constructions.

45a. Compare the active and passive constructions in the following examples:

ACTIVE	The mayor The secretary We	welcomed will read hold	the diplomat. the report. classes	here.
PASSIVE	The diplomat The report Classes	was welcomed will be read are held	by the mayor. by the secretary.	here.

In these examples, the direct object in the active construction becomes the subject in the passive. Often the subject in the active is retained as an agent in the passive, as expressed in the phrases **by the mayor** and **by the secretary**. Sometimes the subject is not retained as an agent, as in "Classes are held here."

The indirect object in an active construction may also become the subject in a passive construction. Compare:

He gave **the boy** a book.
The boy was given a book.

45b. The verb forms in the passive construction are composed of the auxiliary verb **be** in the appropriate tense + the past participle of the principal verb. Examples:

I **am invited.**	We **have been invited.**
He **was invited.**	They **will be invited.**
You **are invited.**	They**'re going to be invited.**[1]

45c. Although the active construction is used more frequently in English than the passive, there are certain situations when the passive seems more effective or appropriate. The passive construction is often used in the following situations:

(1) The speaker considers the *performer* of the act expressed by the verb unimportant or not essential to the meaning he wishes to convey:

Harvard **was founded** in 1636.
The United Nations Charter **was signed** in 1945.[2]
George **was wounded** in the war.

(In these sentences the founders of Harvard, the signers of the Charter, and the agent that wounded George are not particularly important in conveying the information given.)

---

[1] For a list of all tense forms in the passive, see the Appendix, page 246.
[2] Statements such as "World War II **ended** in 1945" or "The doorbell **rang**" are active constructions and should *not* be confused with passive constructions. An agent is neither stated nor implied: "The war (itself) **ended**" and "The doorbell (itself) **rang**."

(2) The speaker wishes to emphasize the *receiver* of the activity expressed by the verb (the subject in the passive construction):

> The man **was hit** by a speeding car.[3]
> The book **was given** to me by my instructor.

(3) The speaker wishes to make a statement seem objective or impersonal:

> It **is believed** that the political situation is critical.
> It **is thought** by experts that the project will fail.

46 | INTRODUCTION to AUXILIARY VERBS

The uses of auxiliary verbs in the formation of tense phrases (**is** going, **has** given, **will** sing) and in the formation of negative statements (He **doesn't** sing) and of questions (**Does** he sing?) have already been described.

Other auxiliary verbs (**can, may,** etc.) or equivalent verb phrases (**be able to,** etc.) add the idea of ability, permission, possibility, probability, obligation, necessity, or preference to the activity or state expressed by the principal verb. For example, in the sentence, "I **can** swim," **can** adds the idea of ability to perform the activity expressed by **swim**. Some of these auxiliaries and verb phrase equivalents and the ideas that they express are described in Sections 47–51.

47 | AUXILIARIES or EQUIVALENT PHRASES that EXPRESS ABILITY TO DO SOMETHING

47a. CAN and COULD

For present or future time: CAN   + simple form
For past time: COULD + simple form

> He **can swim** the length of the pool.
> I **can see** you tomorrow morning.[4]
> She **could drive** a car by the time she was sixteen.
> He said that he **could come** tomorrow.[5]

Cannot (can't) and **could not (couldn't)** express inability:

> He **can't come** today.
> He **couldn't come** yesterday.

47b. BE ABLE TO

For present (or future) time: AM (IS, ARE) ABLE TO + simple form
For past time: WAS (WERE) ABLE TO + simple form
For future time: WILL BE ABLE TO
                                  or   } + simple form
                                AM (IS, ARE) GOING TO BE ABLE TO

---

[3] In the active construction, "The speeding car **hit** the man," the speeding car is emphasized more than the man hit by the car.

[4] **Could** + *simple form* also expresses future time. However, this construction suggests possibility rather than a definite statement of ability. Compare:
> I **can see** you tomorrow.
> I **could see** you tomorrow (if it is important).

[5] In a noun clause following a past tense verb form, the past auxiliary form is ordinarily used to express future or present time. (See Section 44.)

THE PASSIVE CONSTRUCTION AND AUXILIARY VERBS

> I'm **able to drive** in traffic now.
> He **is** now **able to walk** without crutches.
> They **were able to go** after all.
> We're **going to be able to see** you tomorrow.[6]

For future time in a noun clause following a past tense verb form, **would be able to** or **was (were) going to be able to** is ordinarily used:

> He said that he **would be able to help** us move next week.
> They told me that they **were going to be able to leave** on Saturday.

Am not, was not (wasn't) etc. + **able to** and **am, was,** etc. + **unable to** express inability.

> I **am not able to accept** your invitation.
> I **am unable to accept** your invitation.

48 | AUXILIARIES USED in REQUESTING and GIVING PERMISSION TO DO SOMETHING

48a. MAY, CAN, and COULD are used in requesting permission. Although **may** and **can** are used interchangeably in making requests, there are some people who consider **can** unacceptable. **Could** has the effect of softening **can**.[7]

For present or future time: MAY / CAN / or / COULD } + simple form

> **May** I **leave** now?
> **May** I **see** you tomorrow?
> **Can** I **borrow** your book?
> **Could** I **turn** in my paper tomorrow?

The use of **can't** or **couldn't** suggests that the speaker realizes there is some reason why permission may not be given.

> I know the assignment is due today, but **can't (couldn't)** I turn it in tomorrow?

48b. MAY, CAN, and COULD are used in giving permission.

For present or future time: MAY / CAN / or / COULD } + simple form

> You **may leave** now.
> You **may come** back at 5:30.
> You **can hang** your coat here.
> You **could have** an appointment tomorrow.

Cannot (can't) is ordinarily used when permission is *not* given:

> You **can't come** in just now.
> You **can't park** your car here.

---

[6] **Would be able to** + *simple form* also expresses future time. However, this construction suggests possibility rather than a definite statement of ability. Compare:
> We **are going to be able to see** you tomorrow.
> We **would be able to see** you tomorrow (if it is important).

[7] **Could** softens **can** in much the same way as "**Would** you please . . ." softens "**Will** you please . . ." in making requests.

49 AUXILIARIES or EQUIVALENT PHRASES that EXPRESS OBLIGATION and NECESSITY

49a. SHOULD and OUGHT TO express a sense of obligation to do or become something or to feel a certain way about something; that is, the speaker believes that either he or another person is obliged to act or feel a certain way. **Should** and **ought to** are usually interchangeable.

For present or future time: SHOULD or OUGHT TO } + simple form

You **should be** ashamed of yourself.
I **should study** tonight because I'm behind in my homework, but I probably won't.
She **ought to improve** her appearance before she looks for a job.

For unfulfilled obligations in past time: SHOULD HAVE or OUGHT TO HAVE } + past participle

I **should have given** you my telephone number.
He **should have seen** a doctor.
I told him that he **ought to have known** better.[8]

Should is ordinarily used in negative statements and in questions:

(1) In statements, **should not (shouldn't)** expresses a sense of obligation not to do something, rather than absence of obligation:

You **shouldn't smoke** so much.

(2) Questions introduced by **should** and **should not (shouldn't)** are used in asking for advice or offering suggestions:

Should I **ask** Jane now?

(*or:* Do you think that I should ask Jane now?)

Shouldn't you **stay** home when you have a bad cold?

(*or:* Don't you think that you should stay home when you have a bad cold?)

49b. HAD BETTER also expresses a sense of obligation in much the same way as **should** or **ought to.**

For present or future time: HAD BETTER + simple form

You **had better take care** of your cold.
I**'d better be** on my way now.

Had better not expresses obligation not to do something.

You **had better not go** out without a coat.
He**'d better not be** late again.

49c. MUST and HAVE TO express a strong sense of obligation that approaches necessity to do something.

---

[8] **Ought to have** (or **should have**) in the noun clause indicates that the obligation has not been fulfilled; if the obligation might have been fulfilled at or after the time the statement is made, **should** or **ought to** + *simple form* would be used:
I told him that he **should (ought to) see** a doctor.

THE PASSIVE CONSTRUCTION AND AUXILIARY VERBS

For present or future time: MUST
or   } + simple form
HAVE (HAS) TO

> They **must be** there on time.
> I **must remember** to telephone Nancy.
> I **have to go** to the grocery store.
> He **has to study** tonight.

For past time: HAD TO + simple form

> I **had to go** downtown yesterday to see my dentist.
> They **had to leave** the party early last night.

Must not expresses a strong sense of obligation not to do something.

> You **must not disturb** him.

Do (does, did) not have to conveys the idea that it is no longer necessary to do something.[9]

> I **don't have to work** today.
> He **doesn't have to study** tonight.
> We **didn't have to take** the examination.

50 | AUXILIARIES or EQUIVALENT PHRASES that EXPRESS POSSIBILITY and PROBABILITY

50a. MAY and MIGHT are usually interchangeable, but **may** seems to be stronger or more emphatic than **might**. Also, **might** is ordinarily used for future time in a noun clause following a past tense verb form.

For present or future time: MAY
or   } + simple form
MIGHT

> She **may change** her mind.
> I **may be able to go** after all.[10]
> She **might have to move** to Chicago.
> He said that he **might transfer** to another university next fall.

For past time: MAY HAVE
or   } + past participle
MIGHT HAVE

> She **may have tried** to call you yesterday.
> I **might have left** my keys at home.

May not and **might not** express lack of possibility or probability:

> I **may not go** after all.
> They **might not be able to come.**
> They **may not have been** there at all.[11]

---

[9] **Do (does, did) not** + **need to** also conveys the idea that it is no longer necessary to do something.
  Example: We **don't need to** take the exam.
[10] **May** and **might** are combined with the verb phrases **be able to** and **have to,** but not with **can** or **must.**
[11] **May** and **might** are not ordinarily used in questions to express possibility or probability. Compare:
  He **may be** there.   **Is** he **likely to be** there?

50b. SHOULD and OUGHT TO express strong probability that approaches expectation.

For present or future time: SHOULD or OUGHT TO } + simple form

> You **should (ought to) receive** the package by next Tuesday.
>
> (*or:* You can expect to receive the package by next Tuesday.)

For unfulfilled expectation in past time: SHOULD HAVE or OUGHT TO HAVE } + past participle

> He **should (ought to) have arrived** yesterday.
>
> (*or:* We expected him to arrive yesterday.)

50c. MUST also expresses strong probability that approaches expectation.
For present time: MUST + BE
For present or future time: MUST BE + present participle

> He isn't here. He **must be** out to lunch.
> You look happy. You **must be having** a good time.
> According to the telegram, he **must be arriving** tonight.[12]

For past time: MUST HAVE + past participle

> His car is gone. He **must have decided** to go home early.
> You're on time. You **must have got up** early today.

50d. The adverbs **possibly** and **probably** may be used with various auxiliaries to express the idea of possibility or probability.

> He'**d probably be able to help** you.
> He **can possibly see** you tomorrow.
> They **probably had to leave** early.
> She **might possibly have tried to call** you yesterday.

51 AUXILIARIES or EQUIVALENT PHRASES USED in EXPRESSING PREFERENCES and WANTS

51a. WOULD RATHER expresses preference for one thing or one course of action over another.

For present or future time: WOULD RATHER + simple form

> I **would rather have** steak than chicken.
>
> (*or:* I would prefer steak to chicken.)
>
> He **would rather stay** home tonight.

For past time: WOULD RATHER HAVE + past participle

> I **would rather have had** a fur coat than an umbrella for my birthday!
> We'**d rather have gone** to the baseball game.

Would rather not indicates a preference or desire not to do something or follow a course of action:

> We **would rather not talk** about that any more.
> I'**d rather not be put** in charge of the program.

---

[12] In the sentence "He must **not** be arriving tonight," we expect something not to take place.

51b. WOULD is used in expressing wants and desires; *I* or *we* **should** (instead of **would**) is used by some people.

> For present or future time: WOULD + simple form
>> I'm hungry. **I would like** a sandwich. Wouldn't you?
>> **I'd like** to see that movie again sometime.
>> I'm sure that she **would be** glad to help you.
>> He said that he **would like** to see you again.[13]

> For past time: WOULD HAVE + past participle
>> I think that even you **would have liked** that book.
>> **I'd have been** glad to show you around the city.

> **Would not** indicates a negative attitude or feeling about something:
>> I **wouldn't want** to go through that experience again.
>> He **wouldn't like** to hear you say that, I'm sure.

---

[13] There are other ways of indicating wants and desires besides the **would** constructions. Compare:
>> He **would like to see** you again soon.
>> He **wants to see** you again soon.
>> He **wishes that he could see** you again soon.

See Section 53 for constructions with **wish (that)**.

EXERCISES FOR PART XI

EXERCISE 40

Change the following sentences from the active to the passive construction.

    Example: John delivered the package.
               <u>The package was delivered by John.</u>

1. The secretary will read the minutes of the last meeting.

2. The postman brought the mail early today.

3. Fred planted this oak tree five years ago.

4. Our club holds meetings once a month.

5. The messenger will deliver the package right away.

6. The Clays have invited the Bakers to dinner.

7. He will answer your letter soon.

8. Frank Lloyd Wright designed this building.

9. The pianist played the concerto very well.

10. Did the plumber repair the faucet in the kitchen?

11. Mozart composed the music for <u>Don Giovanni</u>.

12. John gave me these records.

13. Eli Whitney invented the cotton gin in 1793.

14. We took our guests for a drive yesterday.

15. Ernest Hemingway wrote <u>A Farewell to Arms</u>.

EXERCISE 41

Answer the following questions. Give responses that include a subject and a verb.

(A) The following questions are for practice in using the passive construction.

> Example: Will the report be ready by the secretary?
> No, it will be read by the chairman.

1. Where is the class held on Friday?

2. Is he going to be invited to the party?

3. When was the United Nations Charter signed?

4. Was that book written by your professor?

5. Is it generally believed that the senator will be defeated in the next election?

6. Where were you born?

7. Have they been asked to go on the tour?

8. When will the next class be held?

9. Was Ruth awarded a scholarship?

10. Why was the class dismissed today?

11. Was anyone hurt in the accident?

12. Where was the last conference held?

13. Are you often asked to give speeches?

14. Was America discovered in 1492 by Columbus?

15. The law of gravitation was formulated by Sir Isaac Newton, wasn't it?

(B) The following questions are for practice in using auxiliary verbs.

> Example: Can Albert drive a car?
> Yes, he can.

1. How fast can you type?

2. Why couldn't you come to class yesterday?

3. Will you be able to get here before 7 o'clock?

4. Did he say that he would be able to work tomorrow?

5. May I be excused from class today?

6. Could I hand in the assignment tomorrow?

7. Which chapters should we study for the examination?

8. Did he say that we ought to do some outside reading?

9. Do you think that I had better explain the situation to her?

10. Do you really have to go now?

11. Must you leave so soon?

12. Can you possibly be there by noon?

13. Do you think that he might resign?

14. Who told you that they might not be able to come?

15. Would you rather have a new car or a trip around the world?

16. Would you rather go out to dinner tomorrow night?

17. What would you like for dinner?

18. What would you like to do tonight?

19. Would you like to meet her?

20. Do you think that you should have spent so much money?

21. What did he have to do?

22. Where could he possibly have gone?

23. Why do we have to leave so early?

24. Did he tell you that he might sell his car?

25. What can I do to improve my pronunciation?

EXERCISE 42

Complete the following sentences:

1. I have forgotten my pencil. Could I _____

2. She can read Greek, but she can't _____

3. It is getting cold. You had better _____

4. This coffee tastes so good. May I _____

5. I'm going to the opera tonight, but I'd rather _____

6. We enjoyed meeting you, and we would like _____

7. When I saw him yesterday, he said that he might _____

8. He doesn't look at all well. He should _____

9. We can stay only a few minutes because we have to _____

10. I finally passed the English course, now I don't have to _____

PART XII | Verb Forms in Clauses Involving Wishes, Demands, and Conditions

52 | INTRODUCTION

Special attention is given here to verb forms in the following constructions:

(1) In clauses following the expressions **wish** and **wish that;**
(2) In clauses following such expressions as **demand that** and **it is necessary that;** and
(3) In clauses of condition when the situation is unreal or contrary to fact.

The time expressed by the verb forms in these clauses does not correspond to the time ordinarily expressed by the various tenses. For example in the sentence, "I wish that you **were** here now," the past form of **be** is used to express present time. These constructions are discussed in the following sections.

53 | WISH (THAT) + NOUN CLAUSE

53a. The simple past or the past progressive tense or an equivalent (past form of auxiliary + simple form) is ordinarily used to express a wish for something in present or future time in a noun clause following **wish** or **wish that.** With the verb **be, were** is used for all persons.

Below are some situations involving wishes in present or future time:

(1) A situation *does not exist,* but we wish that it did:

> I am not an actress, but I certainly wish (that) I **were**.[1]
> He wishes (that) he **were** able to go to college, but he has to work to support his mother.
> We wish (that) you **played** bridge.
> I wish I **could speak** Chinese.

(2) A situation *exists,* but we wish that it were different or that it did not exist:

> She has red hair and freckles, but she wishes (that) she **didn't**.
> I wish (that) you **wouldn't talk** so much about business.[2]
> They wish (that) their children **were not** such poor students.
> I wish there **were** no classes today.

(3) A situation *is in progress* or is of a continuous nature, and we wish that it would change right now or in the near future:

> Don't you wish (that) it **would stop** raining?[3]
> I wish (that) he **would finish** his speech in a hurry.
> I wish (that) I **could stop** coughing.
> We wish you **would change** the subject.[4]

---

[1] This construction requires **were** for all persons.
   The parentheses indicate that the **(that)** is often omitted in actual usage.

[2] This statement is actually another way of making a request.

[3] Wishes may be expressed in question form; the negative question form is often used.

[4] In (3) the past form of an auxiliary + simple form is used; the simple past form of the verb would not be appropriate in these situations.

(4) A situation *cannot exist* right now or in the future because circumstances make it impossible, but we still wish that it could:

> He wishes (that) he **could go** with us tonight, but unfortunately he can't.
> We wish (that) you **were coming** with us, but we know how busy you are.
> I wish I **could meet** you for lunch tomorrow, but I'm going to be out of town.

(5) A situation *is not yet in existence,* and we wish for its realization right now or in the future:

> I wish (that) you **would take** me out to dinner.
> We wish (that) he **would marry** the girl next door.
> Don't you wish the waiter **would hurry up** and bring us our soup before it gets cold?

53b. The past perfect tense or an equivalent (past form of auxiliary + **have** + past participle) is ordinarily used to express a wish for something in past time in a noun clause following **wish** or **wish that.**

Below are some situations involving wishes in past time:

(1) A situation *did not exist,* but we wish that it had:

> He wishes (that) he **had taken** your advice, but he didn't pay attention to you at that time.
> She wishes (that) she **had sent** a telegram.[5]
> They wish they **could have been** here for the class reunion.

(2) A situation *existed,* but we wish that it had been different or that it had not existed:

> She wishes (that) she **hadn't bought** a new car.
> We wish (that) they **hadn't sent** us such an expensive present.
> Paul wishes (that) he **hadn't wasted** his time when he was in college.[6]

54 | EXPRESSIONS such as **DEMAND THAT** and **IT IS NECESSARY THAT** + NOUN CLAUSE

The simple form of the verb is used for all persons in the noun clause after such expressions as **demand that** and **it is necessary that.**

> I demand that I **be allowed** to call my lawyer.[7]
> He demanded that he **be given** the right to express his opinion.
> I ask that I **be given** time to consider the matter further.
> The committee recommends that the budget **be discussed** at the next meeting.
> I move that the meeting **be adjourned.**
> The doctor suggested that the patient **stop** smoking.[8]

---

[5] Whether we use the simple present or the simple past of **wish** depends on the time the wish is made. Compare:

> I **wish** [now or at the present time] that I **had bought** that red hat.
> I **wished** [yesterday or at some time in the past] that I **had bought** that red hat.

[6] The simple past form in a clause that follows **wished** also indicates a wish for something in the past. This construction appears occasionally when the situation did not exist at the time the wish was made in the past.

> I felt so homesick that I **wished** I **were** back home again.

[7] The passive construction is often used in making demands, requests, and so forth, probably because the passive makes the statements seem more objective or impersonal. The verb **be** is used for all persons.

[8] The simple form is used for all persons. Some native speakers use **would** or **should** + simple form in some of these constructions.

> The doctor suggested that the patient **should stop** smoking.

VERB FORMS IN CLAUSES INVOLVING WISHES, DEMANDS, AND CONDITIONS

They have requested that I **sign** the contract and **return** it immediately.
Is it necessary that he **take** an examination?
It is important that you **follow** directions.
It is essential that you **give** me all the information at your disposal.[9]

55 | CLAUSES of CONDITION

Clauses of condition indicate the circumstances under which the situation expressed in the main clause may exist or occur. The clause of condition ordinarily begins with **if.**

For example, in the sentence, "**If he comes,** I'll tell him that you want to see him," the **if**-clause states the circumstances under which the situation in the main clause will occur.

Clauses of condition are of two main types:

(1) those stating real or factual circumstances under which the situation in the main clause can, will be, or is habitually realized;

(2) those stating unreal, contrary to fact, or hypothetical circumstances under which the situation in the main clause might be or might have been realized.

55a. The simple present tense or an equivalent (usually present form of auxiliary + simple form) is used in clauses that state real or factual conditions in present or future time. The verb form in the main clause depends on the meaning expressed.

(1) When a situation will or can be realized under the circumstances stated in the **if**-clause, the future tense form or an equivalent is used in the main clause:

> If I **have** time, **I'll call** for you tonight.[10]
> If Jim **can't go, are** you **going to go** anyway?
> **We'll ask** her about her brother if we **see** her.
> If **I'm not** too tired, I **may go** shopping.

(2) When a request or suggestion is made or an obligation is expressed under the circumstances stated in the **if**-clause, the verb form in the main clause is one of the forms used in making requests:

> If you **leave,** please **turn out** the lights.
> If you **go** by the next post office, **will** you please **get** me some stamps?
> If you **see** her, **would** you please **tell** her to get in touch with me?
> If she **is** there, you **should introduce** yourself to her.
> If you **have** headaches often, I **suggest** that you see a doctor.
> If you **fail,** you **ought to be ashamed** of yourself.

(3) When a situation is habitually or customarily realized under the circumstances stated in the **if**-clause, the simple present tense or an equivalent is ordinarily used in the main clause:

---

[9] While constructions in Section 54 are found in textbooks, newspapers, public lectures, and so forth, there are other ways of expressing these ideas in conversational English. Compare:
> **I ask that I be given time** to consider the matter further.
> **Please give me time** to consider the matter further.
> **I want you to give me more time** to consider the matter further.
> It is important **that you follow directions.**
> It is important **for you to follow directions.**
> **You must follow directions.**

[10] The auxiliary **will** + *simple form* is occasionally used in the **if**-clause.
> If you **will cook** the dinner, I'll wash the dishes.
>   (If you do your part, I'll do mine.)
> If he **won't ask** her, I will.
>   (If he refuses to ask her, I will ask her myself.)

> If she **has** several appointments in the morning, she **goes** out to lunch at 1:30.
>
> If he **has** plenty of time, he usually **does** very well on his exams.
>
> I **can't do** good work if I **have** to work under pressure.

55b. The simple past tense (**were** for the verb **be**) is used in clauses that state unreal, contrary to fact, or hypothetical conditions in present or future time; the verb in the main clause is **would (could, might)** + simple form.

> If I **were** the professor, I **would give** easier tests.
>
> If I **were** you, I **would take** his advice.
>
> If he **wanted** to (do so), he **could find** the time.
>
> If you **took** a trip to Europe, which countries **would** you **visit?**
>
> If I **won** the contest, I **would be** very much surprised.

Occasionally an auxiliary + simple form is used in the **if**-clause.

> If I **could go,** I certainly would do so.
>
> If he **should refuse** to help you, what would you do?

55c. The past perfect tense is used in clauses that state unreal, contrary to fact, or hypothetical conditions in past time; the verb in the main clause is **would (could, might)** + **have** + past participle.

> If I **had been** there, I **would have made** several criticisms.
>
> If they **had asked** him, he **would have been able to help** them.
>
> If you **had told** him, he **might have made** some suggestions.
>
> If the semester **had ended** a week earlier, we **could have gone** to Mexico with my uncle.

Occasionally an auxiliary + **have** + past participle is used in the **if**-clause.

> If you **could have had** your choice, which job would you have taken?
>
> If I **could have seen** her, I would have been able to explain everything.

55d. Besides the **if**-clause, there are other ways of stating conditions. Compare the following:

> He can be charming **if** he wants to.
>
> He can be charming **when** he wants to.
>
> **If** Mortimer Glad is elected, do you think that he will try to reduce taxes?
>
> **Suppose that** Mortimer Glad is elected. Do you think that he will try to reduce taxes?
>
> **If** you were in my shoes, what would you do?
>
> **Supposing** you were in my shoes—what would you do?
>
> **If** Germany had not fought against Russia in World War II, do you think that the outcome of the war might have been different?
>
> **Let's suppose** Germany had not fought against Russia in World War II. Do you think that the outcome might have been different?
>
> I'll accept the invitation **if** you'll go with me.
>
> I'll accept the invitation **provided that** you go with me.

EXERCISES FOR PART XII

EXERCISE 43

Answer the following questions. Give long responses in order to have practice in using the constructions introduced in Part XII.

    Example: If it rains tomorrow, what will you do?
                 I'll stay home if it rains.

1. If you go to the store, will you get me a newspaper?

2. If you have time, don't you think you should answer that letter today?

3. Can he do well on tests if he has enough time?

4. If she telephones, will you please tell her to call back later?

5. If you miss the train, what will you do?

6. What would you do if you lost your job?

7. If you could take a trip next summer, where would you go?

8. If you had the chance, would you go into politics?

9. What would you do if you were in his situation?

10. If your house should happen to catch fire, what would you do?

11. Suppose you had some money to invest. How would you invest it?

12. Suppose you had been asked to select the two best movies of the year. Which ones would you have picked?

13. Where do you wish you were now?

14. Did the doctor recommend that you stop smoking?

15. Is it important that he attend the meeting?

16. If you see Margaret, will you please tell her the news?

17. Do you wish that you were ten years younger?

18. Is it necessary that we turn in the homework today?

19. Has anyone requested that you give a speech about your country?

20. If you lost your wallet, what would you do?

Exercises For Part XII

EXERCISE 44

Complete the following sentences:

    Example: I'm not going on the trip, but I wish that _____ I were _____.

1. He isn't here today, but he wishes _____
   _____.

2. It has been foggy all day. I certainly wish that _____
   _____ tomorrow.

3. Some friends of mine took a trip to Canada last summer. I wish that they _____
   _____.

4. I saw my doctor yesterday, and he insisted that _____
   _____.

5. I am thinking about taking graduate work. What do you recommend that _____
   _____?

6. Mr. McDonald has been working hard all week because it is important that ____
   _____.

7. I'm not a scientist, but if I were, I _____
   _____.

8. He doesn't have a car, but if he had one he _____
   _____.

9. She was not in class yesterday, but if she had been, she _____
   _____.

10. I may be asked to serve on the committee, and if so, I _____

EXERCISE 45

Write a short paragraph answering each of the following questions:

1. If you inherited a million dollars, what would you do with the money?

2. If you were a leading statesman of your country, what proposals would you make?

Exercise 45 (continued)

3. Suppose that a tourist asked your advice about what to see in your country. What place of interest would you suggest that he see?

4. Suppose that you were asked to make three wishes. First, wish that something in the present were different; second, wish that something in the past had been different; third, wish that something in the present would be different in the future. What would your wishes be?

PART XIII Troublesome Verbs

56 SAY and TELL

56a. Both SAY and TELL are used in relating indirectly what someone has said.

>He **says** that you are a very good student.
>He **said** to me the other day that we should have good weather next week.
>
>They **tell** me that you are doing a fine job.
>He **told** Jack that he would meet us for lunch.[1]

(In these constructions, an indirect object follows **tell**; a **to-**phrase, not an indirect object, may follow **say**.)

56b. SAY is used in quoting directly from a spoken or written source.

>In his speech of acceptance last Tuesday, the new director **said,** "I know that I shall enjoy working with all of you."
>In a recent article in a fashion magazine, a well-known dress designer **said,** "Women will wear whatever I decide they should wear."

56c. TELL is used in the following situations:

(1) **Tell**—the truth or a lie:

>Rodney always **tells** the truth.
>He always **tells** us the truth.
>According to legend, George Washington **could** never **tell** a lie.
>He **couldn't tell** a lie to his father.

(In this construction, an indirect object may follow **tell** or a **to-**phrase may follow the direct object.)

(2) **Tell**—a story, a joke, the news, the facts, and so forth:

>Try to **tell** me all the important facts.
>Why **don't** you **tell** Stella the joke you told me yesterday?
>George **has** already **told** the good news to his wife.
>She **is** always **telling** fantastic stories about herself.

(An indirect object may follow **tell** or a **to-**phrase may follow the direct object.)

(3) **Tell**—*about* experiences, plans, and so forth:

>Please **tell** us **about** your experiences in Alaska.
>Denise **has** already **told** them **about** her plans.

(An indirect object may follow **tell.**)

(4) **Tell**—time:

>**Would** you please **tell** me the time?
>**Can** you **tell** me the time?[2]

(An indirect object usually follows **tell** in expressions of this kind.)

---

[1] **Say** and **tell** are also used in referring to the kind of things that someone says about someone or something.
>What **did** he **say?**
>He **said** some nice things about you.
>He **said** some very nice things to her.
>He **told** us many good things about your work.

[2] **Say** is used in the following situation:
>What time do you have?   My watch **says** 2 o'clock.

(5) **Tell**—one thing or person from another [make out or distinguish]:

> **Can** you **tell** one brand of coffee from another?
> I **can't tell** the twins apart.

(Neither an indirect object nor a **to**-phrase follows **tell** in expressions of this kind.)

57 TALK and SPEAK

57a. TALK and SPEAK refer to the act of oral communication and are used in the following types of situations:

(1) **Talk** or **speak**—*to* someone (*about* something or someone):

> I **talked to** her today.
> He **spoke to** Mrs. Perkins this morning.
> He **talked to** us **about** the present-day economic system.
> If I were you, I **would speak to** Mr. Green **about** the situation.

(2) **Talk** or **speak**—*about* something or someone:

> After the lecture, some of the students stayed and **talked about** what the professor had said.
> The lecturer **spoke about** the seriousness of juvenile delinquency throughout the world.
> We **talked about** our old school friends all afternoon.[3]

57b. SPEAK is ordinarily used to refer to the act of making or giving a speech or to the manner in which someone speaks.

> The President **will speak** at the banquet.
> **Did** the football coach **speak** at the rally?
> You **speak** very clearly.
> Mrs. Neeley **speaks** French with a Texas drawl.

58 DO and MAKE

58a. **DO** (as a principal verb) and **MAKE** are not ordinarily interchangeable. In the following examples, **do** means to perform, accomplish, or finish, and **make** means to construct, build, or create.

> He **does** his job well.
> We **did** a number of things today.
> They **did** their homework this afternoon.
>
> He **made** all of the furniture in this room.
> Margaret **makes** her own clothes.
> They **make** costume jewelry for department stores.

---

[3] Although both **talk** and **speak** are used in these constructions, we tend to use **talk** when referring to discussion or conversation on a more informal level, as in the sentence, "We **talked about** (rather than **spoke about**) our friends." Also compare:

> We **talked** for an hour.
> (Our conversation lasted an hour.)
> He **spoke** for twenty minutes.
> (His speech lasted twenty minutes.)

TROUBLESOME VERBS

58b. DO is used in the expressions in boldface type in the sentences below:

You always **do the right thing,** but I always seem to **do the wrong thing.**
Bill always **does his best.**
Will you **do** me **a favor?**
He **does** a lot of **good** for mankind.
Mr. Marks **does the cooking** on Sundays.
We **did the dishes** [washed and dried the dishes] in a hurry.
When we're short of money, we **do without** [get along or go without] cigarettes.
Let's **do away with** [dispense with or get rid of] all this red tape.
He **did** these **paintings** [painted the pictures] when he was in Italy.

58c. MAKE is used in the expressions in boldface type in the sentences below:

I hope I didn't **make** too many **mistakes** in the exam.
Mr. Willis should **make** [give] **the speech** of welcome.
Mrs. Preston **made** [prepared] **the salad** while Mr. Preston broiled the steaks.
The maid **makes** [puts in order] **the beds** every day.
I have to **make** [earn] **a living** somehow.
They are **making** [earning] a lot of **money** in the stock market.
She is **making the arrangements** [organizing] for the party.
Please **make certain** [be sure] that you have not forgotten anything.
It is important to **make a good impression** [create favorable reaction] on people.
Your suggestion **makes sense** [is sensible or practical].
Will his illness **make a difference** [cause a change] in his attitude toward his work?
The organization is **making** steady **progress** [advancing or going forward] toward their goal.
I would like to **make a request** [ask a favor].
Why are you **making fun of** [mocking or ridiculing] me?
I have to **make up my mind** [decide] by tomorrow.
I'll **make up** [invent or think up] some excuse.
Why don't you **make up with** [settle your differences with] Fred?

59 | LIE—LAY; RISE—RAISE; SIT—SET [4]

59a. LIE, RISE, and SIT are not followed by an object.

The old church **lies** [is located] north of the town.
I'm going to lie down for a while.
Your book **is lying** on the hall table.
Mr. Griffin **rose** [got up] from his chair to greet Mrs. Barnes.
The cost of production **has risen** [has gone up] 40 per cent.
The water in the river **is** still **rising** after the storm.
Please **sit** in this chair.
She **sat** in the chair by the window and watched the parade.
I **have been sitting** at my typewriter all day.

---

[4] The principal parts of these verbs are—

lie	lay	lain	lying
lay	laid	laid	laying
rise	rose	risen	rising
raise	raised	raised	raising
sit	sat	sat	sitting
set	set	set	setting

59b. LAY, RAISE, and SET are followed by an object.[5]

Please **don't lay** [don't put] that hot dish on the table without a mat under it.
He **laid** the evening paper on the desk when he came in.
My brother **was laying** [was placing in position] bricks in the patio when we arrived at his house.
Mrs. Loomis **raises** [grows] prize roses.
My landlady **raised** [increased] my rent.
He **is raising** [is putting up] the window shade to let in the sun.
Mr. Early always **sets** [puts] his briefcase on the mantle.
Ed **set** [established] a good example for his younger brothers.
She **is setting the table** [is arranging the table for a meal].

---

[5] *Exceptions:* In the examples below, **set** and **lay** are not followed by objects. Notice the meanings of the verbs in these situations.

The sun rises in the east, and it **sets** [goes down] in the west.
The concrete **will set** [will harden] in a few hours.
They **set out** [departed] for the beach about an hour ago.
How often does a hen **set** [brood]?
The hens **are laying** [are producing eggs] well this season.

EXERCISES FOR PART XIII

EXERCISE 46

Read the following sentences, giving the correct word in parentheses. (Also write the forms in the spaces at the right.)

Example: What did he (say, <u>tell</u>) you?   tell
(Read: What did he tell you?)

1. She (says, tells) that the green car belongs to Harry.   _____

2. They (said, told) me they had seen the movie already.   _____

3. Patrick Henry (said, told), "Give me liberty or give me death!"   _____

4. Mr. King (has said, has told) me some interesting things about research.   _____

5. Please (say, tell) me the truth.   _____

6. I wish you (would say, would tell) me all about it.   _____

7. In this light, I (can't say, can't tell) whether this suit is navy blue or black.   _____

8. Mr. Lane always (says, tells) good after-dinner jokes.   _____

9. This clock (says, tells) 12:15.   _____

10. Would you please (say, tell) me the time?   _____

11. He (talks, speaks) English with an accent.   _____

12. The governor (will talk, will speak) at the convention.   _____

13. They (did, made) four assignments over the weekend.   _____

14. Mrs. Kelly (did, made) the curtains out of unbleached muslin.   _____

15. I'll try to (do, make) my best.   _____

16. Would you please (do, make) me another favor?   _____

17. Mr. Price (does, makes) a good living for his family.   _____

18. It (doesn't do, doesn't make) any difference to me what we do.   _____

19. After breakfast we did the dishes and (did, made) the beds.   _____

20. I (did, made) only one mistake on the last quiz.   _____

21. Why don't you (lie, lay) down for a while if you're tired.   _____

22. My father (is sitting, is setting) on the porch.   _____

23. Several students (rose, raised) their hands to answer the question.   _____

24. The postman (lay, laid) the package on the steps.   _____

25. The shopping district (lies, lays) south of the Civic Center.   _____

EXERCISE 47

Answer the following questions. Whenever possible, give long responses in order to have practice in using the constructions introduced in Part XIII.

    Example: What time is it?
             My watch _says_ 2:35.

1. What did you talk to him about?

2. Did he tell you about his latest plans?

3. What shall we tell him to do?

4. How did you do on the last exam?

5. Are you making fun of me?

6. What did you do today?

7. Are you making progress in learning English?

8. How long does it usually take you to do your homework?

9. Did she make a good impression on you?

10. Have you made up your mind about where you're going on your vacation?

11. Can't you do without desserts in order to lose weight?

12. Have you made all the arrangements for the program?

13. Would you mind doing the dishes?

14. Have you made certain that the doors are locked?

15. Do you know how to make spaghetti?

REVIEW EXERCISES FOR VERBS (UNIT 2)

EXERCISE 48

Answer the following questions. Give long responses (or short responses followed by an explanation) in order to have practice in using the various verb forms introduced in Unit 2.

1. How long do you plan to stay here?

2. What are you going to do next summer?

3. Which books did you have to get for this course?

4. Have you ever appeared on a radio program?

5. Are you studying anything besides English at this time?

6. What would you like to do this evening?

7. What were you doing at this time last year?

8. Does it rain a great deal in this part of the country?

9. How many years have you studied English?

10. Can either of your parents speak English?

11. If you were ill, where would you go for medical care?

12. Did you say that you would not be able to meet us for lunch?

13. Would you rather go swimming or play tennis?

14. If someone asked you how to get to the library, what would you tell him?

15. Didn't you know that we were going to have a quiz today?

16. How long does it take to get from here to your house?

17. Do you think it might rain tonight?

18. What do you want for your birthday?

Exercise 48 (continued)

19. Is it necessary that we write all our papers in ink?

20. If Bill had asked you for some money, would you have given it to him?

21. Should a person tell his friends how much money he is making?

22. Where were you born?

23. Would you tell me how to say "thank you" in your language?

24. Do you know anyone who would help me make some costumes for the play?

25. How long have we been studying verbs?

26. Could you give me two ways of asking permission to do something?

27. Is it important that we be on time for the meeting tonight?

28. If the store is open, will you please get me some typing paper?

29. Shall we leave in a few minutes?

30. Would you suggest that I do more reading?

31. Where would you like to be right now?

32. Your father is an architect, isn't he?

33. Where did you put your hat?

34. What were you doing a few minutes ago?

35. How long does it usually take you to get downtown from your house?

36. Can you tell me the name of a good restaurant?

37. What time do you have?

38. How many people were invited to the reception?

39. How long did it take you to do the last assignment?

40. Shouldn't we do the next exercise now?

Review Exercises For Verbs (Unit 2)

EXERCISE 49

Place in the spaces at the right the letter indicating the correct form:

Example: He (A) said (B) told the truth.   B

1. I (A) am living (B) have lived here for six months.

2. Mr. Smith (A) went (B) has gone to Mexico many times.

3. Professor Brown (A) teaches (B) is teaching a course in Old English this semester, isn't he?

4. Did he say that he (A) will arrive (B) would arrive next week?

5. Dr. Anderson (A) gave (B) has given a speech on the cardiac cycle, didn't he?

6. Would you mind if I (A) turn (B) turned on the radio?

7. Mrs. Bennett will come to see us when she (A) has (B) will have enough time.

8. Why haven't you been able to (A) make (B) do any progress?

9. He (A) use to practice (B) used to practice the piano three hours a day.

10. (A) Did you tell (B) Did you say Mrs. Green the news?

11. I know that you (A) can make (B) can do a wise decision.

12. My roommate (A) is sitting (B) is setting downstairs.

13. You (A) had better go (B) would rather go to bed early tonight because you look tired.

14. They will not be able to wait until Harry (A) arrives (B) will arrive.

15. Is it necessary that the student (A) return (B) returns the book by 4 o'clock?

Exercise 49 (continued)

16. The conference (A) ended (B) has ended (C) had ended with a banquet last night. _____

17. They wish that you (A) were (B) had been (C) would have been there last week. _____

18. He (A) must go (B) would go (C) should have gone to the last meeting. _____

19. Did they say they (A) will telephone (B) have telephoned (C) would telephone me tomorrow? _____

20. The tired man felt better after he (A) has rested (B) had rested (C) was rested a while. _____

21. The children (A) have gone (B) went (C) had gone to the circus yesterday. _____

22. I (A) should go (B) should have gone (C) had to go to the dentist yesterday, but I was not able to get there. _____

23. There were ten people in the room. I (A) never saw (B) had never seen (C) am never seeing five of them before. _____

24. Yesterday we (A) went (B) had gone (C) have gone to visit my uncle for the day. _____

25. I wish that I (A) will go (B) would go (C) could go with you. _____

26. He (A) must go (B) should go (C) had to go back because he had forgotten his briefcase. _____

27. Please hand in your paper after you (A) will correct (B) have corrected (C) corrected the spelling errors. _____

28. Mr. Johnson said that he (A) might go (B) can go (C) may go to Afghanistan next year. _____

29. He would get over his cold if he (A) would take (B) would have taken (C) has taken the medicine the doctor gave him. _____

30. We would like to go with you if we (A) would have had (B) had (C) would have the time. _____

Review Exercises For Verbs (Unit 2)

EXERCISE 50

Read the following sentences, giving the correct form of the verbs in parentheses. (Also write the forms in the spaces at the right.)

    Example: We (be) here two years.   have been
                 (Read: We have been here two years.)

1. This is one of the most interesting articles I (read) in a long time.   _____

2. She (play) the violin well, doesn't she?   _____

3. I checked the data carefully before I (turn) in my lab report.   _____

4. You (fly) in an airplane before, haven't you?   _____

5. She (do) her homework when I called her last night.   _____

6. I'll keep on working on this problem until I (solve) it.   _____

7. The President (speak) over the radio next Sunday.   _____

8. The Walkers (be) in Europe three or four times.   _____

9. I certainly wish that you (hear) the lecture last night.   _____

10. I'll read that book when I (find) the time.   _____

11. We cannot proceed until the committee (make) a decision.   _____

12. The representatives of twenty-nine Asian and African nations (meet) in Bandung, Indonesia, in April, 1955.   _____

13. This morning the sun (shine) when I got up, but it began to rain while I (eat) my breakfast.   _____

14. It is not raining now, but when I (come) to school this morning, it (rain) very hard.   _____

15. He has never read Mark Twain's novel Huckleberry Finn, but he (want) to read it very much.   _____

EXERCISE 51

Fill in the blanks with correct forms of the verbs in parentheses:

1. It is Friday afternoon. Mr. Jones _____ (work) in his garden. He usually _____ (do) his gardening on Saturday, but this Saturday his old friend, John Small, whom he _____ (not see) for five years, is coming to visit him.

2. When I came home last night, I _____ (notice) that the lights were on in my room. I was puzzled because I felt certain that I _____ (turn) them off when I left the house.

3. This morning I ran into Bob White, whom I _____ (not see) for several years. I don't think that you _____ (ever meet) Bob, but you _____ (hear) me talk a lot about him.

4. Yesterday I bought a television set. I _____ (think) about buying a set for a long time, but until last week I couldn't make up my mind whether or not I wanted one. However, last week while I _____ (look) at television at my aunt's house, I _____ (realize) that there were worthwhile programs and that I would enjoy having a set of my own.

5. Mr. Duncan has been a newspaper man for over twenty years. He _____ (start) out as a reporter for a paper in a small town. After he had worked there for two or three years, he _____ (get) a job as a reporter on a big city paper. Since then he _____ (live) and and _____ (travel) in many parts of the world as a foreign correspondent.

Review Exercises For Verbs (Unit 2)

EXERCISE 52

Fill in the blanks with correct forms of the verbs in parentheses:

Dear John:

I haven't written to you for such a long time that I _____ (not know) where to begin.

Some very exciting things _____ (happen) to me this year. First, Uncle Charlie, whom you surely must have met during one of your visits with us, _____ (give) me $5000 for my last birthday. He said that he _____ (think) it was about time for me to see something of the world. So I _____ (plan) to take a trip around the world.

I'll leave New York in two weeks and fly to San Francisco, where I _____ (spend) a few days seeing old friends and soaking up the atmosphere of that wonderful city. Then on September 10th I'll leave by ship for Honolulu. I _____ (never be) there and I'm looking forward to swimming at Waikiki Beach. After a week there, I _____ (be) off for the Orient. I _____ (send) you some postcards along the way. I _____ (send) along my itinerary and hope that you will drop me a line now and then.

As you can imagine, I'm very busy these days. Yesterday I _____ (spend) all morning getting my papers in order, and in the afternoon I _____ (have) to see my doctor to get a smallpox vaccination. Last week I _____ (have) my typhoid shots. So long now.

I wish you _____ (go) along.

                                            Sincerely,

                                            George

EXERCISE 53

Complete the following sentences:

    Example: He said that he __was here__ last night.

1. They wish that Marian _____ tomorrow.

2. _____ while I was making coffee.

3. Did he wish that _____ last Saturday?

4. If you had been there, _____
_____

5. If you were I, what _____
_____?

6. Let's try to finish our homework before they _____
_____

7. If you eat too much food, you _____
_____

8. After we had finished the experiment, we _____
_____

9. Would you have come if you _____
_____?

10. Before he went home, _____
_____

11. When he arrived at the office, _____
_____

12. The committee requested that the speaker _____
_____

UNIT 3 | VERBALS

PART XIV | Verbals

60 | INTRODUCTION

The three forms called verbals are the *infinitive*, the *gerund* [or **ing-**form], and the *participle*.

The *infinitive* may be a noun equivalent or a modifier, depending on its function in the sentence.

    I like **to swim.**   (noun equivalent—direct object)
    He worked hard **to get ahead.**   (modifier of **worked**)
    He gave me a book **to read.**   (modifier of **book**)

The *gerund* is a noun equivalent. It has the same form as the present participle.

    Swimming is good exercise.   (noun equivalent—subject)
    I am fond of **swimming.**   (noun equivalent—object)

The *participle* is a modifier. Both the present and past participle forms are used as modifiers of nouns.

    We read an **interesting** book.
    The **pleased** customer returned the following day.

61 | INFINITIVES and GERUNDS as OBJECTS of VERBS

Certain verbs may be followed by infinitives and gerunds as objects. In this construction the infinitive or gerund is equivalent to a noun or pronoun object. Compare:

    I want **a book.**
    I want **to borrow** a book.[1]

In this section verbs are listed according to whether they are followed by gerunds or infinitives.

61a. Verbs that are followed *only* by an infinitive fall into three groups: (1) those followed directly by the infinitive; (2) those followed by a noun or pronoun + infinitive; (3) those followed either by the infinitive directly or by a noun or a pronoun + infinitive.

---

[1] Infinitives and gerunds, like verbs, may be followed by objects. In this sentence, **a book** is the object of **to borrow;** the whole phrase **to borrow a book** is the object of the verb.

(1) VERB + INFINITIVE

care	I **don't care to see** him again.[2]
decide	We **have decided not to go**.[3]
deserve	You **deserve to win** the scholarship.
endeavor	The club **endeavored to raise** $5000 for charity.
forget	I **have forgotten to telephone** Jim.
hope	We **hope to see** you soon.
learn	George **is learning to drive** a car.
mean [intend]	I **didn't mean to hurt** your feelings.
plan	We're **planning to leave** tomorrow.

(2) VERB + (pro)noun + INFINITIVE

advise	I **advise** you **to see** a lawyer.
cause	He **caused** me **to be** late.
command	The guard **commanded** us **to halt**.
encourage	They **encouraged** me **to study** abroad.
force	The committee **forced** Mr. White **to resign**.
get	We finally **got** him **to accept** the offer.

Other verbs in this group include **instruct, invite, oblige, order, persuade, remind, teach, tell, urge, warn**.[4]

It is possible to state most of the sentences in (2) in passive constructions without changing the meaning to a great extent. The (pro)noun preceding the infinitive in the original sentence becomes the subject in the passive construction. Compare:

The committee **forced** Mr. White **to resign**.
Mr. White **was forced to resign** by the committee.

The subject of the original sentence may or may not be included as agent in the passive construction. Compare:

The guard commanded us to halt.
We **were commanded** to halt **by the guard**.
We **were commanded** to halt.

(3) (a) VERB + INFINITIVE   (b) VERB + (pro)noun + INFINITIVE

ask	She **asked to come**.	She **asked** us **to come**.
beg	The child **begged to go**.	The child **begged** me **to go**.
expect	We **expect to leave** tonight.	We **expect** them **to leave** tonight.
promise	I **promised not to tell**.	I **promised** him **not to tell** you.
want	They **want to visit** you soon.	They **want** you **to visit** them soon.
wish	I **wished to stay**.	They **wished** me **to stay**.

---

[2] **Care** usually appears in negative statements or in questions.
  I don't care to go.
  Do you care to dance?

[3] Whether **not** is placed before the infinitive or the main verb or both depends on the meaning to be expressed.
  I have decided **not** to go.
    (I have made a decision, and my decision is not to go.)
  I **haven't** decided to go.
    (I have not made a decision as to whether or not I will go.)
  I **haven't** decided **not** to go.
    (I have not made a decision—a decision not to go.)

[4] After **warn, not** usually precedes the infinitive.
  I **warned** you **not to do** that.

VERBALS

The sentences with **ask, beg,** and **expect** in (3b) may be stated in passive constructions without changing the meaning to a great extent. Compare:

> She **asked** us **to come** early.
> We **were asked to come** early.
>
> We **expect** them **to leave** tonight.
> They **are expected to leave** tonight.

61b. The verbs listed below are followed by gerunds only: VERB + GERUND

admit	He **admitted taking** the key.
appreciate	We **would appreciate hearing** from you.
avoid	I **have avoided meeting** him so far.
consider	I **considered buying** a car.
deny	He **denied taking** the key.
enjoy	We **enjoyed meeting** you.
escape	He **escaped being** hurt in the accident.
finish	I **have** just **finished typing** my paper.
imagine	**Imagine winning** the Irish sweepstakes!
keep	**Keep trying!**
miss	I'm sorry that I **missed seeing** you.

Other verbs in this group include **postpone, practice, quit, resent, resist, suggest, stop.**[5]

The expressions **do you mind** and **would you mind** are followed by a gerund.

> **Do you mind closing** the window?
> **Would you mind waiting** for me?

The verbs in some constructions may be followed by a (pro)noun or a possessive form of a (pro)noun + the gerund or **ing**-form.

> Imagine **John** (him) winning the Irish sweepstakes!
> Imagine **John's** (his) winning the Irish sweepstakes![6]

61c. The verbs listed below may be followed by either an infinitive or a gerund with little or no change in meaning:

begin	The woman **began to laugh.**
	The woman **began laughing.**
continue	The traffic **continued to move** slowly.
	The traffic **continued moving** slowly.
dislike	We **dislike to play** bridge.
	We **dislike playing** bridge.
dread	I **dread to think** about it.
	I **dread thinking** about it.
intend	They **intend to call** her tomorrow.
	They **intend calling** her tomorrow.

---

[5] **Stop** may be followed by an infinitive, but the infinitive in this case is a modifier indicating purpose.
  I **stopped to talk** to him.
    (I **stopped in order to** talk to him.)
  Also see Section 64.

[6] According to an "age-old" rule, the gerund or **ing**-form should be preceded by a possessive form. However, both forms are used in present day English.

like	I **like to drive** your car. I **like driving** your car.[7]
neglect	He **neglected to file** his income tax return. He **neglected filing** his income tax return.
plan	I **plan to take** German next year. I **plan taking** German next year. (*or:* I **plan on taking** German next year.)
prefer	He **prefers to type** his own letters. He **prefers typing** his own letters.
start	She **starts to teach** tomorrow. She **starts teaching** tomorrow.

The auxiliary **can't** + **bear** or **stand** may also be followed by either the infinitive or gerund.

I **can't bear to see** her cry.
I **can't bear seeing** her cry.

I **can't stand to hear** that again.
I **can't stand hearing** that again.

The verbs **remember** and **try** may be followed by either an infinitive or a gerund, but the meaning is usually different. Compare:

He **remembers to write** to her every week.
  (*or:* He doesn't forget to write to her every week.)

He **remembers writing** to her every week.
  (*or:* He recalls that he wrote to her every week.)

Try to get some sleep.
  (*or:* Make an attempt to get some sleep.)

Try getting some sleep.
  (*or:* Why don't you get some sleep? That's what you need.)

The verbs **allow** and **permit** may be followed by a noun or pronoun + infinitive or by a gerund directly. Compare:

They **allow** (permit) us **to smoke** here.
They **don't allow** (permit) **smoking** here.

62 | INFINITIVES as COMPLEMENTS

Infinitives sometimes appear as complements after **seem** and **appear**.

You **seem to be** tired.
Josephine **appeared to be** in good spirits.

63 | THE GERUND as OBJECT of a PREPOSITION

The gerund is used as the object of a preposition.

He earns his living **by selling** brushes.
In taking the cake out of the oven, I burned my hand.
The child was saved **from drowning** by the lifeguard.

---

[7] After the verbs **dislike, like,** and **prefer** the meaning expressed by the gerund is sometimes different from that expressed by the infinitive. Compare:
  I like **to swim** and **to play** tennis. (the activities)
  I like **swimming** and **tennis.** (the sports)

The same principle applies when a preposition is combined with a verb to form a fixed phrase, such as **object to**.[8]

> He **objected to going** there.
> I **am accustomed to working** late.
> I **am used to getting** up early.
> We **are opposed to having** a meeting without him.
> They **are looking forward to seeing** you.
> They **went on talking** for hours.
> Let's **keep on working** for a while.
> I **put off doing** my assignment until the last minute.
> He **is interested in taking** this course.[9]

64 THE INFINITIVE and GERUND in EXPRESSIONS of PURPOSE

The infinitive as a modifier of the *verb* usually expresses *purpose*. The meaning is "in order to."

> I **must leave** now **to get** there on time.   [in order to get there on time]
> You **will have to make** an appointment **to see** him.   [in order to see him]

When purpose is expressed by **for,** the **gerund** is used.

> This exercise is good **for reducing** the waist line.

65 THE PRESENT and PAST PARTICIPLES as ADJECTIVES

The present participle or the past participle may precede the noun as a modifier or may follow the verb as a complement. The meanings expressed by the present and the past participles usually differ. Compare:

> This is **tiring** work.
>   (The work is tiring to us.)
> He is a **tired** boy.
>   (The boy himself is tired.)
> He is the most **boring** speaker I have ever heard.
>   (He is boring to me.)
> The **bored** student looked out of the window.
>   (The student himself was bored.)
> He is a very **interesting** person.
>   (He is interesting to us.)
> He is **interested** in our plans.
>   (He himself is interested in our plans.)

When the present participle or the past participle *follows* the noun that it modifies, it carries with it the idea of the activity that would be expressed if the participle were expanded into a clause. Compare:

> The man **speaking** is my uncle.
>   (*or:* The man **who is speaking** is my uncle.)
> The interest **shown** was not very encouraging.
>   (*or:* The interest **that was shown** was not very encouraging.)

---

[8] In the phrase **object to, to** is a preposition in form, although according to function it is sometimes described as an adverb, an adverb-preposition, a particle, etc. In any case, it should not be confused with the infinitive with *to*.

[9] See Part XVII for lists of verb + preposition combinations.

66 INFINITIVES and PARTICIPLES FOLLOWING COMPLEMENTS or OBJECTS

Infinitives and participles frequently follow complements or objects. Below are some of the patterns in which they appear:

(1) Verb + { COMPLEMENT / OBJECT } + { INFINITIVE / PRESENT PARTICIPLE / PAST PARTICIPLE }

    I am **happy to be** here.
    It is **time to go** now.
    That is **John sitting** over there.
    These are the **facts gathered** by the committee.
    I gave John some **coffee to drink.**
    The police caught **him stealing** a car.
    We found **her tired and depressed.**

(2) Verbs GET and HAVE + OBJECT + PAST PARTICIPLE

    They **got their car washed** at the garage.
        (They took their car to the garage and had it washed.)
    I **had my suit pressed** yesterday.
    He **has his shoes shined** every day.

(3) Verbs HELP, LET, MAKE + OBJECT + SIMPLE FORM

    They **helped me do** my assignment.
    He **let me drive** his car.
    The instructor **made us repeat** the sentence several times.

Occasionally **help** is followed by the infinitive. Compare:

    I **helped** her **overcome** her fear of speaking in public.
    I **helped** her **to overcome** her fear of speaking in public.

(4) Verbs FEEL, HEAR, SEE, WATCH + OBJECT + { SIMPLE FORM / PRESENT PARTICIPLE }

Compare:

    I **felt the car move.**
        (The car moved, and I felt it.)
    I **felt the car moving.**
        (The car was moving, and I felt it.)
    I **heard the rain fall** all night long.
    I **heard the rain falling** all night long.
    We **saw them come** across the street.
    We **saw them coming** across the street.
    We **watched him mow** the lawn.
    We **watched him mowing** the lawn.

67 | PERFECT and PASSIVE FORMS of INFINITIVES, GERUNDS, and PARTICIPLES

67a. The *perfect forms* of the verbals ordinarily indicate that the activity expressed by the verbal existed or occurred *before* the activity or state of the verb in the clause or sentence.

Perfect Infinitive: TO HAVE + past participle

>I am glad **to have met** you.
>I seem **to have misplaced** my key.

Perfect Gerund: HAVING + past participle

>Your **having had** that experience will be to your credit.

Perfect Participle: HAVING + past participle

>**Having finished** my shopping, I went home.

After + the gerund is often substituted for the perfect participle construction.

>**After finishing** my shopping, I went home.

67b. The *passive forms* of the verbals have the same purpose as passive tense forms; that is, the *subject* refers to the *receiver* of the activity expressed by the verbal.

Infinitive: Present Passive: TO BE + past participle
Perfect Passive: TO HAVE BEEN + past participle

>He wanted **to be nominated** for president.
>I am honored **to have been asked** by the committee to speak.

Gerund: Present Passive: BEING + past participle
Perfect Passive: HAVING BEEN + past participle

>I can't imagine his **being elected** president.
>Your **having been arrested** several times for speeding should make you cautious.

Participle: Present Passive: BEING + past participle
Perfect Passive: HAVING BEEN + past participle

>**Being tired,** I went to bed early.
>**Having been caught** in that situation before, I knew exactly what to do.

EXERCISE 54

Answer the following questions. Give responses in which you use an infinitive after the verb.

    Example: What do you want to do?
               I want <u>to go</u> home now.

1. What have you decided to do this evening?

2. Where are you planning to go for your vacation?

3. Did you forget to do that assignment?

4. Where do you want to go for dinner?

5. When did you learn to drive a car?

6. Do you hope to get an <u>A</u> in this course?

7. Who advised you to take this course?

8. What caused you to be late?

9. Who taught you how to drive a car?

10. Did you tell him to meet us for lunch?

11. Did you ask her to go with you?

12. When do you expect to receive your degree?

13. Do you want to see me after class?

14. Have you been asked to join a fraternity?

15. Why was he forced to resign?

16. What kind of radio do you advise me to buy?

17. Who made her promise not to tell?

18. Why are you encouraging them to take a trip?

19. Did you persuade your friend to go with us tonight?

20. Did the policeman warn you not to cross the street in the middle of the block?

EXERCISE 55

Answer the following questions. Give responses in which you use a gerund after the verb.

1. Did she admit losing the key?

2. Did he appreciate your pointing out his mistakes?

3. Have you considered applying for a scholarship?

4. Does she deny saying that?

5. Do you enjoy listening to popular music?

6. Why did he postpone taking the examination?

7. Has she quit worrying about her grades?

8. When did he stop smoking?

EXERCISE 56

Answer the following questions. Give responses in which you use either an infinitive or a gerund verb, as indicated by the question.

1. Has it begun to rain yet?

2. Do you like to play golf?

3. When did he start working?

4. Have you tried calling her today?

5. Do you dislike getting up early?

6. Will you continue to study English after this course?

7. Does he intend to invite her to go with us?

8. Do you remember seeing that man before?

9. Do you prefer swimming to tennis?

10. Will they allow us to park here?

11. Did you remember to tell her about the change in plans?

12. Don't they allow smoking in the theatre?

Exercises For Part XIV

EXERCISE 57

Read the following sentences, giving appropriate <u>verbal</u> forms of the verbs in parentheses. (Also write the forms in the spaces at the right.)

    <u>Example</u>: They asked me (come) over right away.   to come
               (Read: They asked me <u>to come</u> over right away.)

1. I want to swim, but they do not allow (swim) in this lake.   _____

2. Did you plan on (finish) this letter before the mailman came?   _____

3. She tried (see) the manager in order to discuss the matter.   _____

4. We avoided (drive) over the unpaved road by taking the new highway. _____

5. I have to leave the house at seven o'clock (get) to work on time.   _____

6. I should get my coat (clean). _____

7. That boy earns his living by (sell) papers. _____

8. The policeman made us (stop) our car. _____

9. Joseph wants to save his money (travel) next year. _____

10. I asked the man if he would mind (turn) off the radio. _____

11. The farmer risks (lose) his crop if there is a drought. _____

12. They hope (build) a house at the beach next year. _____

13. We are very glad (be) here. _____

14. When questioned, the students denied (play) the practical joke. _____

15. I often dream of (go) on a trip to Spain. _____

16. Why do they object to (smoke) here? _____

17. The manager let us (leave) work early the day before the holiday. _____

18. Do you see the man (talk) to Mr. Hall? _____

19. I must start soon (get) there before dark. _____

20. We aren't accustomed to (get) up so early. _____

EXERCISE 58

Draw a circle around the correct form in each pair of parentheses below:

1. While walking down the street toward my dentist's office, I muttered (encouraged, encouraging) words to myself (to keep, keeping) up my courage. Like most people, I avoided (to face, facing) the dentist's drill and endeavored (to postpone, postponing) the (feared, fearing) ordeal as long as possible. But yesterday, when a molar started to ache, I decided it was time (to see, seeing) a dentist. If I postponed (to keep, keeping) my appointment again, I would risk (to lose, losing) a tooth.

2. The tennis champion has been asked (to play, playing) an exhibition game at the Tennis Club next Sunday. Everyone (interested, interesting) in this sport should certainly plan on (to attend, attending). Watching a fine player is a good way of (improving, improve) one's own game. In addition, there is much pleasure in (seeing, see) someone do something expertly. I am certainly looking forward to (watching, watch) the champion (to play, play).

3. On a noon broadcast today I heard the news of a (damaged, damaging) earthquake in Greece. (Hear, Hearing) that made me wonder about how the people there might have acted during the earthquake.

   I imagined men (to work, working) in factories and could see them (to leave, leaving) their machines and (to rush, rushing) outside. They would be worrying about whether or not their families were safe. They would want (to get, getting) home, but they would find the buses not (to run, running). I could see mothers (to try, trying) (to comfort, comforting) their (frightened, frightening) children. I could hear (excited, exciting) teachers (to tell, telling) the school children (to march, marching) outside calmly.

UNIT 4 | ARTICLES

PART XV | Definite and Indefinite Articles

68 | INTRODUCTION

The *definite* article is **the**; the *indefinite* articles are **a** and **an**. **A** is used before words beginning with a consonant sound (**a book, a chair, a hotel, a university**); **an**, before words beginning with a vowel sound (**an apple, an egg, an hour, an onion**).[1]

It is usually difficult for students to know when and where to use articles. Some general principles and special uses are explained and illustrated in this unit to serve as a guide for students who have difficulty in mastering usage.

69 | ARTICLES with SINGULAR COUNTABLE NOUNS

An article is used with a *singular countable noun* (a noun that stands for a person or thing that can be counted as a single unit or item). It is either **a book** or **the book, an apple** or **the apple, a boy** or **the boy, a teacher** or **the teacher.**

69a. In a few situations, **a** or **an** has approximately the same meaning as the number **one.**

> I'll be here for **an** hour or two.
> (*or:* I'll be here for **one** or two hours.)

More often **a** or **an** has the meaning of **one** in the sense of a single unit or item. In situations of this kind, **one** cannot be substituted for the indefinite article without changing the meaning. Compare:

> I have **a** black dress.
> I have only **one** black dress.
> I ate **an** egg for breakfast.
> I ate only **one** egg for breakfast today, but I usually eat two.

69b. The main use of **the** is to single out a specific or particular person or thing. Before a singular countable noun, **the** has much the same meaning as the demonstrative **that**, although **that** is more emphatic in pointing something out. Compare:

---

[1] *Pronunciation notes:*

  (a) The letter **h** is pronounced as the consonant sound [h] in words like **a hotel** and **a home**; in some words like **an hour** and **an honor**, it is a silent letter. The letter **u** is usually pronounced as a vowel sound, but at the beginning of some words like **a university** and **a union**, it is pronounced as the consonant sound [j] + the vowel [u]; in these cases, **an** is used.

  (b) The article **a** is ordinarily pronounced as the weak vowel [ə]; **an** may be pronounced as [æn], but it is often weakened to [ən]; **the** is ordinarily pronounced [ðə] before words beginning with a consonant sound and [ðɪ] before those with a vowel. Thus, we usually say:

> **a** [ə] book   (not [e])
> **the** [ðə] book   (not [ði])
> **the** [ðɪ] apple   (not [ði])

See the Appendix, page 250, for a list of American-English sounds.

Did you take **the** book to Mary?
Did you take **that** book to Mary?

In the above example, the speaker has in mind a specific book, and he assumes that the person to whom he is talking also has in mind the same book. If necessary, the speaker might further identify the book by adding a qualifying word, phrase, or clause, such as—

the French book
the book **that was on the table**
the book **on mountain climbing**

69c. Whether a definite or indefinite article is used before a singular countable noun may be further illustrated by the following sentences:

I ate **an egg.**
  (a single item)
I ate **the egg.**
  (a specific egg, for example, **the** egg **in the dish,** etc.)

Sometimes we begin with an indefinite article and then shift to the definite article as soon as the identity of the person or object has been established.

There is **a letter** for you at the office. Would you like me to bring **the letter** to you?

A man and **a woman** were sitting in front of me on the bus. They were arguing about where they should go for dinner. **The woman** wanted to go to a Chinese restaurant, but **the man** said that he didn't like Chinese food.

70 | ARTICLES with PLURAL COUNTABLE NOUNS

Because a plural countable noun refers to more than one person or thing, the *indefinite* article *cannot* be used. It is either **books** or **the books, apples** or **the apples,** and so forth.

70a. Indefinite *articles* are not used with plural nouns, but indefinite *adjectives*, such as **some, any, several, many, few, a few, fewer,** may be used to indicate an indefinite number.

She put **flowers** in the vase.
  (*or:* She put **some** flowers in the vase.)
There aren't **any** napkins on the table.[2]
There aren't **many** students here.
He ate **a few** sandwiches.
I made **fewer** mistakes today.

70b. An article is not used before a plural noun that refers to persons or things as a group or in general.

Clerks are often called white-collar workers.
I like to read **books** based on history.[3]

---

[2] **Some** is used in affirmative statements; **any,** in negative statements. Either form may be used in questions. Also see Section 13b for further explanation of uses of indefinite adjectives with plural nouns.

[3] As shown in this sentence, a modifier following a noun does not necessarily make it specific.

DEFINITE AND INDEFINITE ARTICLES

70c. **The** singles out or identifies specific or particular persons or things. Before a plural countable noun, **the** has much the same meaning as the demonstrative **those,** although **those** is more emphatic. As with singular countable nouns, a qualifying word, phrase, or clause is often used to identify further the persons or objects.

> Please give me **the books.**
> **The carpenters** got a raise, but **the plumbers** didn't.
> She put **the flowers** that I brought her in a vase.
> **The students** in the next room are taking an examination.

71 | ARTICLES with NON-COUNTABLE NOUNS

The indefinite article is *not* used with a non-countable noun (a noun that stands for something that cannot be counted as a single unit or item). It is either **water** or **the water, truth** or **the truth, music** or **the music.**

71a. The following types of nouns are generally considered non-countable. The indefinite article is *not* used with these nouns.

(1) *Mass nouns*, such as **water, air, oil, ice, coffee, tea, ink, oxygen:**

> Would you like **coffee** or **tea?**
> Water is composed of **hydrogen** and **oxygen.**

Indefinite adjectives, such as **some, any, much, little, a little, less,** may be used with mass nouns to indicate indefinite quantity.

> Do you want **some** coffee?
> There isn't **any** sugar on the table.
> Would you give me **a little** meat, please?
> Try putting **less** cream in your coffee.[4]

Countable units of measure may be used with mass nouns to indicate definite amounts. Compare:

> I'd like **a cup of** coffee.   I'd like some coffee.
> He wants **a glass of** milk.   He wants milk.
> I need **a pound of** sugar.   I need sugar.
> Here is **a bottle of** ink.   Here is some ink.
> Where is **the can of** oil?   Where is the oil?

(2) *Abstract nouns*, such as **liberty, justice, honesty, kindness, life, truth, beauty, democracy:**

> **Honesty** is the best policy.
> We believe in **liberty** and **justice** for all.
> What is **life?**

(3) Names of general areas of subject matter, such as **history, art, science, engineering, chemistry, music, economics, English:**

---

[4] See Section 13b for further explanation of uses of indefinite adjectives with mass nouns.

He is taking courses in **English, French, mathematics, history,** and **political science.**
He teaches **violin** and **piano.**[5]

The name of an area of subject matter that functions as a modifier may be preceded by an article. The use of the article is governed by the noun modified. Compare:

He is studying **English.**
He is studying **the English language.**
He is taking **geology.**
He is taking **a geology course.**

(4) Names of sports or recreational activities, such as **baseball, tennis, golf, bridge, dancing, sailing, singing:**

He plays both **football** and **baseball.**
Do you like **folk dancing?**

The name of a sport or recreational activity that functions as a modifier may be preceded by an article. Compare:

He plays **baseball.**
Have you seen **a baseball game** lately?

71b. **The** before a non-countable noun limits or restricts; that is, our attention is directed to a particular portion or part. The noun may be further limited or restricted by a qualifying word, phrase, or clause.

The coffee was all right, but **the cream** was sour.
The oil in my car needs to be changed.
I will never forget **the kindness** you have shown me.
We studied **the history** of Western Europe.

71c. Some nouns ordinarily considered as non-countable nouns may also function as countable nouns. For example, a noun that is abstract and non-countable in one situation may be a countable noun in another situation. Compare:

Japanese often drink **tea.**   (a mass noun)
The teas of India are of several varieties.   (a plural countable noun meaning "the types of tea")
"**Beauty** is **truth**" is a line from a poem by John Keats.   (abstract nouns)
Mary is **a beauty.**   (a singular countable noun meaning "a beautiful girl")
The truths at stake in the decision are many.   (a plural countable noun meaning "the principles")
What is **democracy?**   (an abstract noun)
What is the difference between a republic and **a democracy?**   (a countable noun meaning "a form of government")
Science has contributed much to human progress.   (a general area of subject matter)
Would you call psychology **a science?**   (a countable noun meaning "a branch of science")

---

[5] In this example, **piano** and **violin** refer to areas of study. However, **piano** and **violin** are countable nouns when they refer to musical instruments.

He has **a piano** and **a violin,** but he doesn't own **a flute.**
The violin is on top of **the piano.**

Also, **the** is ordinarily used when referring to the type of instrument played.

He plays **the piano, the violin,** and **the flute.**

DEFINITE AND INDEFINITE ARTICLES

He teaches **history**. (a general area of subject matter)
The doctor wrote **a history** of the case for the medical journal. (a countable noun meaning "an account or report")

71d. There are also the following groups of nouns that are used as either countable or non-countable nouns, depending on the meaning to be expressed.

(1) **Breakfast, lunch, dinner, supper, tea,** etc. Compare:

Mrs. Oglethorpe always serves **lunch** at one o'clock.
That was **a good lunch.**

Have you had **dinner** yet?
The dinner I had at that restaurant was excellent.

(2) **School, church, market, town,** etc. Compare:

Roger went to **church** this morning.
We parked our car in front of **the church.**

We must go to **town** this afternoon.
I drove for two hours before I reached **the town.**

72 | SUMMARY of ARTICLES with COUNTABLE and NON-COUNTABLE NOUNS

The chart below summarizes the use of articles with the different types of nouns covered in Sections 69, 70, and 71.

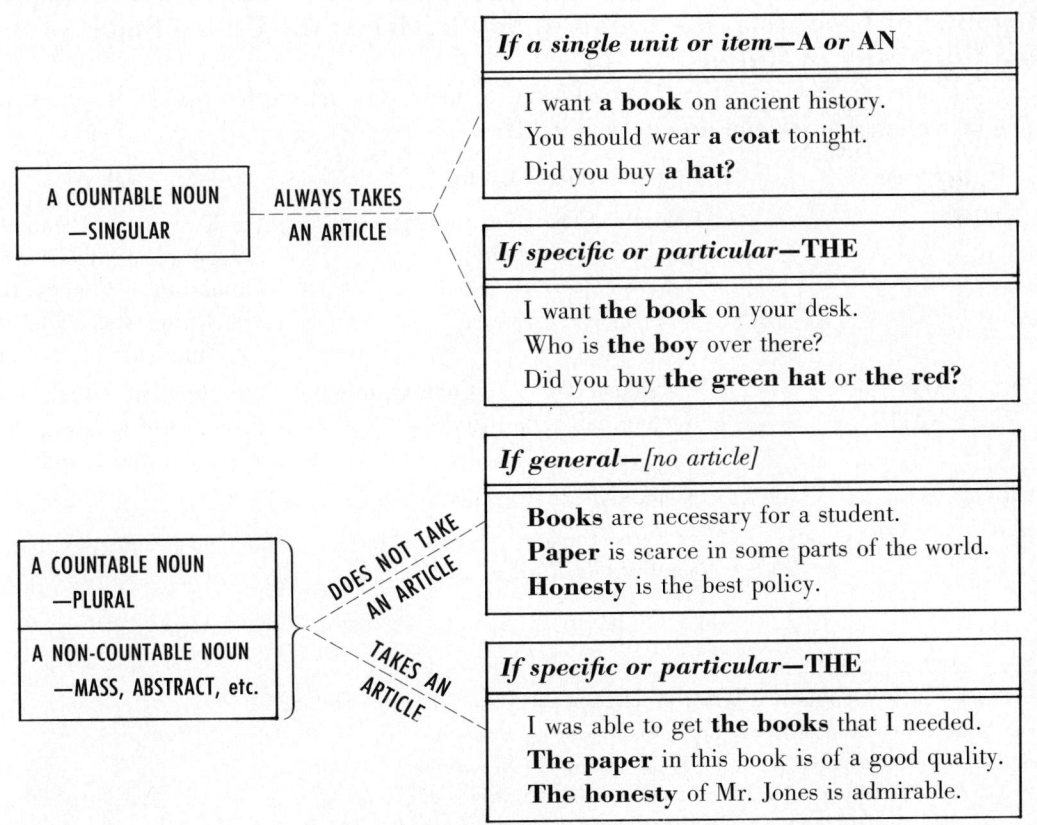

73 ARTICLES with PROPER NAMES[6]

73a. As with common nouns, **the** before a proper name singles out or identifies a specific or particular person, place, or thing. In general, when the proper name is sufficient in itself to establish identification, no article is required before the name. The name *Henry Potter*, for example, is ordinarily all that is necessary to identify the individual with that name. **The** would be used only in a situation where the identification was not clearly established. Compare:

> I know **Henry Potter** very well.
> **Mr. Potter** had lunch with **Major Cory**.[7]
> **The Henry Potter** that I went to school with is now editor of a newspaper.[8]

The is required when a person is referred to by a title composed of what would ordinarily be considered a common noun + an identifying phrase.

> **The President** (of the United States)[9] will hold a press conference tomorrow.
> **The Queen of England** has traveled extensively since her coronation.
> **The Secretary of State** flew to Paris for the conference.

73b. In general, the two principles that apply to the names of persons also apply to the names of places (including geographical areas, institutions, businesses, etc.) and other proper names.

(1) No article is required when the name serves to identify a place in the same way that a proper name identifies a person. Examples are **Iran, South America, New York, Lincoln Street, Harvard University.**

(2) **The** is required before a name composed of a noun that would ordinarily be a common noun + an identifying phrase (usually introduced by **of** or **for**). Examples are **the Republic of Indonesia, the Union of South Africa, the United States of America, the University of Illinois.**

However, the number of exceptions to these two principles makes it necessary to list types of names that do and do not require **the.**

Type of Name	Without Article	With THE
(1) COUNTRIES	Colombia, Thailand, Canada, Russia, England, Lebanon	the Republic of Colombia, the Kingdom of Thailand, the Dominion of Canada, the Soviet Union, the United States (of America)[10]
(2) STATES, PROVINCES, COUNTIES, CITIES	Oklahoma, Quebec, Cook County, Boston, Salt Lake City	the State of Oklahoma, the Province of Quebec, the City of Boston, the Hague
(3) CONTINENTS	Africa, North America	
(4) GEOGRAPHICAL AREAS	Eastern Europe, North Africa, Southern California	the North Pole, the South Pole

---

[6] By *proper name* we mean the name of a person or the name of a particular place or thing.

[7] No article is required when a rank or title precedes the name of a person.

[8] Notice that **the** is usually required before the plural form of a family name.
> **The Potters** [the Potter family] are away on vacation.

[9] The full title is "the President of the United States," but it is often shortened to "the President" when the reference is clear.

DEFINITE AND INDEFINITE ARTICLES

Type of Name	Without Article	With THE
(5) EMPIRES, DYNASTIES, etc.		the Ottoman Empire, the Ming Dynasty, the British Commonwealth of Nations
(6) STREETS	Maple Street, Fifth Avenue, Elderberry Road, Sunset Boulevard [11]	
(7) PARKS	Central Park, Hyde Park, Kruger Park	
(8) ISLANDS, LAKES, and MOUNTAINS	—*Singular:* Wake Island, Lake Geneva, Mount Whitney	—*Plural:* the Canary Islands, the Great Lakes, the Andes Mountains
(9) OCEANS, SEAS, RIVERS, CANALS, DESERTS, and FORESTS		the Atlantic Ocean,[12] the Red Sea, the Tigris River, the Suez Canal, the Sahara Desert, the Black Forest
(10) UNIVERSITIES, COLLEGES, SCHOOLS, INSTITUTES	Yale University, New York University, Wellesley College, San Francisco State College [13]	the University of Maryland, the College of Holy Names, the State College of Washington
(11) MUSEUMS, LIBRARIES		the Metropolitan Museum, the Louvre, the Library of Congress, the Huntington Library
(12) BUILDINGS	Independence Hall, Carnegie Hall, Wheeler Auditorium	the Empire State Building, the Medical-Dental Building, the Civic Auditorium
(13) BUSINESSES (stores, restaurants, firms, etc.)	Penney's, Joe's Cafe, Mary's Beauty Shop,[14] Sears Roebuck (and Company), Hotel Ambassador	the J. C. Penney Company, the All-Nite Grocery Store, the Feather Mattress Company, the Fox Theatre, the Statler Hotel
(14) HOLIDAYS	Christmas, Thanksgiving, New Year's Day, Washington's Birthday	the Fourth (4th) of July
(15) CHARTERS, CLUBS, COMMITTEES, DOCTRINES, etc.		the United Nations Charter, the Rotary Club, the Foreign Relations Committee (of the Senate), the Monroe Doctrine

---

[10] We do not usually refer to countries, states, and so forth by their official titles; that is, we refer to **France,** rather than to **the Republic of France.** However, **the United States, the Soviet Union,** and **the United Kingdom** are commonly used titles.

[11] Although most names of streets are not preceded by **the,** there are a few exceptions, such as **the Avenue of the Americas** in New York City.

[12] The word **ocean** is often omitted; **sea, river,** and **desert** are often omitted when the place is well-known.
   The Panama Canal connects **the Atlantic** and **the Pacific.**
   The Nile flows into **the Mediterranean.**

[13] An article is usually not required when the identifying proper name precedes **School, College,** etc. There are a few exceptions such as **the Johns Hopkins University.**

[14] A business title with a possessive form of a personal pronoun does not usually require an article. When the possessive form would not be a proper name if it were not in the title, **the** is usually required.
   There is a sale in **the Tot's Shop.**
   The Farmers' Market is on Eighth Avenue.

73c. Whether or not an article is used with the *names of nationalities* depends on the way the name is used.

(1) When the name of a nationality functions as a *noun*, the principles governing the use of articles with countable nouns apply.

> There is **a Belgian** in my class.
> He is **the Frenchman**[15] I told you about.
> Are they **the Italians** who own this store?

In referring to an *entire group* of people, no article is required if the name has a plural form; **the** may be used to single out one group from another.

> **Americans** like sports.
> **Norwegians** usually make good sailors.
> He said **the Italians,** not **the Americans,** were fond of opera.

The is ordinarily used if the name does not have a plural form.

> **The British** drink a lot of tea.
> **The French** are noted for their fine cooking.

(2) When the name of a nationality functions as an adjective complement, no article is used.

> Werner is **German**.
> The Pinsons are **French**.
> The Katos are **Japanese**.

74 ARTICLES with NOUNS MODIFIED by PROPER NAMES and POSSESSIVES

When a proper name is used as a modifier of a noun, the use of the article depends on the *noun modified*. Compare:

> Here is **a dictionary**.
> Here is **a Spanish dictionary**.
>
> **The earthquake** caused a great deal of damage.
> **The San Francisco earthquake of 1906** caused a great deal of damage.
>
> He is studying **art**.
> He is studying **Japanese art**.
>
> He collects recordings of **ballads**.
> He collects recordings of **South American ballads**.

This same principle applies when a noun is modified by the possessive form of a common noun. Compare:

> **A coat** was left in the car.
> **A boy's coat** was left in the car.
>
> **The coat** was left in the car.
> **The boy's coat** was left in the car.
>
> This store does not sell **shoes**.
> This store does not sell **boys' shoes**.

---

[15] **Frenchman** or **Frenchwoman** is used in referring to an individual; **Frenchmen**, to two or more individuals or to the French people as a whole.

DEFINITE AND INDEFINITE ARTICLES

When the possessive form of a *proper noun* is a modifier, an article is not used except with the possessive of a plural family name.

> Someone ran into **a car** while it was parked on First Street.
> Someone ran into **John's car** while it was parked on First Street.
> Someone ran into **the Smiths' car** while it was parked on First Street.

No article is used when the possessive form of an abstract noun functions as a modifier.

> **The rewards** are many.
> **Honesty's rewards** are many.
> **Life's rewards** are many.

75 | SOME SPECIFIC USES of the DEFINITE ARTICLE

75a. **The** is ordinarily used with names of things that are automatically singled out because of their *obvious identification*. For example, when we say "Has **the** postman come yet?" we mean "the particular postman who brings mail to our house." The people in each locality (from an area to a home) refer to many things in this manner.

> I am going to { **the** store. / **the** post office. / **the** city. / **the** country. / **the** beach. }

On a universal scale we refer to **the moon, the earth, the world, the universe, the equator, the north, the south, the east, the west, the northeast,** and so forth.[16]

This principle may also be said to apply to names of monuments or places considered unique in that the name is associated with only one monument or place. Examples are **the Acropolis, the Sphinx, the Taj Mahal, the White House.**

75b. **The** is used in the following *expressions of time:* in **the** morning (afternoon, evening), on **the** third of March, in **the** middle of **the** week, **the** day before yesterday, **the** week after next, and so forth.

No article is used in the following expressions of time: at 10 o'clock, at noon (night, midnight), on Monday, in July, last week, next week, and so forth.

75c. **The** is required when **first, second, third,** and so forth *precede* a noun.[17] *No* article is required when **one, two, three,** and so forth *follow* a noun. Compare:

> Read **the first chapter** for tomorrow.
> Read **Chapter One** for tomorrow.

> He fought in **the Second World War.**
> He fought in **World War II.**

---

[16] In giving the general location of one place in relation to another, **the** is omitted. Compare:
   The wind is blowing from **the north.**
   The river is **east** of the city.

[17] This principle does not apply to names of streets such as **First Street, Tenth Avenue,** etc.

EXERCISES FOR PART XV

EXERCISE 59

This exercise is designed to develop your ability to <u>hear</u> the articles - a step in learning to use the articles correctly in speaking and writing. Listen as your instructor reads these passages aloud. If you hear an article (a, an, or the), write it in the space provided. If you do not, leave the space blank.

(1) We learn in _____ geography courses that _____ valley surrounding _____ Nile River is one of the most fertile in _____ world. The reason for the richness of the valley is that annual floods of _____ Nile bring minerals to _____ soil. In the old days, _____ rich land of _____ Egypt attracted many people, and so Egypt became the first known civilized country; sometimes it is referred to as "_____ Cradle of Civilization."

(2) _____ Library of Congress, _____ national library of _____ United States, is situated near _____ Capitol in Washington, D.C. The primary purpose of _____ Library is to serve _____ members of _____ legislative branch of _____ government, but it is also open to _____ public as _____ reference library. _____ scholars come from all parts of _____ country to make use of its facilities.

_____ Library contains _____ copy of every book copyrighted in _____ United States. In _____ Library there are also collections of _____ musical instruments, recordings, maps, photographs, and documents. Perhaps _____ document of _____ most interest and significance to Americans who tour _____ Library is _____ first draft of Lincoln's Gettysburg Address.

In 1939 _____ five-story annex was added to _____ main building, constructed in 1837, in order to accommodate _____ vast amount of material that has been collected throughout _____ years.

Exercise 59 (continued)

(3) _____ Yellowstone National Park lies on _____ Continental Divide. The main area of _____ park is on _____ broad plateau, which is chiefly of _____ volcanic origin. The presence of hot springs and geysers gives evidence of _____ volcanic activity in _____ area today. Among the many attractions of _____ park are _____ geysers, which shoot columns of water into _____ air at _____ periodic intervals.

(4) Soon after _____ close of _____ Spanish-American War in _____ year 1898, _____ dreaded disease, yellow fever, broke out among _____ American troops that were stationed in Cuba. _____ commission composed of Major Walter Reed, Dr. James Carrol, Dr. J.W. Lazear, and Aristides Agramonti was appointed to investigate _____ causes and _____ transmission of _____ disease.

Major Reed determined to test _____ theory which had been advanced years before that _____ disease was transmitted by _____ mosquitoes. To do this, it was necessary to use _____ human beings for the test, for _____ animals appeared to be immune. _____ volunteers were called for. Every man who volunteered knew he was likely to die. Many of _____ brave volunteers did die in the experiment, but at last _____ theory was proved.

Once _____ cause was known, it was possible to stamp out yellow fever, _____ disease that had caused countless deaths. _____ effect of this event on _____ history and world progress has been revolutionary. _____ Panama Canal became _____ reality, and shorter trade routes were open to all ships of _____ world.

Exercises For Part XV

EXERCISE 60

(A) Insert <u>a</u>, <u>an</u>, or <u>the</u> in the blanks before the singular countable nouns in the following sentences:

1. Do you usually eat _____ egg for breakfast.

2. Do you want me to make _____ reservation for you on _____ next plane to Chicago?

3. Have you studied _____ lesson for today?

4. Did you read _____ book that I recommended to you?

5. We want to buy _____ lamp that she liked for her birthday.

6. There is _____ piano in _____ auditorium.

7. Is there _____ radio in _____ kitchen?

8. There is some paper and _____ bottle of ink on _____ desk in my room.

9. I must have _____ extra key made for _____ front door.

10. I received _____ letter this morning; _____ letter was from my brother.

(B) Insert <u>the</u>, where needed, in the blanks before the plural countable nouns and the non-countable nouns in the following sentences.

1. Our instructor has not returned _____ assignments that we turned in last week.

2. Ernest likes to watch _____ football on television.

3. Mr. Olsen likes _____ sugar, but not _____ cream, in his coffee.

4. I have plenty of _____ time but not enough money.

5. I have to go to _____ town this afternoon to pick up _____ supplies that I ordered by telephone this morning.

6. Today there will be a lecture on _____ history of Mexico.

7. Have you enjoyed _____ baseball games that you've gone to this year?

8. _____ meat that we bought yesterday has spoiled.

Exercise 60 (continued)

9. _____roses in your garden look healthier than mine.

10. Would you like to have_____dinner in_____town with us tonight?

(C) Insert <u>the</u>, where needed, in the blanks before the proper names in the following sentences.

1. Do you know where_____Caroline Islands are?

2. _____Tunisia is located in_____North Africa.

3. _____Max's Cafe is located in_____Tower Building at the corner of_____ _____Scott Street and_____Tenth Avenue.

4. Mr. Hale did his undergraduate work at_____University of Virginia, and then went to law school at_____Columbia University.

5. _____Lake Erie is smaller than_____Lake Michigan. They are two of _____Great Lakes located between_____Canada and_____United States.

6. _____Professor Johnson was elected president of_____Chemical Society of America.

7. _____Panama Canal, which connects_____Atlantic Ocean and_____Pacific Ocean, was built on land leased from_____Republic of Panama.

8. _____Charter of the United Nations was signed at_____San Francisco Conference on June 26, 1945.

9. _____Kelleys own a summer cottage at_____Crater Lake.

10. They usually stay at_____Biltmore Hotel when they are in Los Angeles.

Exercises For Part XV

EXERCISE 61

In the following sentences, place <u>a</u>, <u>an</u>, or <u>the</u> in the blanks if an article is needed. If an article is not needed, leave the space blank. (This exercise is intended as a review of the various principles and types of examples given in Part XV.)

1. I saw _____ friend on the way to _____ school today.

2. Is _____ fourteenth chapter long?

3. Were you able to get _____ books that you needed?

4. Would you care for _____ cup of coffee and _____ piece of cake?

5. Mr. Cotton bought _____ new car _____ last week.

6. _____ President likes to play _____ golf.

7. I'm going to take _____ course in economics and _____ art course that is given by Professor Schaeffer this semester.

8. He isn't _____ professional musician, but he plays _____ violin very well.

9. Mr. Preston collects _____ stamps from _____ Oriental countries.

10. Last night we saw _____ movie that was filmed in _____ Tahiti.

11. The professor said that _____ student who wrote this paper had _____ mediocre mind.

12. Thailand was called _____ Siam before _____ World War II.

13. Take _____ Fifth Avenue bus at _____ next corner.

14. _____ government of _____ United States is one of divided powers and separated authority.

15. _____ Los Angeles River seldom has _____ water in it.

16. _____ people have always had to face many problems during _____ life.

Exercise 61 (continued)

17. Mr. Peters is _____ writer. He has recently written _____ book on fishing.

18. Do you remember _____ name of _____ store which advertised a sale of men's shoes?

19. Modern art is _____ non-realistic type of art.

20. _____ strong wind has been blowing from _____ north all day.

21. Canada is _____ member of _____ British Commonwealth of Nations.

22. In 1922, Albert Einstein was awarded _____ Nobel Prize for his work on _____ quantum theory.

23. _____ Amazon River originates in the Peruvian Andes and flows east to _____ Atlantic.

24. Helen put _____ package that _____ postman brought on _____ dining room table.

25. In _____ days of Copernicus, everybody believed that _____ earth was _____ center of the universe.

26. _____ Irish emigrated to _____ United States in large numbers after _____ potato famine in the 1840's.

27. _____ Secretary of Labor will give a speech in Dallas on _____ Labor Day.

28. Maria wants to learn _____ French language before she goes to _____ Europe next year. She already speaks _____ Spanish and _____ German fluently.

29. This morning _____ sailor and _____ soldier were sitting across from me on _____ streetcar; _____ soldier was showing _____ picture of his wife to _____ sailor.

30. It is generally believed that _____ giraffe is _____ voiceless animal; however, a professor from _____ University of Capetown recently reported that, when he was doing research in the Transvaal, he heard _____ bull giraffe growl.

UNIT 5 | PREPOSITIONS

PART XVI | Basic Uses of Prepositions

76 INTRODUCTION

A preposition shows a relationship between its object and other words in a sentence. The preposition may be in the form of one word (**at, by, in, on,** etc.) or in the form of a phrase that functions as a unit (**in front of, by way of,** etc.).

Some of the relationships that prepositions express are *place* or *position, direction, time, manner,* and *agent.*

The book is **on** the desk.	(place or position)
The boy ran **toward** the house.	(direction)
The man arrived **at** ten o'clock.	(time)
He travels **by** train.	(manner)
The book was written **by** him.	(agent)

A preposition + an object forms a *phrase*. This kind of phrase usually functions as a modifier (adjective or adverb).

The report **of the meeting** was read.	(adjective)
We go to class **at ten o'clock.**	(adverb)

77 PREPOSITIONS of PLACE or POSITION

77a. The following sentences and illustrations show some of the relationships of place or position expressed by various prepositions:

The paper is { on / in / by / beside / near / against / under } the desk.

He is sitting { behind / in back of / in front of / beside / near / by } her.

Jack is { in / inside / outside / in front of / in back of / behind / underneath / on top of } the car.

They walked { *across* the park. / *around* the park. / *under* the bridge. / *down* the street. / *up* the street. / *over* the hill. / *through* the park. / *on* the sidewalk. }

PREPOSITIONS

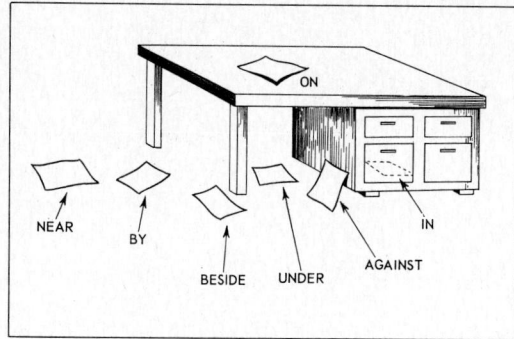

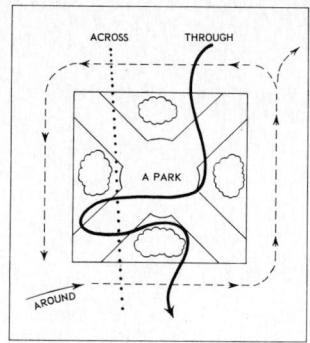

FIGURE 20

FIGURE 21

77b. Below is a list of some prepositions that indicate relationships of place or position:

1.	at	Elizabeth is **at** the store.
		Is Mary **at** home?
2.	to	Elizabeth went **to** the store.
	from	Mr. MacDonald is **from** Scotland.
3.	in	Mr. Brown is sitting **in** the leather chair **in** the lobby.
	on	Put a stamp **on** the envelope.
		Please sit **on** the sofa.
4.	by	The matches are over there **by** the cigarettes.
	beside	The napkin is placed **beside** the plate.
	near	They are sitting **near** the window.
	against	Don't lean **against** the stove.
5.	over	Our apartment is directly **over** yours.
		A plane flew **over** our house at noon.
	under	The box is **under** the table.
	beneath	The closet is **beneath** the stairs.
	underneath	Put a pad **underneath** the rug.
	on top of	The carpenter is **on top of** the house.
6.	behind	The chair is **behind** the desk.
	in back of	John is standing **in back of** Harry.
	in front of	There is a car parked **in front of** the house.
7.	up	I saw Mr. Jones walking **up** the street.
	down	There is a service station about two miles **down** the road.
8.	across	They live **across** the street from us.
	around	Let's take a walk **around** the block.
	through	I took a walk **through** the park yesterday.
9.	between	Martha is sitting **between** George and Jim.
	among	The letter is somewhere **among** these papers.
10.	inside	These plants should be kept **inside** the house.
	outside	The chairs were left **outside** the house all night.
11.	after	Put a question mark **after** each question.
	before	In giving dates, we usually place the month **before** the day.
12.	above	This city is three thousand feet **above** sea level.
		His name is **above** mine on the list.
	below	This land is **below** sea level.
		Your grade is **below** average.
13.	at the top of	Your name is **at the top of** the waiting list.
	at the bottom of	His name is **at the bottom of** the list.
	at the head of	He is now **at the head of** his class.

BASIC USES OF PREPOSITIONS

77c. Compare **in—on, on—at, at—in** in the situations described below:
(1) IN—ON
In general, **in** means beneath the surface; **on** means touching the surface.

> There is a grease spot **on** my coat and a moth hole **in** my sweater.
> We had to drive a large nail **in** the ceiling in order to hang the picture **on** this wall.

(2) ON—AT
In an address, **on** is used with the name of the street; **at,** with the house number + the name of the street.

> He lives **on** Green Street.
> He lives **at** 1236 Green Street.

(3) AT—IN
In referring to location, **at** ordinarily indicates a specified location; **in,** a location within a house, building, city, and so forth.

> I'll meet you **at** the library.
> I'll meet you **at** the information desk **in** the lobby of the hotel.
> She is **in** the kitchen preparing dinner.

In is also used in referring to a location within a country.

> They own a house **in** Sweden.
> He is **in** Peru, South America, now.

In is ordinarily used in referring to cities.

> He lives **in** Hartford, Connecticut.
> They will arrive **in** Bangkok next month.

At is sometimes used in referring to the arrival of a train, and so forth.

> The train will arrive **at** Philadelphia at 8:10 p.m.

78 | PREPOSITIONS of DIRECTION [1]

78a. The following sentence shows some of the relationships of direction expressed by various prepositions:

> The dog ran { **into** / **out of** / **toward** } the building.

78b. Below is a list of some prepositions that indicate relationships of direction:

> into   I walked **into** the room and sat down by the fireplace.
> out of   They ran **out of** the burning building.
> toward   He walked **toward** the City Hall.
> by way of   You can go **by way of** the Panama Canal.

78c. Compare **in—into** in the following situations:
In ordinarily refers to place or position.

> He is **in** his office now.

Into ordinarily refers to motion or action, although **in** is often used interchangeably with **into** in situations of this kind.

---

[1] The prepositions listed in this section are those usually thought of as indicating direction. However, there is some overlapping of place and direction in such prepositions as **from, to, through, up, down, over, under,** etc.

PREPOSITIONS

I saw him go **into** (in) the director's office a few minutes ago.
They went **into** (in) the building an hour ago.

79 PREPOSITIONS of TIME

79a. The following sentence shows some of the relationships of time expressed by various prepositions:

Please arrive $\begin{Bmatrix} \textbf{at} \\ \textbf{by} \\ \textbf{before} \\ \textbf{after} \end{Bmatrix}$ 10 o'clock.

79b. Below is a list of some prepositions that indicate relationships of time:

1. at   The baseball game will start **at** 2:30 p.m.[2]
         This cafe opens **at** noon and closes **at** midnight.
   by   Try to be there **by** 2 o'clock.[3]

2. in   The train will arrive **in** an hour.
         I must leave **in** a few minutes.
         He goes to work early **in** the morning.[4]
   on   Ray's birthday is **on** November 18.

3. for   They stayed **for** three weeks.
   during   We saw them often **during** the summer.
   since   We have been here **since** 1955.

4. after   Call me again **after** 10 o'clock.
   before   He always gets home **before** 6 o'clock.

5. until   Why don't you stay **until (till)** Sunday?
   (till)   I'll be here **till (until)** 5 o'clock.

6. at the beginning of   I'll call you **at the beginning of** the week.
   at the end of   You will receive your check **at the end of** the month.
   in the middle of   Let's have lunch sometime **in the middle of** the week.

79c. Compare **on—in** and **for—during—since** in the situations described below:

(1) ON—IN

In giving dates, **on** is used before days of the week or before months + the day of the month; **in,** before months not followed by the day and before numbers indicating the year.

On Saturday they left for Europe.   They took a trip **in** June.
The store opened **on** May 23, 1950.   They moved to Boston **in** July, 1955.
On May 10th they left for Europe.   They took a trip to Japan **in** 1954.

(2) FOR—DURING—SINCE

In expressions of time, **for** refers to a period of time, frequently stated in terms of the number of hours, days, weeks, and so forth, and in such expressions as **for a long (short) time, for several (a few) minutes, for a little while,** and so forth.

We waited **for** $\begin{Bmatrix} \text{fifteen minutes.} \\ \text{two hours.} \\ \text{several hours.} \\ \text{a long time.} \end{Bmatrix}$

---

[2] **At 2:30 p.m.** = at exactly or precisely 2:30 p.m.
[3] **By 2 o'clock** = not later than 2 o'clock.
[4] The definite article is used in the expressions **in the morning (afternoon, evening),** but not in **at noon (night, midnight).** (Also see Section 75b.)

BASIC USES OF PREPOSITIONS

During also refers to a period of time, frequently stated as a block of time **(during the summer, during the year, during the semester, during my vacation,** etc.).

It rained a great deal **during** { the winter.
the year.
the spring semester.
April.
1955. }

In many cases **for** refers to something more or less *continuous*; **during,** to something *intermittent*. **For** is followed by the indefinite article; **during,** by the definite article. Compare:

It rained **for a day or so.**
   (It rained almost continuously for a day or so.)
It rained **during the day.**
   (It rained sometime during the day or perhaps off and on during the day.)

Since refers to a period of time that extends from a point of time in the past to the present or to another point of time in the past. The verb tense is usually the present perfect or past perfect.

I have been here **since** { five o'clock.
May 10th.
June, 1952. }

We had been there **since** noon.

Compare:

We haven't seen him **for** two or three years.
We saw him several times **during** our trip South.
We haven't seen him **since** 1954.

They have lived in London **for** two years.
They have met many people **during** the two years [two year period] they have been in London.
They have lived in London **since** 1950.

In addition, note the following expressions:

(1) ON TIME—IN TIME
   On time means "on schedule"; **in time** usually means before an appointed time (often with time left over to do something).

Were you late for your appointment?
No, I was there **on time.**   (I was there at the appointed time.)
No, I reached the office **in time** to have a cup of coffee before my appointment.

(2) FROM . . . TO — FROM . . . UNTIL
   These expressions have approximately the same meanings and are usually interchangeable in expressions of time.

He works **from** 8:00 **to** 5:00.   He works **from** 8:00 **until** 5:00.

However, only **from . . . to** is used in referring to *place* or *position*.

We drove **from** Boston **to** New York in four hours.

(3) AROUND—ABOUT
   Around and **about** (sometimes preceded by **at**) are used to indicate approximate time.

I'll pick you up **around** 7 o'clock.
It is now **about** 5 o'clock.

80 PREPOSITIONS of MANNER

1. by   You can go **by** bus (car, train, ship, plane, foot).
2. on   He went **on** foot (horseback).
   I like to travel **on** a train (ship, plane).
3. in   We came here **in** a car (taxi).
   Please write **in** ink (pencil).
   He speaks **in** a low voice.
   He left **in** a hurry.
4. with   I accept your invitation **with** pleasure.
   She greeted him **with** a smile.
   The car started **with** a jerk.
5. like   He walks **like** an old man.
   You speak **like** an authority on the subject.

81 SOME OTHER TYPES of PREPOSITIONS

(1) AGENT (or INSTRUMENT)—**by** and **with**

     This poem was written **by** Walt Whitman.
     The door is opened **by** a mechanical device.

     Try opening the door **with** this key.
     I can write better **with** my own pen.

(2) ACCOMPANIMENT—**with**

     He went **with** her to the store.
     Try some of this sauce **with** your meat.

(3) PURPOSE—**for**

     This door is **for** emergency exits only.
     I need to go to the store **for** a loaf of bread.

(4) ASSOCIATION—**of**

     The new wing **of** the building is almost completed.
     We heard the news **of** your promotion from Bill.

(5) MEASURE—**of** and **by**

     I want three quarts **of** milk and a pound **of** cheese.
     One-third **of** the students are from South America.
     Coffee is sold **by** the pound, but ribbon is sold **by** the yard.

(6) SIMILARITY—**like**

     You look **like** your brother.
     This material feels **like** silk.
     It looks **like** rain.

(7) IN THE CAPACITY OF—**as**

     He got a job **as** an elevator operator.
     Mr. Kingsley will serve **as** chairman of the committee.
     She appeared **as** Desdemona in *Othello*.

EXERCISES FOR PART XVI

EXERCISE 62

<u>Draw a circle</u> around the correct preposition in parentheses in the exercises below:

(A) <u>Place or Position or Direction</u>

1. Do you live (at, on) Bay Street (in, on) Newport?

2. I hung the picture (above, on) the fireplace.

3. She walked (in, into) the kitchen and put her packages (on, over) the table.

4. Is Jane (at, in) home? No, she is (on, at) the library.

5. Mary is sitting (in, on) the sofa (at, in) the living room.

6. Michigan is situated (in, between) Lake Michigan and Lake Huron.

7. While waiting for my train, I took a walk (around, across) the station.

8. A formation of twelve airplanes flew (over, on top of) our house.

9. The artist spends many hours (in, on) his studio (on, at) 50 Charles Street.

10. John found a note pinned (in, on) his door which said: "Meet me (at, in) the corner of Pine and Fifth Streets."

11. The Blake family lives (at, on) Third Street (in, on) Cleveland, Ohio.

12. Don't forget to put your return address (in, on) the envelope.

13. He sat (near, against) the camp fire.

14. Mr. Flanagan, who is (from, of) Ireland, is staying (at, to) his sister's home in Boston.

15. Someone has spilled ink (in, on) this rug and has burned a hole (in, on) that one.

16. The door was locked; so I shoved the letter (under, around) the door.

17. He piled the books (above, on top of) the table.

18. He arrived (in, at) Switzerland last week.

19. You are ahead of me. Your name is (above, at the top of) the list.

20. Your score on the examination is well (above, over) average.

Exercise 62 (continued)

(B) Time

1. Does the movie begin (at, on) 6:30? No, it will not begin (until, for) 9:00; so do not arrive (before, by) that time.

2. He asked me to come (at, in) 11:30, not (at, in) noon.

3. We will go to Florida (since, during) the month of January.

4. The stores stay open (on, in) Mondays (until, for) 9:00 p.m.

5. Mary has been in the United States (for, during) a year.

6. John has lived in France (for, since) two years.

7. I read (for, during) three hours, (at, from) 9:00 p.m. (until, by) 12:00.

8. Did you meet Mr. Green (at, during) your stay in Savannah?

9. No, I did not see him because I was there (for, during) only two hours.

10. The train is (on, in) time. It will arrive (in, by) three hours.

11. Is your birthday (in, on) April? Mine is (in, on) April 7.

12. Come (by, on) 8:00 if you can; no one will be seated at the theater (after, since) 8:30.

13. I try to get to school (in, on) time to have a cup of coffee before my first class.

14. He will leave for Thailand (at, in) the end of August. There will be a farewell party for him (in, on) the twentieth of August.

15. Columbus discovered America (in, on) 1492.

16. The projector broke down twice (for, during) the showing of the film.

17. He had been waiting here (during, since) noon.

18. I received my bill (to, in) the middle of the month.

19. Can you be ready (by, on) six o'clock?

20. We plan to finish this project (around, until) the first of the year.

Exercises For Part XVI

Exercise 62 (continued)

(C) <u>Miscellaneous</u>

1. We accept your kind invitation (by, with) pleasure.

2. I should like to read that book (by, of) Ernest Hemingway.

3. These oranges are sold (of, by) the dozen.

4. The door (of, at) the house is painted red.

5. He says he can communicate (by, of) mental telepathy.

6. Always sign important papers (by, in) ink.

7. Would you rather write (by, with) a pen or pencil?

8. Over one-third (of, in) the oranges are spoiled.

9. The first speech will be given (by, of) Mr. Steele.

10. Do you like to travel (by, in) bus?

11. He toured the country (in, by) a station wagon.

12. How would you like to go (by, with) us (by, in) our car?

13. This liquid smells (like, as) turpentine.

14. This cake is (for, to) lunch.

15. We always buy olive oil (of, by) the gallon.

16. The sound (of, by) rain lulls me to sleep.

17. It looks (like, as) a nice day.

18. It will take four yards (of, by) material to make this dress.

19. He always speaks (in, by) a loud voice.

20. Stanley took a temporary job (as, like) a chauffeur.

EXERCISE 63

<u>Draw a circle</u> around the correct **preposition** in **parentheses** in the following paragraphs:

1. John Doe, who graduated (of, from) the University of North Carolina two years ago, is now doing graduate work (in, on) engineering (at, to) Georgia Tech. He expects to receive his Master's degree (by, in) next June. After that, he plans to accept a job (as, like) a technician (by, with) an oil company (in, at) South America.

2. Jim was walking (across, over) the campus (in, at) noon when he met a friend whom he had not seen (since, during) summer. They stopped (in front of, around) the gymnasium and sat down (in, on) the steps. After they had talked (for, during) about ten minutes, Jim said, "I must go (toward, to) the library and take out some books. I have a test in history (in, on) Friday. I am living (to, in) Jefferson Hall this semester. Why don't you drop by some afternoon (over, after) classes?"

3. Mr. Hill arrived in New York (on, in) May 10 (at, on) eight o'clock (in, on) the evening. He decided to call on his uncle who lived (on, in) Fifth Avenue. He got on a bus (at, of) the station and put his fare (on, into) the farebox. The bus was very crowded, so Mr. Hill had to stand up all the way.

When he reached 85th Street, Mr. Hill got off the bus and walked a short distance (in, to) the apartment building (in, of) which his uncle lived. He knocked (at, in) the door, (of, on) his uncle's apartment. He waited (for, during) a few minutes, but no one came (to, at) the door. He was disappointed to find no one (to, at) home. He didn't know where to go because his uncle had promised to reserve a room for him (at, by) a downtown hotel. He saw a bench (at, to) the end of the hall, and he sat down (on, in) it to wait for his uncle.

Exercises For Part XVI

EXERCISE 64

Insert an appropriate preposition in the blanks in the following sentences:

1. They arrived _____ Bombay _____ 8:00 p.m. _____ July 30.

2. Charles lives _____ College Avenue _____ an apartment.

3. Phoenix is located _____ the state _____ Arizona.

4. John asked me to go _____ him to buy a pair _____ shoes.

5. Put a pad _____ the hot dish to protect the table.

6. Mr. Walker has _____ a grey suit today.

7. This story was written _____ Conan Doyle.

8. My aunt stayed at our house _____ two weeks.

9. Mary is a good housekeeper; she always sweeps _____ the bed.

10. They had to drive _____ the block four times before they found a parking place.

11. There is an ink spot _____ the collar _____ your shirt.

12. Please write _____ ink, and don't forget to write _____ every other line.

13. Did you receive a letter _____ your brother yesterday?

14. The bus will not leave _____ fifteen minutes.

15. Elections are held _____ the first Tuesday _____ November.

16. Maximo always entertains us _____ stories of his experiences.

17. Does this bus go _____ Central City?

18. Mr. and Mrs. Simpson have lived _____ Chestnut Street _____ six years.

19. Dr. Parks has been living _____ Mobile _____ October. His home is _____ Magnolia Avenue.

20. He dived _____ the lake and swam _____ the boat.

EXERCISE 65

Fill in the blanks with appropriate prepositions in the following paragraphs:

1. Would you please tell me how to get _____ the baseball park? Certainly. You go down Arch Street two blocks and turn left _____ King Street. Stay _____ King Street _____ about two miles. You will go _____ a bridge and _____ a tunnel. You will come to Ocean Avenue about four blocks after you leave the tunnel. Turn right _____ Ocean Avenue, and _____ the middle of the block you will see the main entrance _____ the ball park. I would suggest that you drive your car _____ the block and park _____ the parking lot behind the field.

2. _____ June 13 the Circle Players will open _____ Star Theatre _____ a revival _____ George Bernard Shaw's play, <u>Major Barbara</u>. When the play opened _____ Philadelphia a week ago, the critics gave the Circle Players enthusiastic reviews. Good reviews are not unusual for the Circle Players, who have thrilled audiences _____ their performances _____ the past decade. In fact, they were so loudly acclaimed _____ London for their performance of <u>Major Barbara</u> that the play ran _____ three years.

Tickets are now on sale _____ the box office _____ the Star Theatre _____ the three week engagement. There will be a performance every night, except Sunday, _____ 8:30 p.m., and a matinee _____ Wednesday and Saturday _____ 2:30 p.m. Reservations may be made _____ mail or telephone.

PART XVII | Prepositions in Phrasal Combinations

82 INTRODUCTION

Many of the words listed as prepositions in Part XVI appear in various phrasal patterns. One pattern is a *verb* + such words as **in, on, up, over;** in these combinations the prepositions modify the verbs in much the same way as adverbs and are often referred to as *preposition-adverbs*. The difference between the prepositions described in Part XVI and preposition-adverbs may be shown by the following examples:

(1) The child looked **over** the table.

(The preposition **over** shows a relationship of position; other prepositions, such as **on** or **under,** would indicate different positions.)

(2) The student **looked over** his notes.

(The combination of the verb **look** + the preposition-adverb **over** conveys the meaning of "review" or "go over"; the verb **look** + the preposition-adverb **for,** for example, would convey the meaning of "seek.")

Another group of verbs are followed by specific prepositions. Examples are **arrive in, approve of, laugh at.** The prepositions in these combinations do not change the meaning of the verb to the extent that the preposition-adverbs do in the combinations **look over** and **look for.**

Whether the word following the verb is a preposition-adverb or a preposition is not particularly important here, because the combinations in either case must be learned as fixed phrases. The two groups are given in separate lists, however, because it is necessary in most cases to define the meaning of the *verb* + *preposition-adverb* combinations.

In addition to the types of combinations described above, prepositions are found in other kinds of fixed phrases such as **to be afraid of, to have confidence in, in addition to, at once.**

83 VERB and PREPOSITION-ADVERB COMBINATIONS [1]

Although verb and preposition-adverb combinations are regarded as units, some combinations may be separated by an object. Combinations that may appear either followed or separated by an object are listed in group (1) below; those always followed by an object, in (2); those without objects, in (3).

(1) VERB + Preposition-Adverb + Noun OBJECT *or* VERB + Pronoun OBJECT + Preposition-Adverb [2]

1. **bring back**
    a. [recall] Your story **brings back** pleasant memories.
    b. [return] You may borrow my car if you will **bring** it **back** by five o'clock.

---

[1] In this unit, we do not attempt to offer complete lists of combinations; nor do we give all of the meanings of a particular combination. For more complete lists and detailed definitions of *verb* + *preposition-adverb* combinations, consult a standard dictionary or a word study manual.

[2] A noun object may also be placed between the verb and preposition-adverb in most situations; however, in learning to use the combinations on this list, it may be simpler to place the noun object *after* the preposition-adverb because there seems to be a tendency to place it in this position.

2. **bring up**
    a. [rear (children)] They **brought up** their children in the country.³
    b. [introduce or mention (a subject)] Why don't you **bring up** your proposal at the next meeting?
3. **call back** [telephone again]
    Why don't you **call** him **back** in an hour?
4. **call in** [to ask (someone) to come in (for a purpose)]
    We **called** him **in** to ask his advice.
5. **call up** [telephone]
    Why don't you **call** her **up** now?
6. **check off** [mark (an item on a list) for identification or verification]
    As each person arrives, **check** his name **off** the list.
7. **check out** [withdraw (a book, etc.)]
    When did you **check out** these books?
8. **cheer up** [put (someone) in good spirits or in a good mood]
    Try to **cheer** her **up**; she hasn't been feeling well lately.
9. **cross off** [remove (an item from a list)]
    Cross my name **off** the list, please.⁴
10. **cross out** [remove by drawing a line through]
    When you misspell a word, **cross** it **out** and write it correctly.
11. **do over**
    a. [do again] Your composition was poorly organized; you must **do** it **over**.
    b. [redecorate] We are planning to **do over** our living room soon.
12. **drop off** [leave (someone or something at a place)]
    I'll **drop** you **off** at the post office.
13. **figure out** [solve or reason out]
    I just can't **figure** it **out**.
14. **hand in** [submit or turn in]
    Bill forgot to **hand in** his homework today.
15. **look over**
    a. [review] You'd better **look over** this lesson again.
    b. [examine] We'd like to **look over** the clothes on sale.
16. **look up**
    a. [search for (in a reference book, etc.)] You can **look up** population figures in an almanac.
    b. [pay a visit to] **Look** me **up** whenever you're in town.
17. **pick out** [select]
    Please help me **pick out** a new hat.
18. **pick up**
    a. [collect] Can you **pick** me **up** about 4:30?
    b. [learn by chance] We **picked up** some new ideas at the conference.
19. **point out** [call attention to]
    I want to **point out** several important facts to you.
20. **put on**
    a. [don (clothing)] You should **put on** a raincoat because it has started to rain.
    b. [start (coffee, radio, etc.)] Should I **put on** the coffee now?

---

³ This sentence may also be expressed in the passive. In the passive construction, the object **the children** becomes the subject, and there is no object after **brought up**.
    Their children were **brought up** in the country.

⁴ When **cross off** and **check off** (see item 6.) are followed by **the list, the page,** etc., the noun object is placed between the verb and the preposition-adverb.

PREPOSITIONS IN PHRASAL COMBINATIONS

21. **take off** [remove (clothing)]
    Why don't you **take off** your coat and stay a while?
22. **take out**
    a. [escort] John **took** Mary **out** last Saturday; they had dinner together and then went to see the play at the Star Theatre.[5]
    b. [extract] The dentist **took out** two of my wisdom teeth last week.
23. **take up**
    a. [become interested in (a subject, a hobby, etc.)] Walter has **taken up** flying.
    b. [discuss] We'll **take** that **up** again tomorrow.
    c. [introduce] Mr. Martin **took up** a new subject in class today.
24. **think over** [give thought to or (re)consider]
    Think it **over** a little longer.
25. **try on** [test the fit or appearance]
    I'd like to **try on** these two suits, please.

Additional combinations are listed below:

ask for	= request	**take on**	= assume responsibility; undertake something (a job, a project, etc.)
bring out	= reveal		
call down	= scold	**take over**	= assume control of
call off	= cancel	**talk over**	= discuss
carry out	= complete; accomplish	**think through**	= think about until reaching a conclusion
give up	= surrender; lose hope		
hang up	= put (a coat, etc.) on a hook	**think up**	= invent or plan by thinking
pay back	= repay	**throw away**	= discard
put across	= cause to be understood	**try out**	= test or experiment
put away	= store or set aside	**turn down**	= reject
put off	= delay; postpone	**turn in**	= hand in
put out	= extinguish (cigarette, lights, etc.)	**turn off**	= shut off (a radio, gas, etc.)
save up	= put aside money (for a purpose)	**turn on**	= put on (a radio, gas, etc.)
take back	= regain possession; retract a statement of promise	**turn out**	= extinguish (lights, etc.)
		turn over	= change the position; transfer (goods, responsibility, etc.)

(2) VERB + Preposition-Adverb + (Pro)noun OBJECT

1. **call for** [go to get]
   I always **call for** my laundry on Friday afternoon.
2. **call on** [pay a visit]
   We **called on** the Miltons the last time we were in Detroit.
3. **come across** [find by chance]
   Mr. Watson **came across** an interesting old bookstore on Palm Street recently.
4. **come to**
   a. [equal] These groceries **come to** five dollars.
   b. [appear suddenly] The idea **came to** me while I was watching television.
5. **get into, out (of)** [get inside, leave (a car, a taxi, etc.)]
   We **got into** a taxi at the station and **got out** at the Ritz Hotel.
6. **get on, off** [board, leave (a train, a bus, etc.)]
   Get on the bus at Third Street and **get off** at Broadway.
7. **get over** [recover from]
   It took Mr. Brown a long time to **get over** pneumonia.
8. **go over** [review]
   Let's **go over** this exercise again.

---

[5] In this sentence, it seems more natural to place the noun object between the verb and preposition-adverb.

9. **keep on** [continue]
    He **kept on** working there for thirty years.
10. **look after** [watch or take care of]
    I had to **look after** my young cousins yesterday.
11. **look for** [search for or try to find]
    Several students are **looking for** summer jobs.
12. **look into** [investigate]
    It would be a good idea to **look into** the business further before you invest all your money in it.
13. **put up with** [tolerate]
    Some people can't **put up with** noise when they are trying to concentrate.
14. **run out of** [exhaust a supply]
    Some people never **run out of** things to say.
15. **take after** [resemble]
    John **takes after** his father both in looks and in character.

Additional combinations are listed below:

become of	= befall or happen to	**get through with**	= be finished with
catch on	= understand	**go through**	= search or look through
catch up with	= overtake	**happen to**	= befall or become of
come along with	= accompany	**keep up with**	= maintain a standard
check out of	= leave (a hotel)	**look down on**	= regard as inferior
check up on	= investigate	**look in on**	= pay a brief visit to
drop in on	= visit informally	**look out for**	= watch or be careful of
drop out of	= discontinue attendance or participation (in a school, a club, etc.)	**look up to**	= admire
		look forward to	= anticipate
		run across	= come across, meet by chance
get along with	= cooperate; come along with	**see about**	= find out about
get behind in	= fall behind in	**talk back to**	= answer rudely
get through	= manage to finish	**wait on**	= serve

(3) Some combinations are not followed by objects; others, some of which appear in groups (1) and (2), may be used without an object.

1. **check out** [pay the bill and leave a hotel]
    What time do you have to **check out?**
2. **cheer up** [get in good spirits]
    Try to **cheer up!** It does no good to sit around worrying.
3. **get along** [adjust; progress]
    How are you **getting along?**
4. **get back** [return]
    When did you **get back?**
5. **get in** [arrive]
    When does the next train **get in?**

Additional combinations are listed below:

come along	= get along	**turn up**	= make an appearance
drop in	= visit	**keep off**	= do not touch or step on
get through	= manage to finish	**keep out**	= do not enter
get up	= arise	**lie down**	= recline
give up	= lose hope	**look out**	= be careful
hang up	= end a telephone call	**sit down**	= be seated
keep on	= continue	**stand up**	= get up on one's feet
take off	= depart (as a plane, etc.)	**wake up**	= rouse from sleep

PREPOSITIONS IN PHRASAL COMBINATIONS

84 | VERB and PREPOSITION COMBINATIONS

(1) VERB + Preposition + (Pro)noun OBJECT

1. **agree on** (or upon)
   We all seem to **agree on** the definition of the terms.
2. **agree with**
   We **agree with** you on that point.
3. **approve of**
   She doesn't **approve of** smoking.
4. **argue with**
   He **argued with** the taxi driver about the fare.
5. **arrive at** (a place), **arrive in** (a country, city)
   He **arrived at** the airport in time to have dinner before the flight.
   They **arrived in** Rangoon in January.[6]
6. **belong to**
   That tennis racquet **belongs to** Harold.
7. **believe in**
   The Rogers certainly **believe in** having a good time.
8. **care for**
   I don't **care for** cream in my coffee, thank you.
9. **complain about** (or **of**)
   The students are always **complaining about** the assignments.
10. **consent to**
    The management has **consented to** the wage increase demanded by the union.

Additional combinations are listed below:

comment on	hear from	pay for	think about (or of)
consist of	laugh at	rely on	vote for
count on	listen to	succeed in	wait for
decide on	look at	talk to	wish for
depend on	object to	talk about (or of)	work for
hear about (or of)			

(2) VERB + (Pro)noun OBJECT + Preposition + (Pro)noun OBJECT

1. **add** something **to** (or **with**) something
   Now, **add** this number **to** that number.
2. **blame** someone or something **for** something
   The policeman **blamed** Mrs. Read **for** the accident.
3. **compare** one thing **with** (or **to**) another
   Compare this product **with** the one you have been using.
4. **congratulate** someone **on** (or **for**) something
   We **congratulate** you **on** your promotion.
5. **explain** something **to** someone
   Please **explain** this math problem **to** me.

---

[6] **Arrive at** sometimes precedes the name of a city in referring to the arrival of a train, bus, etc. (Also see Section 77c.) Compare:

    The train will **arrive at** Miami at 5:30 p.m.
    We will **arrive in** Miami tomorrow.

6. **excuse** someone **for** something
    Please **excuse** me **for** being late.
7. **introduce** someone **to** someone
    I **introduced** him **to** my sister.
8. **keep** something **for** someone
    Would you **keep** this money **for** me?
9. **prefer** one thing or person **to** another
    I **prefer** this painting **to** that one.
10. **remind** someone **of** someone or something
    She **reminds** me **of** my cousin.
    Please **remind** me **of** my appointment.
11. **thank** someone **for** something
    Thank you **for** telling me about your plans.
12. **subtract** something **from** something
    Subtract this figure **from** the total.

(3) There are other combinations that ordinarily appear in fixed phrases.
1. **fall in love with**
    Anthony **fell in love with** Cleopatra.
2. **get in touch with** [reach or make contact with]
    Try **to get in touch with** Mr. Downs when you get to Minneapolis.
3. **make up one's mind** [decide] [7]
    Have you **made up your mind** yet whether or not to accept the job?
4. **spend money (time, energy, effort) on** something
    I have **spent** a great deal of **time, money,** and **energy on** my garden.
5. **take care of** [watch over or look after]
    Will you please **take care of** my dog this weekend?
6. **take charge of** [assume responsibility for]
    Mr. Brown will **take charge of** the office after the first of the year.
7. **take** something **into consideration**
    You should **take** all expenses **into consideration** before building a house.
8. **waste money (time, energy, effort) on** something
    We are **wasting** too much **time on** this problem.

85 | COMBINATIONS WITH BE AND HAVE

(1) There are many phrasal combinations of **be** + *adjective complement* + *preposition*. (The verb and adjective may be separated by **not** or by an intensifier.)
1. **be afraid of**
    He says that he **is** not **afraid of** anything.
2. **be aware of**
    We **are** well **aware of** the situation.
3. **be certain of**
    Are you **certain of** the date?
4. **be composed of**
    A molecule **is composed of** atoms.
5. **be delighted with** (or **by**)
    I **am delighted with** the gift.

---

[7] See Section 58 for further expressions with **make** and **do**.

PREPOSITIONS IN PHRASAL COMBINATIONS

6. **be different from**
    This car **is** very **different from** the one I usually drive.
7. **be disappointed in** (or **by**)
    Are you **disappointed in** the results of the election?
8. **be familiar with**
    They **are** not **familiar with** this type of work.
9. **be famous for**
    This restaurant **is famous for** its charcoal broiled steaks.
10. **be fond of**
    They **are** especially **fond of** Mexican food.
11. **be frightened by**
    The Senator **is** not easily **frightened by** the threats of his opponents.
12. **be happy with**
    The Russells **are** very **happy with** their new television set.
13. **be interested in**
    Floyd **is interested in** skiing.
14. **be known for**
    This town **is known for** its pleasant climate.
15. **be made of** (or **out of, from**)
    These shoes **are made of** the finest leather.

Additional combinations are listed below:

be opposed to   **be surprised by** (or **at**)
be relevant to   **be thankful for**
be satisfied with   **be thrilled by** (or **with**)
be sensitive to

Other patterns with **be** are as follows:

be an authority on
    Professor Keyes **is an authority on** labor relations.
be an opportunity for
    That **should be an** excellent **opportunity for** you to say what you think.
be no doubt about
    There **is no doubt about** the accuracy of the report.
be in charge of
    Mr. Hicks **is in charge of** the sales department.
be in favor of
    I **am in favor of** having supper after the play.
be in love with
    He says that he **is** very much **in love with** her.
be out of date
    The information in that book **is out of date.**
be out of order
    The telephone **is out of order.**
be (or **look**) **out of place**
    This large sofa **would be (look) out of place** in a small room.

(2) There are some combinations of **have** + *noun* + *preposition*. (Modifiers of the noun may separate the verb and noun.)

1. **have access to**
    The accountant **has** complete **access to** the files.
2. **have ability in**
    He **has** outstanding **ability in** the field of clinical psychology.

3. **have confidence in**
   We **have** a great deal of **confidence in** your judgment.
4. **have faith in**
   You must **have faith in** your own abilities.
5. **have influence over**
   His father doesn't **have** much **influence over** him.

86 OTHER PREPOSITIONAL COMBINATIONS

Prepositions are also found in fixed phrases. Some are used as unit-prepositions and are followed by an object; others are used as modifiers (generally of the verb or whole sentence).

(1) Combinations used as unit-prepositions: [8]

1. **according to**
   Answer the questions **according to** the instructions.
2. **along with**
   Let's consider these questions **along with** the others.
3. **as far as**
   Let's walk **as far as** Madison Avenue.
4. **at home in**
   He is **at home in** any country.
5. **at** (or **on**) **the point of**
   We were **at the point of** discussing Mr. Baker's proposal when the meeting was adjourned.

Other combinations are listed below:

ahead of	in addition to	in (or with) reference to
at the time of	in between	in regard to
because of	in care of	in search of
by means of	in case of	in spite of
except for	in common with	in terms of
for fear of	in contrast to (or with)	instead of
for the purpose of	in the course of	on account of
for the sake of	in exchange for	on the point of

(2) Combinations used as modifiers:

1. **as yet**
   We haven't **as yet** reached a decision.
2. **at all**
   I don't like that hat on you **at all**.
3. **at any time**
   Please feel free to call on us **at any time**.
4. **at first, at last, at length, at once**
   At first, we were very disappointed in our progress.
5. **at the time, at the present time, at this (that) time**
   At the time, we were delighted with the idea of living abroad.

Other combinations are listed below:

by this (that) time	in fact
by the way [incidentally]	up to now
in any case	up to the present time
in any event	

---
[8] See Part XVI for additional combinations that function as prepositions of place, time, and so forth.

EXERCISES FOR PART XVII

EXERCISE 66

Place an appropriate preposition-adverb or preposition in the blanks in the following exercises.

   Example: Did he bring __back__ the book that he borrowed?

(A) Refer to Section 83 if necessary.

1. You may check my name _____ the list.

2. Look _____ your notes before the test.

3. He picked _____ four ties to go with his new suit.

4. Tomorrow we will take _____ a new subject.

5. The doctor called _____ a brain specialist for consultation.

6. I can't read his writing. Can you figure _____ what this says?

7. He dropped me _____ at the corner drugstore.

8. If you don't know the meaning of the word, look it _____

9. Would you like to try _____ some suits?

10. Are you looking _____ the information desk?

11. If you come _____ any information that I could use in my report let me know.

12. He got _____ the ship in New York and got _____ at Rotterdam.

13. How much do these groceries come _____?

14. I think we'd better look _____ the matter further before reaching a decision.

15. He got _____ a taxi in front of the hotel and _____ at the station.

(B) Refer to Section 84 if necessary.

1. He doesn't expecially care _____ opera.

2. What is he complaining _____ now?

3. I don't want to argue _____ you about it.

Exercise 66 (continued)

4. Few people believe _____ ghosts these days.

5. Will her father consent _____ her marriage?

6. We seem to agree _____ many things.

7. When do you expect to arrive _____ Washington, D.C.?

8. He doesn't approve _____ the way we spend our money.

9. Please explain the procedure _____ him.

10. Will you keep these books _____ me while I'm away?

11. I prefer football _____ baseball.

12. You will see a great difference in quality if you compare this camera _____ that one.

13. If you subtract this sum _____ the total, you should get the same answer as I have.

14. Please excuse me _____ interrupting you.

15. Allow me to congratulate you _____ your marriage.

(C) Refer to Section 85 if necessary.

1. Is he aware _____ the seriousness of his illness?

2. Are you familiar _____ this subject?

3. I don't want you to be disappointed _____ me.

4. This design is composed _____ angular shapes.

5. This suitcase is made _____ cowhide.

6. Are they interested _____ going with us this week-end?

Exercises For Part XVII

Exercise 66 (continued)

7. Is he an authority _____ the subject?

8. He is a genius. There is no doubt _____ it.

9. He has a great deal of confidence _____ himself.

10. We don't have access _____ that information.

(D) Refer to Section 86 if necessary.

1. Take these books along _____ you.

2. According _____ this newspaper, the baseball game has been cancelled.

3. You can write to me in care _____ my brother.

4. The Lakes have many interests in common _____ the Peppers.

5. The price of this chair is not unreasonable in terms _____ the design and the quality of the wood.

6. I don't know him _____ all.

7. _____ fact, I know very few people here.

8. The weather has been perfect _____ to now.

(E) Refer to all sections in Part XVII if necessary.

1. Let's try _____ the new machine.

2. In which country were you brought _____?

3. My argument consists _____ four points.

4. Please remind me _____ the appointment.

5. He is afraid _____ his own shadow.

6. I don't approve _____ your smoking. I wish you would give _____ that habit.

7. Clara is very sensitive _____ criticism.

8. We are in favor _____ postponing the examination.

9. He is very interested _____ world affairs.

10. The children laughed _____ the boy because his clothes were different _____ theirs.

11. You can depend _____ me for help.

12. Mr. Pong will take charge _____ the discussion.

13. The committee was opposed _____ the proposal.

14. The picnic was called _____ because of rain.

15. I have to go downtown to see _____ getting some tickets to the opera.

EXERCISE 67

In the blank space on the left-hand side of the page, put the **letter** of the expression in the right-hand list that has the same or a similar meaning to the underlined word or expression in the sentence.

(A)

_____ 1. Some patients <u>recover from</u> an operation quickly.	a.	bring up
	b.	call up
_____ 2. Why did you <u>raise</u> that question during the discussion?	c.	call for
	d.	get in
	e.	get through with
_____ 3. I seldom <u>meet</u> anyone from my home town.	f.	get over
	g.	look over
	h.	look for
_____ 4. Did John <u>telephone</u> Mary last night?	i.	look up
	j.	run across
	k.	see about
_____ 5. The highway patrol is going to <u>experiment with</u> a new method of traffic control.	l.	think over
	m.	think of
	n.	try out
	o.	try on

_____ 6. Scholars <u>search for</u> truth.

_____ 7. When did you <u>finish</u> your engineering problems?

_____ 8. Did you <u>find out about</u> rooms at the housing office?

_____ 9. We have to <u>review</u> the first five lessons before the quiz.

_____ 10. Won't you please <u>reconsider</u> the offer our firm has made to you?

(B)

_____ 1. They will <u>board</u> the ship in Genoa.	a.	catch up with
	b.	get in
_____ 2. I want to <u>call</u> your <u>attention to</u> the painting on this wall.	c.	get on
	d.	keep off
	e.	keep on
	f.	look out for
	g.	look up to
_____ 3. We had to <u>postpone</u> our trip to Miami.	h.	point out
	i.	put across
	j.	put off
_____ 4. Don't you want to <u>remove</u> your coat?	k.	run across
	l.	take off

_____ 5. He will <u>continue</u> working here until June.

_____ 6. Can't we <u>overtake</u> him in the car?

_____ 7. When does the train <u>arrive</u>?

_____ 8. <u>Be careful of</u> that rock in the middle of the road.

Exercises For Part XVII

EXERCISE 68

Answer the following questions orally. In your answer, use the phrasal combination given in the question.

Example: When did you drop out of school?
I dropped out of school in March.

1. How are you getting along these days?

2. When does your plane take off?

3. Do you think that Jack will turn up before the meeting ends?

4. Shall I call for you at 5:30?

5. Do you want me to cross your names off the list?

6. Have you figured out the answer yet?

7. Did you drop Nancy off at her house?

8. Would you please point out the administration building to me?

9. Has Katherine taken up photography as a hobby?

10. Have you ever had a wisdom tooth taken out?

11. When shall I put on the roast?

12. Why did you ask for two tickets?

13. Have you been able to think up anything interesting to do tonight?

14. Did you turn out the lights in the hall?

15. Why did you hang up on me?

16. Does this coat belong to you?

17. Don't you care for sugar in your coffee?

18. Does he work for an oil company?

19. He wastes a lot of money on horse races, doesn't he?

20. You'll make up your mind by tomorrow, won't you?

Exercises For Part XVII

EXERCISE 69

The following exercise is given for review of prepositions and preposition-adverbs presented in Parts XVI and XVII. Fill in the blanks with appropriate prepositions or preposition-adverbs.

Several years ago I became acquainted with a man who had roamed the world _____ search _____ adventure. He had sailed the Atlantic and the Pacific and had spent many months _____ some of the South Sea Islands. One time he was lost _____ a week _____ an outrigger canoe (boat) trying to go _____ one island _____ another _____ a tropical storm. Another time he was sailing _____ the China Coast _____ a Chinese junk (boat) when pirates attacked. The newspapers commented _____ the bravery of his crew, and a private company gave him and his crew a substantial reward _____ capturing the pirates.

While _____ an African safari expedition, he was captured _____ an African tribe. They were interested _____ his money rather than his life and permitted him to communicate _____ English officials _____ South Africa. However, _____ means _____ a clever trick, his party managed to escape. _____ that he took precautions against being captured so easily and hired several body guards.

_____ this experience he was _____ the point _____ returning to his home when he heard _____ an archeological expedition scheduled to cross the Sahara Desert _____ camel. In less than two weeks, he found himself lost _____ the middle of the Sahara. The leader of the expedition tried to get _____ touch _____ headquarters, but the radio sending set was out _____ order. They could think _____ no means of getting back and were about to give _____ hope when an airplane flew _____ the caravan.

Fortunately, the pilot saw them and landed. They were indebted to him _____ saving their lives. My friend returned to Switzerland _____ delay. _____ that time, he has been living _____ Geneva. He seems out _____ place living _____ a conventional style, but he has decided against making further expeditions _____ some time to come.

UNIT 6 | NOUNS and PRONOUNS

PART XVIII | Noun and Pronoun Forms

87 | NOUN FORMS

Most nouns have singular and plural forms. In addition, nouns that refer to persons and animals have singular and plural possessive forms.[1]

SINGULAR	PLURAL
a **student**	two **students**
a **student's** grades	the **students'** grades

87a. A plural form of a noun is regularly formed by adding **s** or **es** to the singular.

| book | books |
| dish | dish**es** |

(1) Most nouns add **s** to the singular form:

girl	girl**s**	chair	chair**s**
page	page**s**	belief	belief**s**
month	month**s**	tree	tree**s**

(2) If the singular form ends in the letters **s, x, z, ch,** or **sh,** the plural is formed by adding **es** to the singular:

bus	bus**es**	wish	wish**es**
class	class**es**	church	church**es**
quiz	qui**zzes**[2]	box	box**es**

(3) If the singular form ends in **y,** preceded by a *consonant*, the plural is formed by changing **y** to **i** and adding **es:**

| lady | lad**ies** | duty | dut**ies** |

If the singular form ends in **y,** preceded by a *vowel*, the plural is made by adding only **s.**

| day | day**s** | monkey | monkey**s** |

(4) The plural of some nouns ending in **o,** preceded by a consonant, is made by adding **es.**

| hero | hero**es** | echo | echo**es** |
| potato | potato**es** | tomato | tomato**es** |

---

[1] The possessive forms ordinarily function as modifiers of other nouns. (See Section 13.)

[2] The spelling principle governing the doubling of consonants for plural nouns is the same as that given for the third person singular forms of verbs. (See Section 24.) When the word ends in a single consonant preceded by a single vowel, the consonant is ordinarily doubled before **es** is added. In some cases, there are two acceptable spellings (**buses, busses**).

Some exceptions:

piano	pianos	soprano	sopranos
concerto	concertos	dynamo	dynamos

The plural of nouns ending in **o,** preceded by a vowel, is made by adding **s.**

folio	folios	radio	radios

(5) With some nouns, final **f** is changed to **v** before adding **s** or **es.**

knife	kni**ves**	self	sel**ves**
life	li**ves**	shelf	shel**ves**
wife	wi**ves**	half	hal**ves**
leaf	lea**ves**	loaf	loa**ves**

When the **f** changes to **v,** the pronunciation also changes: The voiceless / f / in the singular becomes voiced / v / in the plural.

Some nouns retain the **f** in the plural form.

safe	safe**s**	roof	roof**s**
belief	belief**s**	chief	chief**s**
grief	grief**s**	proof	proof**s**

(6) Compound nouns that are written as one word ordinarily form the plural by adding **s** or **es** to the singular. With *hyphenated* compound nouns, the general practice is to add the plural ending to the *first* word of the combination. Compare:

roommate	roommate**s**	mother-in-law	mother**s**-in-law
bookshelf	bookshel**ves**	son-in-law	son**s**-in-law
landlady	landlad**ies**	sister-in-law	sister**s**-in-law
drugstore	drugstore**s**	maid-of-honor	maid**s**-of-honor
cupful	cupful**s**	lady-in-waiting	lad**ies**-in-waiting
streetcar	streetcar**s**	court-martial	court**s**-martial
classroom	classroom**s**	hanger-on	hanger**s**-on
bystander	bystander**s**	passer-by	passer**s**-by

The principles governing the pronunciation of regular plural endings are the same as those for the pronunciation of third person singular forms of verbs. (See Section 24.) Some are pronounced /s/, some /z/, and some as a separate syllable [ɪz] or [əz]. Compare:

/s/	/z/	[ɪz] or [əz]
beliefs	chairs	pages
shirts	ladies	houses [3]
trips	lives	boxes

The following nouns have *irregular* plural forms; that is, **s** or **es** is not added to the singular:

man	**men**	foot	**feet**
woman	**women**	tooth	**teeth**
child	**children**	goose	**geese**
ox	**oxen**	mouse	**mice**

Many nouns taken from other languages form the plural by adding **s** or **es** to the singular. However, the following types of nouns should be noted:

(1) Some nouns have kept the foreign plurals. Examples:

crisis	crises	alumnus	alumni
basis	bases	agendum	agenda
thesis	theses	datum	data
hypothesis	hypotheses	criterion	criteria
analysis	analyses	phenomenon	phenomena

---

[3] The voiceless / s / in **house** may remain / s / or change to / z / when the plural ending is added.

NOUN AND PRONOUN FORMS

(2) Other nouns have kept the foreign plurals, but the regular plural forms (**s** or **es** endings) are also used. Examples:

formula	formulas	or	formulae
curriculum	curriculums	or	curricula
syllabus	syllabuses	or	syllabi
stimulus	stimuluses	or	stimuli
index	indexes	or	indices
memorandum	memorandums	or	memoranda
plateau	plateaus	or	plateaux

In these cases, there is a tendency toward the use of the regular plural endings, although the foreign plurals are preferred in certain academic situations.

There are certain nouns that are not regularly used in both the singular and plural forms.

(1) The singular form of mass nouns (non-countable nouns) and nouns referring to abstract concepts is ordinarily used.

> I'd like two pounds of **coffee.**
> Have you gathered all of the necessary **information?**
> **Courage** is one of his qualities.

(2) The plural form of certain nouns is ordinarily used.

(a) Nouns such as **scissors, tongs, pants, trousers, slacks, shorts** are ordinarily used with the plural of the verb.

> My **scissors need** sharpening.
> Bermuda **shorts are** fashionable in some places.

(b) Nouns such as **the United States, news, measles, mumps** are ordinarily used with the singular form of the verb.

> No **news is** good news.
> **The United States is** composed of 48 states.
> **Mumps is** a childhood disease.

(c) Nouns such as **mathematics, statistics, economics, politics, physics, acoustics** are used with the singular form of the verb when they refer to an area of study or an activity that is thought of as a unit.

> **Statistics is** a required course for majors in **economics.**
> **Politics is** his major field of interest.

When these nouns refer to component parts of an activity or condition, the plural form of the verb may be used.

> These **statistics** [data or figures] on population **are** interesting.
> His **politics** [methods or procedures] **are** unethical.

(3) The same form of a few nouns is ordinarily used as both a singular and a plural noun. Examples are **deer, sheep, fish, trout, series, species, Chinese, Japanese, Swiss.**

> We caught several **fish,** including a **trout** and three **salmon.**
> Answer this **series** of questions today; answer the next three **series** by next week.

87b. Possession may be indicated by two methods: (a) by using the possessive forms of nouns, and (b) by placing an **of**-phrase after a noun. In general, the type of noun determines the method used.

(1) Nouns referring to persons or animals ordinarily form the possessive by adding an apostrophe (') to plural nouns that end in **s** or **es** and by adding ('**s**) to all other nouns, singular or plural.[4] Examples:

ADD (')	ADD ('s)
the boys' club	the boy's book
the horses' stable	the horse's stable
the Smiths' home	Mary Smith's home
the ladies' club	a lady's glove
the wives' discussion	his wife's idea
my roommates' plan	my roommate's plan
	a woman's way
	the women's program
	his son-in-law's business
	his sons-in-law's business [5]

The **of**-phrase may also be used with nouns of this kind in some situations. Compare:

the **men's** clothes	the clothes **of the men**
people's dreams	dreams **of people**
Pharoah's daughter	the daughter **of Pharoah**
my **roommate's** wardrobe	the wardrobe **of my roommate**
the **horse's** stable	the stable **of the horse**
Aristotle's philosophy	the philosophy **of Aristotle**
Shakespeare's sonnets	the sonnets **of Shakespeare**

In some of these situations, the relationship indicated by the **of**-phrase may be one of association, origin, or source, rather than possession.

(2) Nouns referring to things, places, and concepts are often followed by an **of**-phrase to indicate relationships such as association, measure, or portion.

the lower drawer **of the desk**
the handle **of the cup**
the town **of Milpitas**
the performance **of a lifetime**
three pounds **of hamburger**
half **of the chapter**
a box **of stationery**

In some cases the object in the **of**-phrase may be placed before the noun as a modifier. In this construction, the noun may still suggest a relationship such as association, but its function is primarily that of a descriptive modifier. (The possessive form of the noun is *not* used.) Compare:

the **barn** door	the door **of the barn**
the **desk** drawers	the drawers **of the desk**
the **table** top	the top **of the table**
the **hill**top	the top **of the hill**

When the **of**-phrase indicates measure or portion, there is a change in meaning if the object of the **of**-phrase is placed before the noun. For example, when we talk about **a cup**

---

[4] The possessive of singular nouns ending in **s** may be formed by adding either (') or ('s). If it is difficult to pronounce the word with an additional **s**, only the apostrophe (') is ordinarily used.

James' report *or* James's report
(*but:* Euripides' play)

[5] The possessive form of most hyphenated compound nouns, singular or plural, is made by adding ('s) to the last word in the combination.

of coffee, we mean a measure of coffee, but when we talk about **a coffee cup,** we mean a cup that is used for the purpose of serving or drinking coffee. Also compare:

an **ink** bottle	a bottle **of ink**
a **sugar** bowl	a bowl **of sugar**
a **shoe** box	a box **of shoes**

In some cases the possessive form of nouns that refer to *things* or *places* may be used to indicate such relationships as possession, association, or source. Compare:

the galley **of the ship**	**the ship's** galley
the rays **of the sun**	**the sun's** rays
the natural resources **of Canada**	**Canada's** natural resources

(Nouns that refer to things and places are frequently personified, that is, thought of as having characteristics of persons.)

The possessive form of certain nouns indicates measure or source.

a **dime's** worth	two **weeks'** pay
a **day's** work	**life's** best moments

Compound nouns and nouns that modify other nouns should not be confused with constructions that show source or origin. Neither the **of-**phrase nor a possessive form of a noun would be used in place of the following combinations:

symphony music	grocery store
(*not:* music of symphony or symphony's music)	income tax
telephone book	night shift
English lesson	entrance exam
physics laboratory	tuition fee

88 | PRONOUN FORMS

88a. Most pronouns, unlike nouns, have different subject and object forms.

SUBJECT FORMS	OBJECT FORMS
I	me
he	him
she	her
we	us
they	them
BUT:	
it	it
you	you

The subject forms are used as subjects and complements; the object forms are used as objects of verbs or prepositions.

He told **us** a joke, and **we** laughed at **it.**

In present day English, both the subject and object forms of pronouns are used as *complements* following **it is (was), this is (was), that is (was),** although some people consider the object forms unacceptable.

Who is it?
It is **I.** *or* It's **me.**

What's happened to the Smiths?
That's **they** at the door now.
 or That's **them** at the door now.

88b. There are two possessive forms for most pronouns: one for use as a modifier and another for use alone as a subject, an object, or a complement.

FORMS USED AS MODIFIERS	FORMS USED ALONE
my book	**mine**
his book	**his**
her book	**hers**
its color	**its**
our house	**ours**
your house	**yours**
their house	**theirs**

Compare the uses of these forms:

This is **my** book.
This book is **mine**.
Her lessons are all in, but **yours** are not.
Our club has **its** [6] finances in order.

88c. The following pronouns are combinations of possessive forms and **self** or **selves**.

myself   ourselves
yourself   yourselves
himself   themselves
herself
itself

These forms are used for emphasis:

I **myself** am going to speak to them.
The theory in **itself** sounds fine.
John built his house **himself**.

These pronouns are also used when the object refers to the same person as the subject. Compare:

I bought a present for **myself**.
I bought a present for **them**.

He accidentally hit **himself** on the head.
He accidentally hit **her** on the head.

The child can now dress **herself**, but sometimes her mother dresses **her**.

89   A NOTE on GENDER

Nouns or pronouns that refer to female beings are of *feminine* gender: **girl, woman, she, her.**

Nouns or pronouns that refer to male beings are of *masculine* gender: **boy, man, he, him.**
Nouns that refer to inanimate objects are of *neuter* gender: **desk, chair, it, its.**

89a. Many nouns may refer to *either male or female* beings: **student, teacher, lawyer, doctor.**

May I bring a **friend** to the party?
You should see a **doctor**.

---

[6] Do not confuse **its**, the possessive pronoun, with **it's**, the contraction of **it is**.

NOUN AND PRONOUN FORMS

With nouns of this type, the sex of the person may be established by another noun or pronoun.

> She goes to a **woman doctor.**
> She invited two of her **girl friends** and three of her **boy friends** to the party.
> The **student** handed in **her** paper on time.

Other nouns refer specifically to males or to females:

MALE	FEMALE	MALE	FEMALE
boy	girl	bridegroom	bride
brother	sister	grandfather	grandmother
father	mother	great-uncle	great-aunt
gentleman	lady	stepfather	stepmother
husband	wife	actor	actress
king	queen	duke	duchess
man	woman	emperor	empress
nephew	niece	god	goddess
sir	madam	heir	heiress
son	daughter	hero	heroine
uncle	aunt	prince	princess
		waiter	waitress
		widower	widow

89b. All pronouns (except **she, her, hers, herself, he, him, his, himself**) may refer to *either* males or females.

> **They** (the girls) will be here in an hour.
> We saw **them** (the brothers) at the auto show.

They and **them** may also refer to things.

> Where did you buy **them** (the oranges)?

89c. Sometimes places, things, or concepts may be thought of as having the characteristics of persons and thus be referred to as male or female. This kind of usage occurs particularly in informal conversation or in poetic expression.

> Do you like Paris? Ah yes! **She's** a **queen** among cities.
> How's your old car? Oh, **she's** running like a dream these days.
> The ship sank with all **her** crew on board.
> There is a line in John Milton's *L'Allegro* that runs,
>   "And Laughter holding both **his** sides."

It and **its** are often used in referring to animals.

> The dog ate **its** food.

EXERCISES FOR PART XVIII

EXERCISE 70

Read the following sentences. Give the plural form of the nouns in parentheses. (Also write the forms in the spaces at the right.)

    Example: Study the next three (chapter).   chapters
              (Read: Study the next three <u>chapters</u>.)

1. Can you recommend some good (book)? _____

2. There are several (student) waiting to see you. _____

3. I had to have two (tooth) pulled the other day. _____

4. The weather forecast is for blue (sky). _____

5. How many (church) are there in this town? _____

6. Two of my brothers are (lawyer). _____

7. The (roof) of these houses are tile. _____

8. Get me two (loaf) of bread _____

9. My (foot) really hurt! _____

10. You can always hear (echo) in these mountains. _____

11. They are proud of their (son-in-law). _____

12. Are (postman) employees of the federal government? _____

13. Did you raise these (tomato) in your garden? _____

14. There are twelve (month) in a year. _____

15. How many (day) are there in this month? _____

16. I think we need two (radio). _____

17. Don't you think that (tax) are too high? _____

18. This recipe calls for two (spoonful) of butter. _____

19. How many graduate (thesis) were completed this year? _____

20. We saw several (deer) in the park. _____

EXERCISE 71

Read the following sentences. Give the possessive form of the nouns in parentheses. (Also write the forms in the spaces at the right.)

    Example: This is (John) book.   John's
                  (Read: This is John's book.)

1. Have you seen my (roommate) sweater?

2. Are you (Jim) sister?

3. Do you know where the (Browns) house is located?

4. She doesn't like her (mother-in-law) criticisms.

5. Have you read (William Faulkner) latest novel?

6. Are there many (boys) clubs in this city?

7. Elizabeth Cady Stanton was a leader in the movement for (women) rights.

8. He never does an honest (day) work.

9. There is a (children) program on the radio every afternoon at 4:30.

10. The lecturer spoke about (Brazil) natural resources.

11. We always enjoy your (wife) cooking.

12. My (sister) husband is a news analyst.

13. I'd like to have a few (minute) rest.

14. The (student) excuse was not very good.

15. We are going to meet at (Bill) house.

16. I'd like a (nickel) worth of peanuts, please.

17. The refreshments were prepared by the (professors) wives.

18. Have you met (Mr. Balfour) wife?

19. Is it (Alice) ambition to be a ballet dancer?

20. They say that a dog is (man) best friend.

EXERCISE 72

Read the following sentences. Substitute pronouns for the underlined words.
(Also write the forms in the spaces at the right.)

    Example: This cake is delicious.   It
                   (Read: It is delicious.)

1. Did you see John?   _____

2. Mary is a talented young woman.   _____

3. Did you bring your book this time?   _____

4. Where did you get those apples?   _____

5. Jim and Betty are going to the play with us. _____

6. My watch needs repairing.   _____

7. Have you met John's sister?   _____

8. Where did you put my gloves?   _____

9. Have you seen your aunt recently?   _____

10. The bride's face was radiant at the wedding. _____

11. These magazines are for you.   _____

12. My nephew is in high school now.   _____

13. Do you know where my umbrella is?   _____

14. The children have gone to bed.   _____

15. The prince's tour took five months.   _____

16. Did you enjoy Betty's letter?   _____

17. That actor has a promising future.   _____

18. Mrs. Johnson is a good friend of mine.   _____

19. They sell stoves on the third floor.   _____

20. Mathematics is easy for me.   _____

EXERCISE 73

<u>Draw a circle</u> around the correct form in each of the parentheses below:

    <u>Example</u>: I borrowed (the book of John, (John's book)).

1. On (Tuesday night, the night of Tuesday) several of us gathered at (Bill's house, the house of Bill). For a while we talked about (the world's situation, the world situation). After that we discussed (T. S. Eliot's poetry, T. S. Eliot poetry). Later we listened to recordings of (folks' songs, folk songs) and (music of symphony, symphony music).

2. Before going to my (philosophy's class, philosophy class) this morning, I came across (Stan's brother, the brother of Stan's) near (the campus cafeteria, the cafeteria of campus), and we decided to have (a coffee cup, a cup of coffee). I noticed that Jim had (a chemistry's syllabus, a chemistry syllabus) and I said, "I see that you are taking (a chemistry course, a course of chemistry)." He replied that he was on his way to his (chemistry class, class of chemistry) and that there would be a ten minute quiz at (the period's beginning, the beginning of the period).

    As we were getting up from the table, I knocked my (coffee cup, cup of coffee) off the table and broke it. I spoke to the cashier about it, and he said that there would be no charge for the broken cup.

PART XIX | Agreement

90 INTRODUCTION

In this part, two main areas of agreement are considered: (a) agreement of *subject and verb*, and (b) agreement of a *pronoun with the noun or pronoun to which it refers*.

91 AGREEMENT of SUBJECT and VERB

The verb agrees with the subject in *person and number*.

I am ready.
He is going home.
She has been here before.

We are ready.
They are going home.
They have been here before.

In many cases, agreement is not evident because the same form of the verb is used with all persons, singular and plural.

I will be there.
He went home.
She had never **met** Jim before.
I can be there.

We will be there.
They went home.
They had never **met** Jim before.
We can be there.

91a. The general principle for determining the agreement of a subject and a verb is the rule that "a singular subject takes a singular verb and a plural subject takes a plural verb." Compare:

SINGULAR

The **man drives** to work.
Robert is going fishing.
Mr. Potter has gone to the meeting.

PLURAL

The **men drive** to work.
Robert and I are going fishing.
Mr. Potter and his brother have gone to the meeting.

Along with this rule must go an understanding that the singular or plural form of the subject is not the only factor that determines agreement. *The idea in the mind of the speaker may also be a factor.* For example, some nouns that are singular in form may convey either singular or plural meaning, depending on the idea in the mind of the speaker. Compare:

My **family is** here.
   (family = a unit)
My **family are** here.
   (family = individuals)
Peaches and cream is delicious.
   (peaches and cream = a unit)
Peaches and cream are perishable and should be refrigerated.
   (peaches and cream = separate items)

91b. The following notes on agreement of subject and verb are intended as a guide, not as hard and fast rules:

(1) When the subject is followed by a phrase, the verb ordinarily agrees with the subject, not the noun in the phrase.

> The **package** of cigarettes **is** on the table.
> The **boxes** of candy **are** on the table.

(2) When the subject consists of two or more nouns that are connected by **and**, the principles of agreement are as follows:

(a) If the nouns refer to *different* persons or things, the *plural* form of the verb is used.

> **Jim and Joe are** roommates this semester.
> **The pen and paper are** on the desk.

(b) If the nouns refer to the *same* person or thing, the *singular* form of the verb is used.

> My old **friend and colleague,** George, **is** in town.
> **The author and lecturer is** arriving tonight.

(c) If the nouns are regarded as a *unit*, the *singular* form of the verb is used.

> **Bread and butter was** all he asked for.

(3) When the subject consists of two or more nouns joined by **or, either . . . or,** and **neither . . . nor,** the verb ordinarily agrees with the noun *nearer the verb*.

> John or his **brothers are going** to help me.
> Either your key or my **key is missing.**
> Neither my gloves nor my **hat goes** with this dress.

(4) When a collective noun, such as **family, group, committee, class,** is regarded as a single unit, the *singular* form of the verb is used; when it is regarded as a collection of separate units, the *plural* form of the verb is used. Compare:

> The **committee has agreed** on a plan.
> The **committee have not agreed** on a plan.

(5) When **this** or **that** is the subject, the third person *singular* form of the verb is used; when **these** or **those** is the subject, the third person *plural* form of the verb is used.

> **That is** a good idea!
> **These are** times that try men's souls.

(6) When the subject is an indefinite pronoun, the principles of agreement are as follows:

(a) The following indefinite pronouns, whether singular or plural in meaning, are ordinarily used with the third person *singular* form of the verb: **each, everybody, everyone, everything, any, anybody, anyone, anything, somebody, someone, something, one, no one, nothing, nobody, either, neither, another, the other.**

> **Each arrives** on time.
> **Everybody is having** a good time.
> **Someone is** on the telephone.

It is also possible to use a plural verb with **neither.**

> **Neither are (is)** to blame.
> **Neither** of the answers **are (is)** correct.

(b) The following indefinite pronouns are ordinarily used with the third person *plural* form of the verb: **all, both, few, many, several, some:**

> **All were** satisfied with their grades.
> **Both are** in the closet.
> **Several have** already **written** to me.

AGREEMENT

(c) **None** and **enough** may be used with either the third person singular or plural, depending on the meaning. Compare:

> **None has returned** from the meeting.
> (**none** = no one)
> **None were** on time, for they all missed the bus.
> (**none** = not any of them)
>
> **Enough has been said** on that subject.
> (**enough** = enough discussion)
> **Enough are** here to constitute a quorum.
> (**enough** = enough members)

(7) The title of a book is considered *singular* and is used with the third person singular form of the verb.

> *The Dialogues* of Plato **is** a great classic.
> *The Web and the Rock* **was** Thomas Wolfe's third novel.

(8) The word **people,** meaning many persons, is considered *plural* and is ordinarily used with the third person plural form of the verb.

> The **people were** excited about the news.

The word **peoples,** also plural, refers to races, tribes, or nations.

> The **peoples** of the world **want** peace.

(9) When the expression **the number of** precedes a subject, a *singular* form of the verb is ordinarily used; when the expression **a number of** precedes a subject, a *plural* form of the verb is ordinarily used. Compare:

> **The number of students** in the music class **is limited** to five.
> **A number of books** [several books] **are** on reserve in the library for this course.

(10) A plural noun referring to money, time, or distance that is preceded by an expression of amount or quantity is considered *singular* and is ordinarily used with the third person singular form of the verb.

> **Fifty dollars is** too much to pay for that coat.
> **Three weeks is** a long time to wait to hear from him.
> **Forty miles** on that road **seems** like two hundred!

A noun that is preceded by an expression of fraction or portion (such as **half of, part of,** etc.) may be considered either singular or plural. Whether a singular or plural form of the verb is used depends on whether the noun following **of** is singular or plural.

> *One third of the* **apples are** yours.
> *Half of the* **time was spent** in the country.
> *All of the* **money has been spent.**[1]

91c. The following points concerning agreement in sentences introduced by **it** and **there** are important:

(1) **It** is always used with a *singular* form of the verb.

> **It is** time to go.
> **It was** the Smiths who called us.

---

[1] Also see Section 87a for agreement with nouns such as **scissors, politics, sheep,** etc.

(2) Whether **there** is used with a singular or plural form of the verb depends on whether the *subject* of the sentence is singular or plural. The subject will be found after the verb.

> There **is a man** at the door.
> There **are several people** at the door.

Although both **it** and **there** are used to introduce sentences, they are not used in the same situations.

(1) Uses of **it**:
  (a) As a pronoun:
> He bought a gardenia and gave **it** to me.

  (b) In expressions of time, weather, and distance:
> **It** is 9:00 o'clock.
> **It** is boiling hot today.
> **It** is two blocks to the post office.

  (c) In expressions of identification:
> **It** was Barnaby that won the race.

  (d) In impersonal expressions:
> **It** is true that you should see the movie yourself.
> **It** is strange that she didn't tell you.

(2) Uses of **there**:
  (a) To indicate existence:
> **There** is an interesting exhibit at the museum now.
> **There** were a lot of people at the reception.

  (b) To point out or express place or position:
> **There** is the store I was telling you about.
> Where's May? **There** she is.[2]

The uses of **it** and **there** are sometimes confused in the following situations:

> **There** was a good show on television last night.
>   (*not:* It was a good show . . .)
> **It** is two miles to the station.
>   (*not:* There are two miles . . .)

92 AGREEMENT of PRONOUN with the NOUN or PRONOUN TO WHICH IT REFERS

92a. *Personal pronouns* (**he, she, it,** etc.) agree in gender and number with the (pro)nouns to which they refer.

(1) Agreement of *gender* is not always evident because only the *third person singular* pronouns show gender.

> **Helen** gave **her** ticket to Janet.
> **John** sends **his** regards to you.
> This **vacuum cleaner** is highly recommended for **its** durability.

(2) If a pronoun refers to a singular (pro)noun, a singular form of the pronoun is used; if a pronoun refers to a plural (pro)noun, a plural form is used.

---

[2] Notice the word order in this statement. (Also see Section 16.)

AGREEMENT

> **He** will take **his** car.
> **They** will take **their** car.
> **Bill and Jack** will take **their** cars.
> **We** will take **our** cars.
> **Bill and I** will take **our** cars.
>> (Notice that **our** refers to the compound subject **Bill and I** because the meaning is **we**.)

92b. Some points concerning agreement of *relative pronouns* (**who, which, that,** etc.) with the nouns or pronouns to which they refer are as follows:

(1) **Who** and **whom** refer only to *persons*; **that** and **whose** may also refer to persons.

> The **woman who** spoke to me is Charlie's aunt.
> The two **women who** spoke to me are Charlie's aunts.
> He is the **man that** you should see.
> **Mr. Wright, whose** book you have read, will be the guest speaker.[3]

Which refers only to *things*; **that,** and occasionally **whose,** may also refer to things.

> The new **books, which** look a lot like the old ones, have arrived.
> The **groceries that** I bought are on the table.[4]

(2) The same form of a relative pronoun is used in referring to both singular and plural (pro)nouns, but whether the verb following the relative pronoun is singular or plural depends on whether the (pro)noun is singular or plural.

> The **magazine which is** on the table belongs to me.
> The **magazines which are** on the table belong to me.
> I am the **one that is** at fault.
> They are the **ones that are** at fault.

92c. Problems of agreement with *indefinite pronouns* (**each, all,** etc.)[5] occur primarily when a personal pronoun refers to an indefinite pronoun.

(1) If the indefinite pronoun is considered *singular* in form, the personal pronoun that refers to it is also singular; if the indefinite pronoun is considered *plural* in form, the personal pronoun that refers to it is also plural. Compare:

> **Each** did **his** best to make the program a success.
> **All** did **their** best to make the program a success.
> **Everyone** who is coming has paid for **his** ticket.
> **Several** who are coming have not paid for **their** tickets.

In actual usage, a plural form of a personal pronoun is frequently used with an indefinite pronoun generally regarded as singular when the idea expressed seems plural in the mind of the speaker. Compare:

> **Everybody** did **his** part.
> **Everybody** did **their** part.
> **Each** of the boys made **his** own bed.
> **Each** of the boys made **their** own bed.
> **Each** of us did **his** best.
> **Each** of us did **our** best.

---

[3] **Who** is used as subject of the clause; **whom,** as object; **that,** as either subject or object. **Whose** may modify either the subject or object of the clause. (Also see Section 14.)

[4] **Which** and **that** are used as either the subject or object of the clause. **Whose** may modify either the subject or object of the clause.

[5] See Section 91d for lists of indefinite pronouns.

Some people would consider the plural forms in these sentences unacceptable. However, there is a tendency toward this usage, particularly in situations where the indefinite pronouns and their modifiers strongly suggest the idea of plurality.

(2) When an indefinite pronoun, such as **each,** refers to each member of a group of men, **he, him,** or **his** is used in referring to the indefinite pronoun; when the indefinite pronoun refers to each member of a group of women, **she, her,** or **hers** is used; when the indefinite pronoun refers to each member of a mixed group, **he, him,** or **his** is ordinarily used.

> **Each** (man) paid for **his** own lunch.
> **Each** (woman) paid for **her** own lunch.
> **Each** (man and woman) paid for **his** own lunch.

(3) When indefinite pronouns function as modifiers of nouns (indefinite adjectives), the same points given in (1) and (2) apply.

> **Each boy** made **his** own bed.
> **All students** are expected to turn in **their** papers on time.
> **Every person** in the room expressed **his** disapproval.
>   (*or:* Every person in the room expressed their disapproval.)
> **Every man and woman** at the meeting stated **his** opinion.
>   (*or:* Every man and woman at the meeting stated their opinion.)

EXERCISE 74

Read the following sentences. Give the form of the verb in parentheses that agrees with the subject. (Also write the forms in the spaces at the right.)

    Example: Jim and Joe (is, are) roommates.   are
               (Read: Jim and Joe <u>are</u> roommates.)

1. Knowledge of the facts (is, are) necessary to reach a wise decision. _____

2. This book, that notebook, and this pen (belongs, belong) to him. _____

3. Neither Mildred nor her friends (wants, want) to help on the clean-up. _____

4. The first two parts of the experiment (takes, take) the most time. _____

5. The people (arrives, arrive) early for the lectures. _____

6. The number of books in the library (is, are) large. _____

7. There (is, are) something to be said for both sides. _____

8. Either topic (has, have) the professor's approval. _____

9. These (is, are) the best sea stories I've ever read. _____

10. Everyone (thinks, think) this is a good idea. _____

11. <u>Droll Stories</u> (is, are) a well-known book by Balzac. _____

12. Economics (is, are) John's major field of study. _____

13. My club (has, have) a golf tournament every year. _____

14. There (is, are) twenty students in the class. _____

15. It certainly (was, were) not my friends who said that. _____

16. The report of your grades (is, are) in the office. _____

17. (Is, Are) either of your cousins here? _____

18. The committee (has expressed, have expressed) differences of opinion. _____

Exercises For Part XIX

Exercise 74 (continued)

19. Ray and I (am going, are going) to the opera tonight.

20. All of my brothers (is, are) still in school.

21. My teacher and advisor, Mr. Warren, (is, are) very kind.

22. Don't you think that $60 (is, are) too much rent for this room?

23. It (is, are) unusual for them to be late.

24. One half of these books (belongs, belong) to you.

25. There (has been, have been) several calls for you.

EXERCISE 75

Read the following sentences. Give the pronoun form in parentheses that agrees with the (pro)noun to which it refers. (Also write the forms in the spaces.)

1. Both John and George have turned in (his, their) homework.

2. Janet and I are going to practice (our, their) exercises together.

3. The speaker (who, which) gave the last lecture was excellent.

4. Somebody left (his, their) coat in my office.

5. Mr. and Mrs. Chase have given me (his, her, their) advice.

6. Each person should bring (his, her, their) own lunch.

7. The committee expressed (its, their) unanimous approval of the plan.

8. The United States is a well-developed country, although (its, their) history is relatively short.

9. Several of the group have not paid (his, their) bills.

10. The artist (which, whose) paintings you liked is a friend of mine.

UNIT 7 | ADJECTIVES and ADVERBS

PART XX | Comparison of Adjectives and Adverbs

93 | INTRODUCTION

Most descriptive adjectives have comparative and superlative forms to indicate degree. Compare:

> This is a **wide** street.
> This is a **wider** street than that one.
> This is the **widest** street in town.[1]

In the first sentence, the adjective **wide** describes a particular quality. In the second, **wider** indicates that the street has a higher degree of the quality (**wide**) than the other street. In the third, the superlative form **widest** indicates that the particular street we are talking about has the highest degree of the quality of all the streets in town.

Most descriptive adverbs (usually adverbs indicating manner) also have comparative and superlative forms to indicate degree.

> Don works **hard**.
> Don works **harder** than Dick.
> Don works **hardest** of anyone in the class.

In the first sentence, the adverb **hard** describes how Don works. In the second, **harder** indicates that Don works in the manner indicated (**hard**) to a greater degree than Dick. In the third, **hardest** indicates that Don works in the manner indicated to the greatest degree of all the students in the class.

94 | COMPARATIVE and SUPERLATIVE FORMS of ADJECTIVES and ADVERBS

94a. The comparative and superlative forms of most *adjectives* are formed in the following ways:

(1) The endings **er** and **est** are added to most one-syllable adjectives:

tall	taller	tallest
small	smaller	smallest
large	larger	largest
big	bigger	biggest [2]

---

[1] When the superlative form of an adjective precedes a noun, **the** is ordinarily used. However, when the superlative form follows the verb as a complement, **the** is often omitted if the meaning is general rather than specific.
> He is **the tallest** boy in the group.
> He is **the tallest** of all.
> He is **tallest** of all.

[2] *Spelling note:* When the adjective ends in a single consonant preceded by a single vowel, the consonant is doubled before adding **er** or **est**.

217

ADJECTIVES AND ADVERBS

(2) The endings **er** and **est** are also added to some two-syllable adjectives, particularly those ending in the letters **er, ow,** and **y**:

happy	happier	happiest [3]
pretty	prettier	prettiest
lovely	lovelier	loveliest
clever	cleverer	cleverest
narrow	narrower	narrowest

The comparative and superlative forms of many adjectives ending in **er, ow,** and **y** are also formed by placing **more** and **most** before the adjective.

slender	slenderer / more slender	slenderest / most slender
shallow	shallower / more shallow	shallowest / most shallow
lovely	lovelier / more lovely	loveliest / most lovely

(3) **More** and **most** are placed before most two-syllable adjectives other than those ending in **er, ow,** and **y**.

selfish	more selfish	most selfish
fluent	more fluent	most fluent
useful	more useful	most useful
honest	more honest	most honest [4]

(4) **More** and **most** are ordinarily placed before adjectives of three or more syllables.

difficult	more difficult	most difficult
intelligent	more intelligent	most intelligent
beautiful	more beautiful	most beautiful

(5) **More** and **most** are ordinarily placed before adjectives that have the same form as the past or present participle, regardless of the number of syllables.

hurt	more hurt	most hurt
worn	more worn	most worn
bored	more bored	most bored
frightened	more frightened	most frightened
trying	more trying	most trying
interesting	more interesting	most interesting

94b. The comparative and superlative forms of most *adverbs* are formed in the following ways:

(1) The endings **er** and **est** are added to a few adverbs that have the same form as corresponding adjectives.

hard	harder	hardest
fast	faster	fastest
late	later	latest
early	earlier	earliest
slow	slower	slowest
loud	louder	loudest

---

[3] *Spelling note:* When the adjective ends in a consonant + **y,** the **y** is changed to **i** before adding **er** or **est.**

[4] Logically, there is no higher degree of the qualities expressed by such adjectives as **honest, right, wrong, perfect, correct,** etc. However, in actual usage **more** and **most** are sometimes used with these adjectives. The meaning is "nearer" or "nearest" to the quality.

COMPARISON OF ADJECTIVES AND ADVERBS

(2) **More** and **most** are ordinarily placed before adverbs ending in **ly**.

slowly	more slowly	most slowly
loudly	more loudly	most loudly
quickly	more quickly	most quickly
gracefully	more gracefully	most gracefully

94c. **Less** and **least** may be used with adjectives and adverbs to show a lower degree.

This story is **interesting.**
This story is **less interesting than** that one.
This story is the **least interesting** of all.

He speaks **clearly.**
He speaks **less clearly than** you do.
He speaks **least clearly** of all.

The use of **less** with an adjective or adverb to show a lower degree is somewhat limited in that the same idea is often expressed in other ways. Compare:

This book is **less interesting than** that one.
This book is **not as (so) interesting as** that one.
That book is **more interesting than** this one.

John works **less efficiently than** Tom.
John does **not** work **as (so) efficiently as** Tom.
Tom works **more efficiently than** John.

(The first two sentences in each group have a negative force; the last sentence in each group has a positive force.)

Less is ordinarily not used with adjectives or adverbs that add the **er** ending for the comparative form. The idea is usually expressed in a negative construction.

Bill is **not as (so) tall as** Jim.
Bill does **not** work **as (so) hard as** Jim.

The comparative form of an adjective or adverb with an opposite meaning is often used instead of a negative construction. Compare:

Bill is **not as (so) tall as** Jim.
Bill is **shorter than** Jim.

She **doesn't** type **as (so) fast as** I do.
She types **more slowly than** I do.

94d. A few adjectives and adverbs have irregular comparative and superlative forms.

ADJECTIVES			ADVERBS		
good	better	best	well	better	best
well (health)	better	—			
bad	worse	worst	badly	worse	worst
much } many }	more	most	much	more	most
little	less	least	—	less	least
far	farther	farthest	far	farther	farthest
—	further	furthest	—	further	furthest

Her cake is **good.**
He is **well** now.
This is the **worst** storm of the year.
It's not **far** to my house.

She does that **well.**
He is getting along **better** now.
You sing **worse** than I do.
You drove too **far** down the road.

94e. The comparative and superlative forms are sometimes used to give strength to the expression of an idea rather than to indicate comparison.

> I would be **most** pleased to see you.
>   (I would be very, very pleased to see you.)
> That was the **best** dinner.
>   (That was a very good dinner.)
> The **better** stores are located on Crestway Avenue.
>   (The stores with merchandise of fine quality are on Crestway Avenue.)

95 | CONSTRUCTIONS of COMPARISON

95a. AS + { adjective / adverb } + AS

(1) In the following examples, the quality expressed by the adjective or the manner expressed by the adverb exists to *approximately the same degree in two persons or things*.

> This box is **as big as** that one.
> You are **as tall as** I am.
> I work **as hard as** you do.

(2) In the following examples, the qualities expressed by the adjectives exist to *approximately the same degree in one person or thing*.

> She is **as intelligent as** she is beautiful.
> This room is **as unattractive as** it is uncomfortable.
> This rug looks **as wide as** it is long.

95b. MORE + { adjective / adverb } + THAN *or* Adjective / Adverb with **er** ending + THAN

(1) In the following examples, the quality expressed by the adjective or the manner expressed by the adverb exists to *a greater degree in one person or thing than another*.

> The first problem is **more difficult than** the second.
> You are **taller than** I am.
> John is a **better** swimmer **than** Bill.
> He works **more slowly than** she does.
> He works **harder than** you do.

(2) In the following examples, *more of one quality than another* (expressed by the adjectives) exists *in the same person or thing*.

> He is **more dead than** alive.
> She is **more diligent than** intelligent.
> The book is **more practical than** scholarly.

95c. LESS + { adverb / adjective } + THAN *or* NOT SO (AS) + { adverb / adjective } + AS

(1) In the following examples, the quality expressed by the adjective or the manner expressed by the adverb exists to *a lesser degree in one person or thing than another*.

> He is **less interested** in sports **than** you are.
> She is **not so eager** to leave **as** you are.
> Joe does **less well** in chemistry **than** Jim.
> This knife does **not** cut **as well as** that one.
> He does**n't** speak **as clearly as** she does.

(2) In the following example, *less of one quality than another* (expressed by the adjectives) *exists in the same person or thing*.

> He is **less sincere than** he is ambitious.
> He is **not so interested as** he is curious.
> This lesson is **not so difficult as** it is tedious.

95d. NOT + MORE + $\begin{Bmatrix} \text{adjective} \\ \text{adverb} \end{Bmatrix}$ + THAN

or NOT + $\begin{Bmatrix} \text{adjective} \\ \text{adverb} \end{Bmatrix}$ with **er** ending + THAN

Depending on the point of view of the speaker, these constructions may indicate that a quality expressed by the adjective or the manner expressed by the adverb exists to *a lesser degree in one person or thing than another or to approximately the same degree.* Compare:

> He is **not more interested than** I am.
>   (He is less interested than I am. *or* We have about the same interest.)
> He is **not taller than** I am.
>   (He is shorter than I am. *or* He is about my height.)
> He did**n't** arrive **earlier than** she did.
>   (He arrived later than she did. *or* They arrived about the same time.)

EXERCISE 76

(A) Use the adjective in parentheses in the three ways shown in the example below:

    Example: This tree is (old) that one.
              (1) This tree is <u>as old as</u> that one.
              (2) This tree is <u>older than</u> that one.
              (3) That tree is <u>not so old</u> as this one.

1. Martha is (tall) Janice.

2. Your coat is (heavy) mine.

3. This hall is (narrow) that one.

4. Robert was (interested) James.

5. My assignment was (difficult) yours.

(B) Write the following sentences using the adverb in parenthesis in the three ways shown in the example below:

    Example: Henry can run (fast) Tom.
               (1) Henry can run <u>as fast as</u> Tom.
              (2) Henry can run <u>faster than</u> Tom.
              (3) Henry can't run <u>as fast as</u> Tom.

1. Robert speaks (slowly) James.

2. She sings (well) I do.

3. He came (early) you did.

4. I arrived (late) you did.

5. William studies (much) George does.

EXERCISE 77

Read the following sentences, giving the appropriate form of the adjective or adverb in parentheses. (Also write the forms in the spaces at the right.)

    Example: He is (old) than his brother.   older
              (Read: He is <u>older</u> than his brother.)

1. She is (young) than her sister.

2. He is the (old) member of the family.

3. We drove (far) today than yesterday.

4. Can't you do (well) than you have been?

5. English is not so (difficult) for me any more.

6. This book is as (dull) as it is long.

7. In fact, it is the (dull) book I have ever read.

8. She was (frightened) than hurt.

9. Mr. Gaines is (busy) than anyone else in the office.

10. He is always too (busy) to talk to anyone.

11. Alice has been (happy) here than anywhere else.

12. It is usually (hot) here in August than in July.

13. This gift will be as (useful) as it is decorative.

14. I don't feel as (well) today as I did yesterday.

15. Bob is not so (studious) as his cousin.

16. This cake is (good) than the one I made last week.

17. Please do not talk so (loudly).

18. Mr. Pepper works (efficiently) in the morning than in the afternoon.

19. This problem is the (hard) of all.

20. Enjoy yourself! It is (late) than you think!

UNIT 8 | PUNCTUATION

PART XXI | A Guide to Punctuation

96 | INTRODUCTION

Many points concerning punctuation are largely a matter of style, but there are certain principles that may serve as a guide.

97 | CAPITALIZATION

(1) Every sentence begins with a capital letter.

> **T**he painting on the wall was done by Picasso.

(2) The first person singular subject pronoun, **I,** is always capitalized.

> **I** didn't see her, but **I** called her.

(3) Proper names of people, cities, countries, states, universities, buildings, laws, treaties, and so forth are capitalized.

> I saw **J**ohn, the student from **P**aris, **F**rance.
> The **C**onstitution of the **U**nited **S**tates was signed in **C**onstitution **H**all on September 17, 1787.

(4) Names of languages and adjectives of nationality are capitalized.

> The **F**rench boy and the **G**erman girl speak **E**nglish fluently.

(5) Names of college or university courses, other than languages, are capitalized only when the official title of the course is given.

> I am taking **H**istory 10B and **E**nglish 1B this semester.
> I am taking a **h**istory course and an **E**nglish course.

(6) The names of the days of the week, holidays, and the names of months are capitalized.

> This year her birthday falls on **M**onday, **D**ecember 25, **C**hristmas **D**ay.

(7) Names of the seasons are usually *not* written with a capital letter.

> They live in New York in the **w**inter and in Florida in the **s**ummer.

(8) It is customary to capitalize **East, West, North, South** only when they refer to special sections of the country.

> Betty is from the **E**ast.
> My family lives in the **S**outh.

When **east, west,** and so forth refer to general direction, they are not capitalized.

> The post office is **s**outh of the city hall.
> We drove as far **w**est as Utah.

(9) Names of religions and deities are written with a capital letter.

>He is a **B**uddhist. She is a **C**hristian.
>The **L**ord **G**od spoke to the people, and **H**is words were heard.
>Mohsen prays to **A**llah. The **M**oslem temple was beautiful.

(10) In titles, prepositions, articles, conjunctions, and auxiliary verbs are not capitalized, unless they begin the title. All other words are capitalized.

>My new book is called ***Poetry of the Orient***.
>The title of my composition is "Life in the **T**ropics."
>Longfellow wrote the poem "**T**he Arrow and the **S**ong."

(11) Professional titles used with the name of a person are capitalized.

>I called **L**ieutenant Black, but the **c**orporal answered.
>She works with **P**rofessor Jones and **D**r. Martin.

98 | THE PERIOD (.)

(1) A period is used at the end of statements and commands or requests.

>Robert has traveled a great deal.
>Open the window, please.

(2) A period is used after initials or abbreviations.

>Mr. Robert F. Gordon left his card.
>The train will arrrive at Washington, D. C., at 2:30 p.m.

99 | THE QUESTION MARK (?)

A question mark is used at the end of all *direct* questions.

>Is he there?
>Who said that?
>Will you please help me?

A question mark is *not* used after an *indirect* question.

>He asked what the assignment was.
>She asked whether we went to the show.

100 | THE EXCLAMATION POINT (!)

An exclamation point is used after words, expressions, or sentences to show strong feeling or emotion or to call emphatic attention to the sentence.

>Help! Fire!
>Watch out! Be careful!
>She said she would go, and she went!

101 THE COMMA (,)

(1) A comma is used between two main clauses joined by **and, but, or, nor,** or **for,**[1] particularly when the clauses are long.

> Their oldest son is a lawyer, and their youngest son is a doctor.
> The shops were filled with beautiful things, but I had neither the time to shop nor the money to buy anything.

(2) When a clause that functions as a modifier precedes the main clause, it is usually followed by a comma.

> When he finally arrived at 8 o'clock, the program was well underway.
> After they took off from the airport, we felt very sad.

When a clause that modifies the verb *follows* the main clause, a comma is *not* ordinarily used.

> The fun started when he arrived.
> We felt very sad after he left.[2]

(3) Clauses that modify nouns are set off by commas when they are not absolutely necessary for the clarification or the identification of the noun modified.

> Mary, **who is a good student,** always receives good grades.
> I saw John, **who graduated last term.**
> My father, **whom you met,** is a doctor.

(The clauses in these sentences are set off by commas because they are not necessary to identify **Mary, John,** and **my father.**)

> The girl *who fell down* is Mary.
> The man *that you see over there* is John Smith.
> The man *whom you met* is my uncle.

(The clauses in these sentences are not set off by commas because they are necessary to make clear *which* girl or *which* man is meant.)

(4) An appositive[3] is set off by commas when it merely adds information about the noun that it follows.

> Frederick, **my cousin,** lives in Oslo, **the capital of Norway.**
> He read "Ode on a Grecian Urn," **a poem by John Keats.**

---

[1] Some uses of these conjunctions are as follows:
    and—addition (One idea is added to another.)
        This book is yours, **and** that book is mine.
    but—contrast (One idea is contrasted with another.)
        Marie was here today, **but** Joseph was absent.
    or—choice or alternative (One idea is the alternative of the other.)
        He must return the book today, **or** he will have to pay a fine.
    nor—negative addition (One negative idea is added to another.)
        He has never won a prize, **nor** does he ever expect to win one.
    for—cause (One idea explains or gives a reason for the other.)
        The bill was not passed by Congress, **for** there was too much opposition.

[2] If the clause modifies the whole main clause rather than the verb, it is customary to use a comma between the clauses.
        He did not attend college, *because* he wanted to have a good time.
          (He did not attend college, and the reason was that he wanted to have a good time.)
        I agree that she is very pretty, *although* I don't really like her type.

[3] *Appositives* are words, phrases, or clauses that are used to explain or to describe other nouns.

An appositive that serves to identify the noun that it follows is not ordinarily set off by commas.

>My cousin **Frederick** lives in Oslo.
>He read Keats' poem "**Ode on a Grecian Urn.**"

(5) Side remarks such as **indeed, by the way, I think, incidentally** are usually set off by commas. These and similar expressions are set off because they *interrupt* the main idea of the sentence.

>Indeed, he repeated that sentence twice.
>Mary, by the way, received her degree last fall.
>He is interesting, I think.
>She is, incidentally, my cousin.

(6) If the words **yes, no, well,** or similar introductory words introduce a sentence, they should be followed by a comma.

>Yes, I think so.
>No, don't leave.
>Well, I'll go with you.

(7) Names in direct address are set off by commas.

>**Mary,** where are you?
>Did I remember to tell you, **Bill,** that you had a phone call?
>**Ladies and gentlemen,** it is a privilege to speak to you.

(8) A *direct quotation* is set off by commas. Notice the position of the commas.

>She said, "Come here."
>"Will you," he begged, "come at once?"
>"Wait for me," she called.

(9) Commas are used to separate items in a date.

>Monday, January 5, 1953, was her wedding day.

(10) A comma separates the name of the city from the county and state, and the state from the country.

>He was born in Madrid, Spain, in 1920.
>According to his birth certificate, he was born in Berkeley, Alameda County, California, on June 20, 1928.

(11) Commas are placed between words, phrases, or clauses in a *series*. (Notice that no comma is used between the last adjective and the noun modified.)

>The tall, thin, dark man is our family doctor.
>She bought potatoes, lettuce, meat, asparagus, and pears.

102 | THE SEMICOLON (;)

(1) A semicolon is placed before the following conjunctive adverbs when they join two main clauses: **futhermore, moreover, besides, still, however, nevertheless, otherwise, therefore, consequently, thus, then.**[4] Notice that a comma often follows the conjunctive adverb.

>The pianist was very ill; therefore, the concert was canceled.
>The candidate had great popular support; however, he failed to win the election.

A GUIDE TO PUNCTUATION

(2) A semicolon is sometimes used to join two closely related main clauses.

> The singular form is *mouse*; the plural form is *mice*.
> The rain fell heavily; the thunder and lightning added to the confusion.[5]

103 THE COLON (:)

(1) The colon formally introduces a word, a list, or a sentence. Usually **as follows** or **the following** precedes the list.

> The following words are conjunctions: and, but, or, nor.
> The letter read as follows: "Come at once."

(2) A colon is used after the greeting on a business letter.

> Dear Mr. Jones: Gentlemen: Dear Sir:

(3) A colon is used in the numbers telling the time.

> It is 8:30.   I shall leave at 9:00.

104 QUOTATION MARKS ("........")

(1) The direct words of a speaker are put in quotation marks.

> "I am going for a walk," she said.
> He asked, "Are you going?"
> "She wrote the letter," I replied.

(2) If a quotation is interrupted, an extra set of quotation marks is used. (Notice the use and position of the commas.)

> "Of course," she explained, "he will be here only a few days."
> "If you are ready," she said, "he will go with you."
> "Excuse me," he said. "I believe you are mistaken."

---

[4] Some uses of conjunctive adverbs are as follows:

furthermore, **moreover**, **besides** —addition

> The engineer says that the plan is not practical; **moreover,** / **furthermore,** / **besides,** he has other objections.

still, **however**, **nevertheless** —contrast

> On the way to the station, we were delayed by heavy traffic; **still,** / **however,** / **nevertheless,** we managed to catch the train.

otherwise—choice or alternative
> He did not know you were in town; **otherwise,** he would have called you.

therefore, **consequently**, **thus** —cause

> Our plane was five hours late; **therefore,** / **consequently,** / **thus,** we did not arrive in time for the conference.

then—sequence of events
> George finished his first book in 1950; **then** he started to work on his second.

[5] If a semicolon is not used, the clauses should be written as separate sentences.

> The rain fell heavily. The thunder and lightning added to the confusion.
> (*not:* The rain fell heavily, the thunder and lightning added to the confusion.)

(3) Titles of poems, short musical compositions, stories, and articles are put in quotation marks.

> We read Walt Whitman's "O Captain, My Captain" last night.
> "The Blue Danube" is still a popular waltz.
> "The Talk of the Town" is a weekly article in *The New Yorker*.

(4) When there is a quotation within a quotation, the outside quotation will be indicated by *double* quotation marks; the inside one, by *single* quotation marks.

> He said, "We are studying T. S. Eliot's 'The Hollow Men' now."

(5) When a quotation consists of two or more paragraphs, quotation marks are placed at the beginning of each paragraph and at the end of the last one.

> The Nineteenth Amendment to the Constitution, which gives women the right to vote, reads as follows:
> "The right of citizens to vote shall not be denied or abridged by the United States or by any State on account of sex.
> "Congress shall have power to enforce this article by appropriate legislation."

The following are some notes on the position of quotation marks:

(1) Quotation marks are placed *outside* the comma and the period.

> "Here is the key," she said.
> We sang "Auld Lang Syne."

(2) Quotation marks are placed *inside* the semicolon and the colon.

> The patriotic man sang "The Star Spangled Banner"; however, he forgot to remove his hat.

(3) Quotation marks are placed *outside* the question mark and the exclamation point when the question mark or exclamation point belongs to the quoted matter.

> "Where is Tom?" she asked.
> The boy shouted, "Fire!"

Quotation marks are placed *inside* the question mark or exclamation point when the question mark or exclamation point belongs to the whole sentence or clause that contains the quoted matter.

> Shall we sing "My Old Kentucky Home"?
> How beautifully Madame Tebaldi sang "Vissi d'Arte"!

105 | UNDERLINING

(1) Titles of magazines, newspapers, and books are <u>underlined</u> in handwriting and typewriting, *italicized* in printing.

> An article on modern art appeared in a recent issue of *Life*.
> He was a reporter for *The New York Times* for many years.
> *Soldier's Pay*, William Faulkner's first novel, was published in 1926.

(2) Foreign phrases and words emphasized are underlined in handwriting or typewriting, italicized in printing.

> The Spanish expression *que le vaya bien* means about the same thing as "good luck."
> He ordered *four*, not three, tickets.

106 | THE APOSTROPHE (')

(1) An apostrophe is used in contractions to show omission of letters.

>Don't go.
>He isn't here.
>Can't you run faster?

(2) An apostrophe followed by **s** (**'s**) is used to form the possessive of singular nouns and of plural nouns that do not end in **s**; **'s** is also used to form the plural of numbers and letters.

>Mary's grades were good. She earned 3 A's and 2 B's.
>Do you belong to a women's club?
>There are four s's in the word *possess*.
>Mind your p's and q's. Walk in two's, not three's.

(3) An apostrophe only is added to form the possessive of plural nouns ending in **s** or **es.**

>She read the students' compositions.
>Ladies' hats are on the fourth floor.

(4) An apostrophe is used with the indefinite pronouns **one, other, somebody, nobody, anyone, someone,** and so forth to show possession.

>Here is somebody's book.
>Nobody's lesson was ready.
>This could be anyone's problem.

107 | PARENTHESES (( ))

Parentheses may be used to enclose remarks, comments, explanations, and so forth that interrupt the main thought.

>She invited the two girls (they are cousins, you know) to the party.
>If it rains (and we certainly hope it doesn't), the picnic will be postponed.

108 | BRACKETS ([ ])

Brackets are used to indicate comment or question added to quoted material by someone other than the author.

>"He [Lincoln] gave his famous Gettysburg Address in November, 1863."
>"Shakespeare died in April, 1616 [?]."

109 | TRIPLE DOTS (...)

Triple dots are used to indicate omission from quoted material. (If the omission occurs at the end of the sentence, a period is added.)

>I agree with William Faulkner's statement that "... the young man or woman writing today has forgotten the problem of the human heart in conflict with itself...."

110 THE DASH (—)

(1) A dash is used to indicate an interruption in the expression of an idea or to give an afterthought.

> Believe it or not, we will arrive in Newport—at long last—on October 7th.
> I don't know what I'll do if I fail this course—heaven forbid!

(2) A dash is sometimes used in place of a comma to indicate special emphasis.

> This book is a review of various aspects of English structure—word order, verbs, articles, and so forth.[6]

---

[6] The dash should not be considered a substitute for the comma in all situations.

EXERCISES FOR PART XXI

EXERCISE 78

Complete the capitalization in the following sentences.

Example: I am studying english. (E)

1. Hurry up! do you want to be late?

2. When i saw john on tuesday, i told him that arthur was taking a trip during the spring vacation.

3. is guam east or west of the hawaiian islands?

4. The merchant of venice, a play by william shakespeare, has been translated into french, german, persian, and many other languages.

5. The university of texas is located in austin, texas.

6. Roberto Garcia, a student from mexico, is a graduate student in electrical engineering.

7. Is easter sunday in march or in april this year?

8. On march 16, 1954, doctor bennett opened his office in the medical dental building on broadway.

9. a buddhist temple is being built on washington street.

10. The suez canal, which is about 103 miles long, connects the mediterranean sea with the red sea.

11. The coronation of queen elizabeth II of england was held in london in june, 1953.

12. The first ten amendments to the constitution of the united states are known as the bill of rights.

EXERCISE 79

Insert commas where they are needed in the following sentences:

    Example: Come here, Mary.

1. Yes I shall be glad to go.

2. Kathleen who is Irish lives in Illinois.

3. The chairman said "As soon as the secretary arrives the meeting will begin."

4. George Santayana the poet and philosopher spent the last years of his life in the Convent of the Blue Nuns in Rome.

5. My cousin incidentally plays the piano very well but he does not like to play in public.

6. The girl whom you met is French.

7. On Wednesday June 10 Sam Frank and Robert sailed for Europe but Martha and Jane did not sail until a week later.

8. Mr. Allan who is an architect designed our summer house in Miami Florida.

9. Anyone who has a B average may apply for a scholarship if he needs financial aid.

10. Please send the package to 250 Broadway Los Angeles California.

11. The tall thin man sat down at the desk opened a drawer and took out a large white envelope.

12. Harry where are the keys to my car?

EXERCISE 80

Complete the punctuation in the following sentences. Insert punctuation marks (commas, semicolons, colons, question marks, exclamation points, quotation marks, underlining, etc.) where they are needed.

1. It's up to you, the teacher said, whether or not you learn anything

2. An article entitled Beyond Everest written by Sir Edmund Hillary appeared in the November 1955 issue of The National Geographic Magazine

3. The composition contained many errors in spelling and punctuation however the content was very interesting

4. The woman shouted Help

5. The men gathered wood and built a fire the women unpacked the lunch set the table and made the coffee

6. The French professor explained the meaning of the expression chacun a son gout to us

7. The children saw the following animals at the zoo a giraffe an elephant a kangaroo a rhinoceros and some monkeys

8. Have you read Sandburg's poem The People Will Live On

9. He came he saw he conquered

10. The weather was very bad between Salt Lake City and Denver consequently the flight was delayed

11. It does not matter which word you use both are correct

12. Have you finished reading the article in Life, Marie asked

13. She said Miss Smith, may I present Dr Beck

Exercise 80 (continued)

14. This large red book which I have not had time to read was given to me by my cousin

15. Aunt Ruth exclaimed What a beautiful morning it is

16. "Where are you from she asked "What languages do you speak

17. John Barber wanted to go to Georgetown University in Washington D C to study law however he did not have the qualifications

18. I hope to get all As and Bs this year I shall therefore study my political science Spanish zoology and English courses as hard as I can

19. Shall we now sing that old song When Irish Eyes Are Smiling

20. Please go to the corner drugstore and bring back the following articles a tube of toothpaste a box of aspirins and three bars of soap

21. Do you know which river appears to run backward

22. Yes it is the Chicago River which used to empty into Lake Michigan before engineers reversed its course

23. Before Columbus's historic voyage with the three ships Pinta Nina and Santa Maria most people believed that the earth was flat

24. The highest mountain on the earth is Mount Everest in the Himalayas and the deepest point in any ocean is in the Pacific Ocean between the Philippines and the Palau Islands

25. The Declaration of Independence was adopted by the Continental Congress in Philadelphia Pennsylvania on July 4 1776 the document was signed by John Hancock President of the Continental Congress

Exercises For Part XXI

EXERCISE 81

Complete the capitalization in the following paragraphs:

1. This morning I met john's brazilian friend, haroldo, at the city hall. John said that haroldo was called by the nickname, harry, by most north americans. Haroldo told me that he had come to the united states because he wanted to study engineering. He is taking courses in the university in history, english, chemistry, and physical education, and he is very busy keeping up with his assignments. When he finishes his work for the b.s. degree, he will return to brazil.

2. The north american girl, mary jones, whom you know, lived in paris, france, from july, 1954, until may 12, 1955. She was very happy there and learned to speak french very well. She had to return to the united states to be with her aunt elsie. Although she has many friends in new england, she misses paris very much.

3. george bernard shaw's play <u>pygmalion</u> was first performed in german in berlin in 1913. Its first performance in english was at his majesty's theatre in london, england, on april 11, 1914. In the fall of 1914, on october 12, to be exact, it opened in new york city. In the role of eliza doolittle, the flower girl, was mrs. patrick campbell. henry higgins, the phonetics professor, was played by philip merivale.

EXERCISE 82

Complete the punctuation in the following paragraphs:

1. The other day Mary met Jane an old friend of hers in front of the administration building and Mary said, "Hello, Jane, how are you?

"Fine, thanks, Jane replied but I am very busy trying to get all my work done before vacation begins in June.

"That, said Mary is true of everyone, I guess.

2. A fox looked at his shadow at sunrise and said, I believe I'll have a camel for lunch today.

All morning he went around looking for a camel however at noon when he saw his shadow again he said, A mouse will do!

3. The other day Charles who is from Cincinnati had a long talk with Knut a Norwegian and Alfredo a Bolivian. At one point Alfredo said, "I've just been thinking about the summer vacation and I'd like to know some good places to go. What do you recommend Charles

Well, Charles replied, I think you ought to see as much of the west as you can. Among the places you must visit are the Grand Canyon the Rocky Mountains and Yellowstone Park. By the way how would you two like to go with me on a trip all over the west in my old car this summer

Fine! exclaimed Alfredo and Knut enthusiastically.

Charles continued, There was an article called Along the Trails of the Golden West in a recent Sunday issue of the News Herald. It had a lot of interesting information moreover it contained several good maps. We are less likely to miss the best places if we take the article along and follow the directions that it gives.

GENERAL REVIEW EXERCISES

EXERCISE 83

Place in the blanks the letter indicating the correct form.

Examples: Do you like (A) coffee (B) the coffee?   A
He (A) said (B) told the truth.   B

1. How (A) many pounds (B) much pounds of sugar do you want?   A
2. Did you do all of your (A) homework (B) homeworks?   A
3. Would you please (A) say (B) tell me the time.   B
4. Do you like to travel (A) on bus (B) by bus?   B
5. Please deposit (A) this money (B) these money in the bank.   B
6. Columbus believed that (A) world (B) the world was round.   A
7. They moved to Trenton (A) in July (B) on July.   A
8. We are looking forward to (A) see you (B) seeing you.   A
9. Do you think the grocer (A) will raise (B) will rise his prices?   B
10. There is a scratch on (A) the table's top (B) the top of the table.   B
11. Do you get (A) much news (B) many news from home?   B
12. The (A) tired woman (B) tiring woman sat down to rest.   A
13. Don't forget to put your return address (A) on the envelope (B) in the envelope.   A
14. They (A) went (B) have gone to town yesterday to buy a present for Edith.   A
15. I appreciate (A) a help (B) the help that you have given me.   A
16. They will not be able to wait until Jim (A) will arrive (B) arrives.   B
17. I have already spent my allowance; so I must (A) make without (B) do without cigarettes for the rest of the week.   B
18. Jack was disappointed (A) in the results (B) on the results of his research.   ___
19. This lesson is (A) more easy (B) easier than the last one.   ___
20. Jane has studied Spanish, (A) didn't she? (B) hasn't she?   ___
21. We wish that we (A) can go (B) could go with you tomorrow.   ___
22. Would you mind (A) to open (B) opening the door?   ___
23. (A) Arabic (B) The Arabic is a difficult language to learn.   ___
24. (A) This people (B) These people arrived early.   ___
25. (A) It (B) There has been a long time since I have seen you.   ___
26. Joseph intends to take several courses in (A) Asian history (B) the Asian history.   ___

Exercise 83 (continued)

27. Do you think that the United Nations (A) has made (B) has done much progress in the last ten years?

28. Where is John? He (A) sits (B) is sitting in the chair over there.

29. The auditorium is almost filled, but there are (A) few (B) a few seats left.

30. Robert graduated from (A) Yale University (B) the Yale University in 1949.

31. Both this book and that one (A) was assigned (B) were assigned as outside reading.

32. Francois lived at International House (A) since the two years (B) during the two years he was at the university.

33. It was (A) such a miserable day (B) such miserable day that I decided to stay home.

34. He (A) said (B) told me that I could borrow his car.

35. Last Saturday was (A) so clear that (B) so clear as we could see a hundred miles from the top of the hill.

36. Mr. Sloan has been away (A) for six weeks (B) since six weeks.

37. Has the instructor corrected (A) exercises (B) the exercises that we handed in yesterday?

38. If I (A) had (B) had had her address, I would have written her.

39. The Johnsons (A) are living (B) have lived here since 1950.

40. We waited in the hall (A) during an hour (B) for an hour.

41. Shall we get (A) on the bus (B) in the bus here?

42. I would rather (A) read (B) reading this book.

43. Did you ever find out (A) who (B) whom telephoned you last Sunday?

44. He usually listens to (A) little music (B) a little music after dinner.

45. Mr. Hart lives (A) on 200 Cedar Street (B) at 200 Cedar Street.

46. How long have you been in (A) United States (B) the United States?

47. People (A) must obey (B) should obey the traffic laws, but they don't always do so.

48. The Committee is very interested (A) in the research project (B) on the research project.

49. I (A) was going to leave (B) am going to leave tomorrow, but now I can't.

50. I seem (A) to forget (B) to have forgotten my key again.

51. The instructor suggested that she (A) selects (B) select another topic.

General Review Exercises

Exercise 83 (continued)

52. Professor Polchek is an authority (A) on Egyptian archeology (B) in Egyptian archeology. _____

53. Why don't you (A) lay down (B) lie down for a while? _____

54. He told me (A) whom (B) that he had chosen Mr. Bailey for the position of advertising manager. _____

55. Mr. Brown has worked here (A) during ten years (B) for ten years. _____

56. John has (A) fewer time (B) less time than you for leisure activities. _____

57. Neither the teacher nor the students (A) like (B) likes examinations. _____

58. They want to spend their vacation at (A) the Lake Tahoe (B) Lake Tahoe. _____

59. You should have a good opportunity (A) to advancement (B) for advancement if you take this job. _____

60. I saw (A) a friend (B) the friend on the way to class. _____

61. We hope (A) to see (B) seeing you at the convention in March. _____

62. Mr. Blake (A) talked about (B) said about foreign trade in class today. _____

63. We don't have (A) some examinations (B) any examinations next week. _____

64. He frequently goes to Chicago, (A) does he? (B) doesn't he? _____

65. Joe borrowed (A) a chemistry book (B) a book of chemistry. _____

66. Mr. Barton always (A) makes a good impression (B) does a good impression on people. _____

67. Professor Nichols usually arrives on campus (A) on time (B) in time to have a cup of coffee before his first class. _____

68. If you want to get to the post office from here, take (A) Broadway bus (B) the Broadway bus. _____

69. George (A) didn't have to (B) didn't ought to go there after all. _____

70. Do you mind (A) to pass out (B) passing out these papers? _____

71. The maid was dismissed because she had left dirty dishes (A) sitting (B) setting in the sink. _____

72. Everyone had (A) good time (B) a good time at the picnic. _____

73. (A) Much more workers (B) Many more workers were admitted to the union in 1950 than in 1940. _____

74. When the police asked him where he had been, he (A) was refusing (B) refused to answer. _____

75. I (A) should telephone (B) should have telephoned you last night, but I was too busy. _____

Exercise 83 (continued)

76. That grocery store is (A) on Charles Street (B) at Charles Street.

77. The last two chapters of the book (A) is (B) are very difficult.

78. Jim is now studying (A) architecture (B) the architecture.

79. The cat is sleeping peacefully (A) in the rug (B) on the rug by the fireplace.

80. We are expecting them to arrive (A) on February 10th (B) at February 10th.

81. She (A) looked on (B) looked for the word in the dictionary.

82. I wish that I (A) took (B) had taken your advice.

83. The man (A) which wallet (B) whose wallet we found wants to give us a reward.

84. Parents often make sacrifices (A) so that (B) because their children may receive a good education.

85. He has not worked (A) very hard (B) very hardly this semester.

86. (A) It (B) There is snow on the ground today.

87. The (A) interested (B) interesting lecture will be repeated next week.

88. Does he (A) make his homework (B) do his homework every night?

89. That student usually hands in (A) intelligent (B) intelligently written compositions.

90. I believe every person would find it worth (A) his while (B) their while to see that play.

91. They have finished (A) to practice (B) practicing for today.

92. Do you remember (A) a name of the book (B) the name of the book that the professor recommended?

93. They (A) got off (B) got out of the taxi at the Empire Hotel.

94. High Conquest is (A) a book (B) book about mountain climbing.

95. (A) According to (B) According with my professor, we must make three book reports before the end of the semester.

96. How did you (A) make up (B) make out in the last examination?

97. The number of students in the class (A) is limited (B) are limited to fifteen.

98. Why do you object to (A) follow (B) following the directions?

99. He knew that he (A) will not have time (B) would not have time to finish the report by tomorrow.

100. I have to (A) call on (B) call for my suit before the store closes.

General Review Exercises

EXERCISE 84

Each item in this section contains a group of three statements. <u>Only one</u> is correct. Place in the blank the letter indicating the correct statement.

    <u>Example</u>: A. He said the truth.   C
                       B. He talked the truth.
                       C. He told the truth.

1. A. He gave to me the book last night.   _____
    B. He gave me the book last night.
    C. He gave last night the book to me.

2. A. Is raining now?   _____
    B. Does it raining now?
    C. Is it raining now?

3. A. George is a student, and Bob isn't either.   _____
    B. George is a student, and so is Bob.
    C. George is a student, but Bob is.

4. A. I didn't see someone.   _____
    B. I didn't see no one.
    C. I didn't see anyone.

5. A. Who sent us the flowers?   _____
    B. Who did sent us the flowers?
    C. Who send us the flowers?

6. A. The library is closed today, doesn't it?   _____
    B. The library is closed today, won't it?
    C. The library is closed today, isn't it?

7. A. When he got home, he turned on the radio.   _____
    B. When he got home, he was turning on the radio.
    C. When he got home, he turns on the radio.

8. A. He said me all about his trip.   _____
    B. He talked me all about his trip.
    C. He told me all about his trip.

9. A. This box is more heavy than that one.   _____
    B. This box is heavier than that one.
    C. This is the more heavier than that one.

10. A. When you take the book?   _____
     B. When did you took the book?
     C. When did you take the book?

11. A. Columbus discovered America, didn't he?   _____
     B. Columbus discovered America, did he?
     C. Columbus discovered America, hadn't he?

12. A. They are pleased with your work.   _____
     B. They are pleasing with your work.
     C. They are please with your work.

13. A. Do you rather go to a concert tomorrow night?   _____
     B. Would you rather go to a concert tomorrow night?
     C. Will you rather go to a concert tomorrow night?

14. A. Her hands were so cold that she could not type.   _____
     B. Her hands were so cold as she could not type.
     C. Her hands were so cold for she could not type.

Exercise 84 (continued)

15. A. I'm not ready, and she isn't too.
    B. I'm not ready, and so is she.
    C. I'm not ready, and neither is she.

16. A. Henry is so old as I am.
    B. Henry is as old than I am.
    C. Henry is older than I am.

17. A. They arrived to the airport at 6 p.m.
    B. They arrived at the airport at 6 p.m.
    C. They arrived on the airport at 6 p.m.

18. A. There is in Baker Hall a lecture at 4 o'clock this afternoon.
    B. There is a lecture in Baker Hall at 4 o'clock this afternoon.
    C. There is at 4 o'clock in Baker Hall a lecture this afternoon.

19. A. They didn't know what in New York was his address.
    B. They didn't know was in New York his address.
    C. They didn't know what his address in New York was.

20. A. Please lock the door when you will have left.
    B. Please lock the door when you will leave.
    C. Please lock the door when you leave.

21. A. Mrs. Parks buys a season ticket to the opera for the past ten years.
    B. Mrs. Parks has bought a season ticket to the opera for the past ten years.
    C. Mrs. Parks is buying a season ticket to the opera for the past ten years.

22. A. I wish that it stopped raining before tomorrow.
    B. I wish that it would stop raining before tomorrow.
    C. I wish that it will stop raining before tomorrow.

23. A. There were fewer automobile accidents in the city this month than last month.
    B. There were few automoboile accidents in the city this month than last month.
    C. There were less automoboile accidents in the city this month than last month.

24. A. The room is crowded but there are few seats left.
    B. The room is crowded, but there are a few seats left.
    C. The room is crowded, but there are fewer seats left.

25. A. Is it necessary that he take the examination?
    B. Is it necessary that he takes the examination?
    C. Is it necessary that he is taking the examination?

APPENDIX

A   VERB CONJUGATIONS

As a summary and for reference, verb conjugations of the irregular verbs **be** and **have** and the regular verb **ask** are given here.

(1) Irregular Verb TO BE: BE—WAS—BEEN—BEING

Simple Present

I am	we are
you are	you are
he is	they are

Simple Past

I was	we were
you were	you were
he was	they were

Present Perfect

I have been	we have been
you have been	you have been
he has been	they have been

Past Perfect

I had been	we had been
you had been	you had been
he had been	they had been

Future

I will be	we will be
you will be	you will be
he will be	they will be

Future Perfect [1]

I will have been	we will have been
you will have been	you will have been
he will have been	they will have been

(2) Irregular Verb TO HAVE: HAVE—HAD—HAD—HAVING

Simple Present

I have	we have
you have	you have
he has	they have

Simple Past

I had	we had
you had	you had
he had	they had

Present Progressive

I am having	we are having
you are having	you are having
he is having	they are having

Past Progressive

I was having	we are having
you were having	you were having
he was having	they were having

Present Perfect

I have had	we have had
you have had	you have had
he has had	they have had

Past Perfect

I had had	we had had
you had had	you had had
he had had	they had had

Present Perfect Progressive

I have been having	we have been having
you have been having	you have been having
he has been having	they have been having

Past Perfect Progressive

I had been having	we had been having
you had been having	you had been having
they had been having	they had been having

Future

I will have	we will have
you will have	you will have
he will have	they will have

Future Progressive

I will be having	we will be having
you will be having	you will be having
he will be having	they will be having

Future Perfect

I will have had	we will have had
you will have had	you will have had
he will have had	they will have had

---

[1] The progressive tense forms of **be** have been omitted because they are seldom used.

APPENDIX

(3) Regular Verb TO ASK: ASK—ASKED—ASKED—ASKING

ACTIVE

Simple Present
I ask	we ask
you ask	you ask
he asks	they ask

Simple Past
I asked	we asked
you asked	you asked
he asked	they asked

Present Progressive
I am asking	we are asking
you are asking	you are asking
he is asking	they are asking

Past Progressive
I was asking	we were asking
you were asking	you were asking
he was asking	they were asking

Present Perfect
I have asked	we have asked
you have asked	you have asked
he has asked	they have asked

Past Perfect
I had asked	we had asked
you had asked	you had asked
he had asked	they had asked

Present Perfect Progressive
I have been asking	we have been asking
you have been asking	you have been asking
he has been asking	they have been asking

Past Perfect Progressive
I had been asking	we had been asking
you had been asking	you had been asking
he had been asking	they had been asking

Future
I will ask	we will ask
you will ask	you will ask
he will ask	they will ask

Future Progressive
I will be asking	we will be asking
you will be asking	you will be asking
he will be asking	they will be asking

Future Perfect
I will have asked	we will have asked
you will have asked	you will have asked
he will have asked	they will have asked

PASSIVE

Present
I am asked	we are asked
you are asked	you are asked
he is asked	they are asked

Past
I was asked	we were asked
you were asked	you were asked
he was asked	they were asked

Present Progressive
I am being asked	we are being . . .
you are being asked	you are being . . .
he is being asked	they are being . . .

Past Progressive
I was being asked	we were being asked
you were being asked	you were being asked
he was being asked	they were being asked

Present Perfect
I have been asked	we have been . . .
you have been asked	you have been . . .
he has been asked	they have been . . .

Past Perfect
I had been asked	we had been asked
you had been asked	you had been asked
he had been asked	they had been asked

Future
I will be asked	we will be asked
you will be asked	you will be asked
he will be asked	they will be asked

Future Perfect
I will have been asked	we will have been . . .
you will have been asked	you will have been . . .
he will have been asked	they will have been . . .

APPENDIX

B | LETTER FORMS

B1. *Form for Business Letters.* (The numbers in parentheses refer to notes which follow the form.)

---

                                                                      100 First Street
                                                                      Sausalito, California
                                                                      June 20, 1955   **(1)**

Credit Manager
ABC Company   **(2)**
100 Market Street
San Francisco, California

Dear Sir: **(3)**

    I wish to call your attention to an error in my May bill. On May 10 I purchased a clock in your jewelry department. On May 12 I returned the clock and received a credit slip for the amount of the purchase. However, I am still charged with the purchase of a clock.

    I should appreciate it if you would look into this matter. I shall delay payment of the bill until I hear from you.   **(4)**

                                                          Yours truly,   **(5)**

                                                         John B. Doe
                                                         John B. Doe   **(6)**

---

    (1) The standard, block form illustrated here is customarily used for business letters. The block form, as shown for the inside address (2), also appears on the envelope.

    (2) Standard abbreviations are **Mr., Mrs., Dr.,** and **D. C.** (District of Columbia). Other titles, such as **President, Professor, General,** and so forth should be written out. It is considered better form to write out the names of states, months, and streets.

    (3) Some salutations used in business letters are as follows:

        Dear Mr. Holden: Dear Mrs. White:
        Dear Sir: Dear Madam:
        Gentlemen: Ladies:

A colon (:) is used after the salutation in a business letter.

    (4) The main point of a business letter in English is to convey the desired information as simply and as briefly as possible; therefore, the language used is usually straightforward and direct.

    (5) Some closing expressions used in business letters are as follows:

        Yours truly,   Sincerely yours,
        Yours very truly,   Yours sincerely,
        Very truly yours,

Only the first word of the closing expression is capitalized. A comma is used after the closing expression.

    (6) If the letter is typed, the sender's name should be typed three or four spaces below the closing expression. The sender's signature should be written in the space between the closing expression and the typewritten name.

    (7) It is customary to type a business letter on standard white paper.

B2. *Forms for Social Letters.* The following form is used for *personal letters*. (The numbers in parentheses refer to notes which follow the form.)

International House
500 Riverside Drive **(1)**
New York 27, New York
November 21, 1955

Dear Mary, **(2)**

You will no doubt be surprised to hear from me after all this time. You know how the saying goes, "I have thought of you often, but I just haven't got around to writing." I won't go into everything that has happened since I last saw you, because I hope to have the opportunity to tell you all this in person on December 15th.

I'm going to my uncle's for the Christmas holidays, and I'm delighted to find that I have to change planes in your fair city. I'll have three hours between planes, and I'm hoping you can meet me at the airport for dinner. The plane will arrive there at 5:30 p.m. The other plane is scheduled to take off at 8:30.

I hope to see your smiling face when I get off the plane.

Affectionately, **(3)**

John
(or: *John B. Doe)*

---

(1) It is considered courteous to write your address in the top right-hand corner of the page. It is also customary to include the date.

(2) The salutation in a personal letter is usually followed by a comma. Some salutations used in social letters are as follows:

    Dear Mary,
    Mary dear,
    My dear Mary, (This salutation is somewhat more formal than the preceding examples.)

(3) Some closing expressions used in social letters are as follows:

    Cordially yours,   Sincerely yours,
    Yours cordially,   Very sincerely,
    Yours,   Affectionately,

(4) Personal letters may be written in ink or may be typewritten.

APPENDIX

The following form is customarily used in replying to a *semi-formal* invitation.

> *Dear Mrs. Smith,*
>
> *It gives me great pleasure to accept your kind invitation to dinner on Friday evening, December twelfth, at six o'clock.*
>
> *Sincerely,*
>
> *John B. Doe*
>
> *International House*
> *December the first*

The following form is customarily used in replying to a *formal* invitation.

> *Miss Mary Doe accepts with pleasure Mrs. John Bell's kind invitation to tea on Friday afternoon, December twelfth, at four o'clock.*
>
> *1200 Crescent Drive*
> *December the first*

Replies to social invitations are customarily written in ink.

APPENDIX

C | LIST of AMERICAN-ENGLISH SPEECH SOUNDS

The sounds in the following list are represented by symbols from the International Phonetic Alphabet (**IPA**), from *The American College Dictionary* (**ACD**), and from *Webster's New World Dictionary* (**WWD**). (Some of the spellings which represent the sounds in written English are shown in examples.)

CONSONANTS[2]

	VOICELESS					VOICED			
IPA[3]	ACD	WWD	Other[4]	Examples	IPA	ACD	WWD	Other	Examples
/p/	p	p		pin, apple, pipe	/b/	b	b		be, rubber, robe
/t/	t	t		tea, better, bite, light, liked	/d/	d	d		do, sudden, rode, lived
/k/	k	k		key, can, occur, sick, bake, talk	/g/	g	g		go, egg
/f/	f	f		fan, offer, life, rough, photo	/v/	v	v		vote, give
/θ/	th	th		thin	/ð/	<u>th</u>	*th*		the, bathe
/s/	s	s		so, bless, horse, city, face	/z/	z	z		zoo, buzz, size, sees
/ʃ/	sh	sh		she, sure, session, nation, racial	/ʒ/	zh	zh		measure, rouge, azure
/tʃ/	ch	ch		chest, catch, question	/dʒ/	j	j		joy, age, edge, educate
/h/	h	h		he, who					
/hw/	hw	hw		why	/w/	w	w		we, one
					/l/	l	l		let, all, smile
					/r/	r	r		red, parrot, write
					/j/	y	y		you, use, million
					/m/	m	m		me, simmer, some, palm, limb
					/n/	n	n		no, dinner, done, know
					/ŋ/	ng	ŋ		sing, sink

---

[2] Consonant sounds are classed as *voiceless* (without vibration of the vocal cords during articulation) and *voiced* (with vibration of the vocal cords during articulation). Many of the consonant sounds fall into pairs of voiceless and voiced sounds, as /p/ and /b/. Two sounds representing a pair are placed opposite each other on the list.

[3] The IPA symbols are used in Kenyon and Knott's *A Pronouncing Dictionary of American English*.

[4] This column has been left blank to provide space for those who would like to add another set of symbols.

APPENDIX
VOWELS AND DIPHTHONGS [5]

	VOICELESS					VOICED			
IPA	ACD	WWD	Other	Examples	IPA	ACD	WWD	Other	Examples
/i/	ē	ē		b<u>e</u>, s<u>ee</u>, s<u>ea</u>, f<u>ie</u>ld, dec<u>ei</u>t	/u/	o͞o	o͞o		t<u>oo</u>, r<u>u</u>le, bl<u>ew</u>, tr<u>ue</u>, sh<u>oe</u>
/ɪ/	ĭ	i		<u>i</u>t, c<u>i</u>ty, mon<u>ey</u>	/ʊ/	o͝o	oo		b<u>oo</u>k, p<u>u</u>t, sh<u>ou</u>ld
/e/	ā	ā		d<u>ay</u>, <u>a</u>ge, r<u>ai</u>n	/o/	ō	ō		g<u>o</u>, bl<u>ow</u>, <u>oa</u>t, t<u>oe</u> [6]
/ɛ/	ĕ	e		l<u>e</u>t, <u>a</u>ny, s<u>ai</u>d	/ɔ/	ô	ô		<u>a</u>ll, l<u>aw</u>, <u>o</u>ffer, <u>ou</u>ght
/æ/	ă	a		c<u>a</u>t, pl<u>ai</u>d	/ɑ/	ä	ä,o		c<u>a</u>lm, d<u>o</u>ll, h<u>ea</u>rt
/ʌ/	ŭ	u		<u>u</u>p, d<u>o</u>ne, t<u>ou</u>gh	/ɝ/	ûr	ŭr		h<u>er</u>, f<u>ur</u>, g<u>ir</u>l, w<u>or</u>d, l<u>ear</u>n
/ə/	ə	ə		<u>a</u>way, el<u>e</u>ment, acc<u>i</u>dent, circ<u>u</u>s, cur<u>i</u>ous [7]	/ɚ/	ər	ẽr		lett<u>er</u>, doll<u>ar</u>, act<u>or</u>, treas<u>ure</u> [8]
/aɪ/	ī	ī		<u>I</u>, m<u>y</u>, l<u>ie</u>, b<u>uy</u>	/ɔɪ/	oi	oi		<u>oi</u>l, b<u>oy</u>
/aʊ/	ou	ou		<u>ou</u>t, n<u>ow</u>, b<u>ough</u>	/ɪu/	ū	ū		f<u>ew</u>, y<u>ou</u>, v<u>iew</u>

---

[5] A diphthong is a blend of two vowel sounds into a sound considered to be a separate, distinctive sound, as /aʊ/ in **out**.

[6] /e/ and /o/ are sometimes represented as diphthongs /eɪ/ and /oʊ/.

[7] /ʌ/ occurs in stressed syllables; /ə/, in unstressed syllables. /ə/ occurs very frequently as the vowel in unstressed syllables (**a**lone, **a** day, th**e** book, etc.).

[8] /ɚ/ and /ɝ/ are pronounced with little or no "r-flavor" by some speakers of English, particularly in Eastern and Southern sections of the United States. In such speech, the sounds in **her** and **letter** are usually symbolized by /ɜ/ and /ə/ respectively.

SUBJECT INDEX

Adjectives (*See also* Modifiers):
  comparative and superlative forms, 217
    forming, 217–218
    irregular forms, 219
  descriptive, 28
  indefinite adjectives, 26–27
    with mass nouns, 157
    with plural countable nouns, 156
  modifiers of, 2
  verbs followed by, 1
Adverbs (*See also* Modifiers):
  comparative and superlative forms, 217
    forming, 218–219
    irregular forms, 219
  conjunctive adverbs, 229n
Agent, modifiers indicating, 39
    (*See also* Prepositions)
Agreement:
  of pronoun with noun or pronoun to which it refers, 212–214
  of subject and verb, 209–212
    book title, 211
    collective nouns, 210
    indefinite pronouns, 210–211
    people, 211
    sentences introduced by *it* and *there*, 211–212
    subject followed by phrase, 210
    the number of, 211
    this or *that*, *these* or *those*, 210
    two or more nouns connected by *and*, 210
    two or more nouns joined by *either . . . or, or, neither . . . nor*, 210
Appositives, 227–228
Articles, 26, 155–163
  definite and indefinite, 155
  some specific uses of the definite article, 163
  summary of articles with countable and non-countable nouns, 159
  with non-countable nouns, 157–159
  with nouns modified by proper names and possessives, 162–163
  with plural countable nouns, 156–157
  with proper names, 160–162
  with singular countable nouns, 155–156
Auxiliary verb, 4 (*See also* Verbs)

Clauses:
  noun-equivalent, 1
  of condition, 123–124

Clauses (*continued*):
  set off by commas, 227
  that function as nouns, 103
    sequence of tenses in, 103–104
  that modify adjective or adverb, 42–43
    indicating degree, 42
    indicating frequency, 42
    indicating result, 43
  that modify nouns, 28–29
    sequence of tenses in, 103
  that modify verbs, 41–42
    indicating place, 41
    indicating purpose, 42
    indicating reason, 42
    indicating time, 42
    sequence of tenses in, 101–103
  verb forms in clauses involving wishes, demands, and conditions (*See* Verbs)
Commands, 16–17
Comparison (*See also* Adjectives, *and* Adverbs)
  constructions of, 220–221
Complement:
  single-word modifiers of, 2
  verbs followed by, 1
Contractions, 3, 4
  of *let* plus *us*, 17
  of pronouns and *will*, 84
  of verb and *not*, 6
Conjunctions, 227n
  introducing clauses modifying verbs, 41
Conjunctive adverbs, 228–229

Demonstratives, 26
Direct object, 2

Expressions, 35n

Frequency, modifiers indicating, 36–37

Gender, 202–203
  and agreement, 212
Gerunds in requests or commands, 16, 17 (*See also* Verbals)

Indirect object, 2
Intensifier, 2, 3
Interrogatives, questions introduced by, 13–14

Letter forms, 247–249
  business letters, 247
  social letters, 248
    accepting invitations, 249

Manner, modifiers indicating, 35–36
Modifiers:
  of adjectives, 2
  of nouns, 25–29
    articles, 26
    demonstratives, 26
    descriptive adjectives, 28
    indefinite adjectives, 26–27
    nouns, 28
    numerals, 28
    phrases and clauses, 28–29
    possessives, 26
    series of modifiers, 25–28
    single word modifiers, 25
  participles, 143 (*See also* Verbals)
  phrase formed by preposition + an object, 171
  preposition-adverbs, 183
    prepositional combinations used as unit-prepositions, 190
  single-word, of subject, object, or complement, 2
  of verbs, 3
  of verbs, adverbs, and adjectives:
    clauses that modify an adjective or an adverb, 42–43
    clauses that modify verbs, 41–42
    indicating accompaniment, 39
    indicating agent or instrument, 39
    indicating degree or intensity, 40
    indicating doubt, possibility, denial, affirmation, 40
    indicating frequency, 36–37
    indicating manner, 35–36
    indicating place or position, 35
    indicating time, 37–39
    more than one modifier in sentence, 39
    purpose, expressions of, 40

Noun-equivalent, 1
  gerunds, 143 (*See also* Verbals)
Nouns:
  as modifiers of nouns, 28
  gender, 202–203
  hyphenated compound:
    forming plural, 198
    indicating possession, 200n
  modifiers of, 25–29 (*See also* Modifiers)
  non-countable, 26, 157–159

SUBJECT INDEX

Nouns (*continued*):
  abstract nouns, 157
    functioning as countable, 158–159
    mass nouns, 157, 199
    names of general areas of subject matter, 157–158
    names of sports or recreational activities, 158
  plural countable, 156–157
  plural form of, 197–199
  possession, indicating, 199–201
  possessive nouns, 25, 197n
    indicating relationship other than ownership, 26n
  proper names, 160–162
  singular countable, 155–156
  verbs followed by, 1
Numerals, 28
  position as modifiers, 25

Object:
  direct object + phrase, 2
  indirect + direct, 2
  single-word modifiers of, 2
  verbs followed by, 1
  verbs followed by two objects, 2

Permission, requesting, 17
Phrases:
  as modifiers of nouns, 28–29
  noun-equivalent, 1
  preposition + object, 171
  used as indirect object, 2
  verb phrases, 4
Place, modifiers indicating, 35
Possessives, 26
Prepositions:
  agent or instrument, 176
  described, 171
  gerund as object of, 146–147
  in phrasal combinations:
    combinations with *be* and *have*, 188–190
    used as modifiers, 190
    used as unit-prepositions, 190
    verb and preposition adverb combinations, 183–186
    verb and preposition combinations, 187–188
  in the capacity of, 176
  of accompaniment, 176
  of association, 176
  of direction, 173
  of manner, 176
  of measure, 176
  of place or position, 171–173
  of purpose, 176
  of similarity, 176
  of time, 174
  preposition-adverbs, 183
  prepositional phrases modifying nouns, 28–29
Present participle (*See* Verbs)

Pronouns:
  agreement with noun or pronoun to which refer, 212–214
  as direct object, 2
  contractions with *will*, 84
  gender, 203
  indefinite and agreement, 213
  possessive forms for, 202
    as modifier of possessive noun, 25
  relative pronouns, 213
    introducing phrases that modify nouns, 29
  subject and object forms, 201
  verbs followed by, 1
Pronunciation:
  h and *u* and *a(an)*, 155n
  of *ing* ending of present participles, 64
  of third person singular of simple present, 60
  past tense of regular verbs, 61–62
  plural forms of nouns, 198
  voiced consonant sounds, 60n
  voiceless consonant sounds, 60n
Punctuation:
  apostrophe, 200, 231
  brackets, 231
  capitalization, 225–226
  colon, 229
  comma, 227–228
  dash, 232
  exclamation point, 226
  parentheses, 231
  period, 226
  question mark, 226
  quotation marks, 229–230
  semicolon, 228–229
  triple dots, 231
  underlining, 230
Purpose, expressions of, 40

Question:
  affirmative, word order in, 4–5
  attached to statements, responses to, 15–16
  introduced by interrogatives, 13–14
    responses to, 14
  long and short responses to, 5–6
  separated from statement it follows, 15

Requests, 16–17

Spelling:
  adding *er* or *est*, 217n
  changes in, when *ing* is added, 63
  doubling of consonants for plural nouns, 197n
Statements:
  affirmative, 1–3
  connected, patterns of, 51–53
    affirmative statements, 51

Statements (*continued*):
  connected, patterns of (*continued*):
    connected affirmative and negative statements, 52
    negative statements, 52
    summary, 53
  negative, 3–4
Subject:
  and verb, agreement of, 209–212
  contractions of subject and verb, 6
  single-word modifiers of, 2

Time, modifiers indicating, 37–39

Verbals:
  defined, 143
  gerund, 143
    as object of preposition, 146–147
  infinitive, 143
  infinitives and gerunds as objects of verbs, 143–146
    verbs followed by either infinitive or gerund, 145–146
    verbs followed only by gerund, 145
    verbs followed only by infinitive, 143–145
  infinitives and gerunds in expressions of purpose, 147
  infinitives and participles following complements and objects, 148
  infinitives as complements, 146
  participles, 143
  perfect and passive forms of infinitives, gerunds, and participles, 149
  present and past participles as adjectives, 147
Verb phrases, 4
Verbs (*See also* Word order)
  agreement of subject and (*See* Agreement)
  and preposition-adverb combinations, 183–186
  auxiliary verb, 4
    described, 110
    expressing preference and wants, 114–115
    in affirmative questions, 5
    in negative statements, 4
    in short questions attached to statements, 15
    or equivalent phrases that express ability to do something, 110–111
    or equivalent phrases that express obligation and necessity, 112–113
    that express possibility and probability, 113–114
    used in requesting and giving permission, 111
  followed by complement, 1
  followed by two objects, 2

SUBJECT INDEX

Verbs (*continued*):
  future tense, 62
  forms in clauses involving wishes, demands, and conditions, 121–124
    clauses of condition, 123–124
    demand that and *it is necessary that* + noun clause, 122–123
    wish (*that*) + noun clause, 121–122
  in affirmative questions:
    constructions of auxiliary *plus* principal verb, 5
    simple forms of *be*, 4–5
    simple forms of verbs other than *be*, 5
  in connected statements, 51
  in negative statements:
    simple forms of *be*, 3
    simple forms of verbs other than *be*, 3–4
    with constructions of auxiliary + principal verb, 4
  in negative requests and commands, 16
  in short questions attached to statements, 14–15
  irregular verb forms, 64–65
  modifiers of, 3 (*See also* Modifiers: of verbs, adverbs and adjectives)
  not used in progressive form, 93–94
  passive construction, 109–110
    in making demands and requests, 122n
  past participle of regular verbs, 62
  perfect tenses, 62–63
  present participle:
    forming, 63
    phrases modifying nouns, 29
  principal parts, 59
  principal verb, 4
  progressive tenses, 63–64
  sequence of tenses:
    in clauses that function as nouns, 103–104
    in clauses that modify nouns, 103
    in clauses that modify verbs, 101–103
  simple form of, 3
  simple past tense, 61–62
    adding *t* to simple present, 61
    ending *d*, 61
    ending *ed*, 61
    pronunciation, 61–62

Verbs (*continued*):
  simple present tense, 59–60
    forming the third person, 59
    pronouncing third person singular, 60
  tense:
    and concept of time, 71
    defined, 71
    sequence of, 101
  troublesome verbs, 129–132
    do and *make*, 130–131
    lie—lay, rise—raise, sit—set, 131–132
    say and *tell*, 129–130
    talk and *speak*, 130
  use of future perfect, 95
  use of future perfect progressive, 95
  use of future progressive, 85–86
  uses of future tense to express activities, 84–85
    in future activities, 84
    making requests, 85
  uses of past perfect to express activities that occurred before another activity or point of time in past, 94–95
  uses of past perfect progressive, 95
  uses of past progressive to express activities, 83–84
    in progress at point of time in past, 84
    in progress at time of another activity in past, 83
  uses of present perfect to express activities, 91–93
    completed in past, but closely connected with activities extending into present or future, 93
    completed short time before moment of speaking, 92–93
  present perfect
    that began in past, have continued up to, and may extend beyond moment of speaking, 91
    that have occurred sometime in past, 91–92
  uses of present perfect progressive, 93–94
  uses of present progressive to express activities, 75–76
    in actual progress at moment of speaking, 75
    that began long before and will end long after moment of speaking, 75–76

Verbs (*continued*):
  uses of present progressive (*continued*):
    that will take place in future, 76
  uses of simple past tense for expressing activities, 81–83
    that occurred in the past, 81
    that occurred over period of time in past, 81–82
  uses of simple present for expressing activities, 71–75
    that extend for varying lengths of time beyond moment of speaking, 72–73
    which are relatively permanent, 73–74
    which occur at intervals, 73
    which will take place in future, 74–75
  verbals (*See* Verbals)

Word order:
  affirmative questions, 4–5
  affirmative statements, 1–3
    direct object becomes subject in passive construction, 109
    indirect object becomes subject in passive construction, 109
    modifiers of verbs, 3
    single-word modifiers of subject, object or complement, 2
    statements beginning with *there is*, 3
    verbs followed by complement, 1
    verbs followed by object, 1
    verbs followed by two objects, 2
  long and short responses to questions, 5–6
  modifiers of nouns, 25–29 (*See also* Modifiers)
  modifiers of verbs, adverbs and adjectives (*See* Modifiers)
  negative questions, 6–7
  negative statements, 3–4
  questions:
    introduced by interrogatives, 13–14
    responses to questions introduced by interrogatives, 14
    short questions attached to statements, 14–15
    short question separated from statement it follows, 15
  requests and commands, 16–17
    in form of signs, 17
    requesting permission, 17

WORD INDEX

A (AN), 26, 28
 and **one,** 155
about, 175
above, 172
according to, 190
across, 172
add . . . to (with), 187
after, 42
 indicating place or position, 172
 indicating time, 174
against, 172
agree on, 187
agree with, 187
all as indefinite pronoun, 210
allow, 146
almost, 41
along with, 190
already, 38
always, position of, 36
am in negative statement, 3
among, 172
and, 227n
 in connected affirmative statements, 51
and neither, 52
and . . . not either, 52
and so, 51
another, 27
a number of, 211
any, 27, 156
 before a singular countable adjective, 27n
 with mass nouns, 157
appear, 1
 infinitives as complements after, 146
approve of, 187
are:
 as auxiliary in short questions attached to statements, 15
 in negative statements, 3
aren't, 3
argue with, 187
around:
 indicating place or position, 172
 indicating time, 175
arrive at, 187
as: in the capacity of, 176
as . . . as, construction of comparison, 220
as far as, 190
ask:
 conjugation of, 246
 followed by infinitive, 144–145
as often as, 42
as well as, 42
as yet, 190
at:
 and **in,** 173

at (*continued*):
 and **on,** 173
 indicating time, 174
at all, 190
at any time, 190
at first, 190
at home in, 190
at the beginning of, 174
at the end of, 174
at the time, 190
a week ago, 37

BADLY, position of, 36
be:
 and passive forms of verbals, 149
 conjugation, 245
 followed by a complement, 1
 in affirmative questions, 4–5
 in connected statements, 51
 in forming progressive tenses, 63
 in passive construction, 109
 in short questions attached to statements, 14
 not used in progressive form, 93–94
 phrasal combinations of **be** + adjective complement + preposition, 188–189
 simple forms of, used with **not,** 3
 contractions of, 3
 simple past tense, 61
 simple present tense, 59
be able to as auxiliary, 110–111
be accustomed to, 147
beat, 64
because, 42
become:
 as irregular verb, 64
 followed by a complement, 1
before, 38, 42
 indicating place or position, 172
 indicating time, 174
be going to, 62
 + simple form of verb, 84
behind, 172
believe (that), 103–104
believe in, 187
belong to, 187
below, 172
beneath, 172
beside, 172
besides, conjunctive adverb, 229
be to + simple form, 62
between, 172
bitten (bit), 65
blame . . . for, 187
born, borne, 65n
both as indefinite pronoun, 210

bring, 2
bring back, 183
bring up, 184
but, 227n
 in connected affirmative and negative statements, 52
buy, 2
by:
 indicating agent or instrument, 176
 indicating manner, 176
 indicating measure, 176
 indicating place or position, 172
 indicating time, 174
by way of, 173

CALL back, 184
call for, 185
call in, 184
call on, 185
call up, 184
can:
 as auxiliary:
  expressing ability to do something, 110
  in requesting and giving permission, 111
 in short questions attached to statements, 15
can't, 4, 111
 in short questions attached to statements, 15
 + **bear** or **stand,** 146
care as verb followed by infinitive, 144n
care for, 187
check off, 184
check out, 184, 186
cheer up, 184, 186
children, 198
come as irregular verb, 64
come across, 185
come to, 185
compare . . . with (to), 187
complain about (of), 187
congratulate . . . on, 187
consent to, 187
consequently, 229n
could:
 and clauses of condition, 124
 as auxiliary:
  expressing ability to do something, 110
  softens **can** in requesting and giving permission, 111
couldn't, 4
cross off, 184
cross out, 184

257

DEER, 199
deliver, 2
demand that, 122–123
describe, 2
didn't, 4
do:
  and **make,** 130–131
  in affirmative questions, 5
  in connected statements, 51
  in negative statements, 3–4
  in short questions attached to statements, 14–15
  pronouncing third person singular of simple present, 60
do (does, did) not have to, 113
doesn't, 4
don't, 4
  in negative requests or commands, 16
do over, 184
down, 172
do you mind, 16
  followed by gerund, 17n, 145
  requesting permission, 17
drop off, 184
during, 174
  for and **since,** 174–175
during the summer, 37

EACH of us did his best, 213
economics, 199
either, 27
  and . . . not either, 52
either . . . or and agreement, 210
enough, 27
  as indefinite pronoun, 211
  meaning of, 41
  modifying adjective, 2
  placed after word modified, 40
ever:
  not used in affirmative response, 92n
  position of, 36
every, 27
every day, 73
excuse . . . for, 188
explain, 2
explain . . . to, 187
extremely, 2

FALL in love with, 188
far used with **how,** 14
feel, 1
  and **am feeling,** 75n
  + object + simple form of past participle, 148
feet, 198
few:
  as indefinite adjective, 26
  as indefinite pronoun, 210
  instead of indefinite article, 156
  modifiers used with, 40
figure out, 184
finally, 38

first, 25
fish, 199
fix, 2
for:
  cause, 227n
  indicating purpose, 176
    and gerund, 147
  relationships of time, 174
    during and **since,** 174–175
for a month, 37
for-phrase used instead of indirect object, 2
furthermore, 229n

GEESE, 198
get, 2
  + object + past participle, 148
get along, 186
get back, 186
get in, 186
get into, out, (of), 185
get in touch with, 188
get on (off), 185
get over, 185
give, 2
go over, 185
got (gotten), 65

HAD in past perfect tense, 63
had been, 64
had better, 112
hadn't, 4
hand as verb followed by two objects, 2
hand in, 184
hardly, 41
hasn't, 4
have:
  and perfect forms of verbals, 149
  conjugation, 245
  in perfect tenses, 62
  phrasal combinations of **have** + noun + preposition, 189–190
  + object + past participle, 148
have been, 64
have to, 112–113
haven't, 4
  in negative questions, 6
hear + object + simple form or past participle, 148
he'll, 6
help + object + simple form, 148
he's, 6
his, 26
how:
  introducing question, 13
  words used with, 14
however, 229n

IF and clauses of condition, 123–124
I'll, 6
I'm, 6
immediately, 37

in:
  and **at,** 173
  and **into,** 173–174
  and **on:**
    indicating place or position, 173
    indicating relationships of time, 174
  indicating manner, 176
  indicating relationship of time, 174
in back of, 172
in front of, 172
in order to, 40n
in the middle of, 174
in time, 175
into and **in,** 173–174
introduce . . . to, 188
is in negative statement, 3
isn't, 3
  in negative questions, 6
it:
  agreement in sentences introduced by, 211–212
  as direct object, 2
  uses of, 212
it is I (me), 201
it's, 6
I've, 6

JUST, 41n
  with present perfect tense, 92–93

KEEP . . . for, 188
keep on, 186
know not used in progressive form, 93–94

LATELY, 38
lay, use of, 132
least in forming comparatives, 219
leave, 2
less, 27
  comparative adjectives and adverbs, 219
less . . . than, construction of comparison, 220
let + object + simple form, 148
let's in requests, 16, 17
let's suppose, 124
lie, use of, 131
like:
  followed by infinitive or gerund, 146
  preposition:
    indicating manner, 176
    indicating similarity, 176
  not used in progressive form, 93–94
little:
  as indefinite adjective, 26
  a little, 26
  modifiers used with, 40
live:
  and **am living,** 75n
  have lived, 91n

look, 1
look after, 186
look for, 186
look into, 186
look over, 183, 184
look up, 184

MAKE:
   and **do,** 130–131
   as verb followed by two objects, 2
   + object + simple form, 148
make up one's mind, 188
many, 156
   as indefinite adjective, 26
   as indefinite pronoun, 210
   modifiers used with, 40
      used with **how,** 14
mathematics, 199
may:
   as auxiliary expressing possibility, 113
   as auxiliary used in requesting or giving permission, 111
may I, 17
men, 198
merely, 41
mice, 198
might:
   and clauses of condition, 124
   as auxiliary expressing possibility, 113
more, 2
   and forming comparatives, 218, 219
moreover, 229n
more . . . than: construction of comparison, 220
most forming superlative, 218, 219
much:
   as indefinite adjective, 26
   modifiers used with, 40
      modified by **very,** 3
      used with **how,** 14
much too, 40
must:
   expressing obligation, 112–113
   expressing strong probability, 114
my, 26

NEAR, 172
nearly, 41
neither, 27
   and neither, 52
never, position of, 36, 37n
nevertheless, 229n
news, 199
next week, 37
   with present progressive, 76
   with simple present, 74
nicely, position of, 36
no before a noun, 27
none, indefinite pronoun, 211
nor, 227n

not:
   in negative questions, 6
   in negative requests or commands, 16
   in short questions attached to statements, 14
   with auxiliary + principal verb, 4
   with **do (does)** and **did,** 3–4
   with simple forms of **be,** 3
   with verbs followed by infinitive as object, 144n
not more . . . than, 221
not so (as) . . . as: construction of comparison, 220
now, 37

OBJECT to, 147n
of:
   indicating association, 176
   indicating measure, 176
   indicating possession, 200–201
offer, 2
on:
   and **at,** 173
   and **in:**
      indicating place or position, 173
      indicating relationships of time, 174
   indicating manner, 176
   indicating relationships of time, 174
one, and **a (an),** 155
only, 41n
on time, 175
on top of, 172
or, 227n
other used with **the,** 27n
otherwise, 229n
ought to:
   expressing obligation, 112
   expressing probability, 114
out of, 173
over, 172
oxen, 198

PARTLY, 41
pass, 2
people, peoples, 211
permit, 146
pick out, 184
pick up, 184
please in polite requests, 16, 17
point out, 184
politics, 199
poorly, position of, 36
possibly, 114
prefer not used in progressive form, 93–94
prefer . . . to, 188
probably, 114
provided that in clauses of condition, 124
put on, 184
put up with, 186

RAISE, 132
rarely, position of, 37
read, 2
recently, 37
remember, followed by infinitive or gerund, 146
remind . . . of, 188
return, 2
rise, use of word, 131
run, irregular verb, 64
run out of, 186

SAY, 2
   and **tell,** 129–130
   pronouncing **says,** 60
says (that), 103–104
scarcely, 41
scissors, 199
see + object + simple form or past participle, 148
seem, 1
   infinitives as complements after, 146
seldom, position of, 36, 37n
sell, 2
send, 2
series, 199
set, 132
several, 156
   as indefinite pronoun, 210
shall and **will,** 62n, 85
sheep, 199
she'll, 6
she's, 6
should:
   expressing obligation, 112
   expressing probability, 114
shouldn't, 4
   in negative questions, 6
shown (showed), 65
simply, 41
since, 42, 174
   for and **during,** 174–175
sit, 131
smell, 1
so far that, 43
some, 156
   as indefinite adjective, 26
   as indefinite pronoun, 210
   in questions, 27
   with mass nouns, 157
so many that, 43
so much that, 43
soon, 37
so that, 42
sound, 1
speak and **talk,** 130
spend money on, 188
still:
   as modifier indicating time, 38
   conjunctive adverb, 229n
stop followed by infinitive, 145n
subtract . . . from, 188
such a . . . that, 43
suppose that, 124

TAKE, 2
take after, 186
take care of, 188
take charge of, 188
take . . . into consideration, 188
take off, 185
take out, 185
take up, 185
talk and **speak,** 130
taste, 1
teach, 2
teeth, 198
tell, 2
   and **say,** 129–130
than with comparative adjectives and adverbs, 42–43
thank . . . for, 188
that:
   and **the,** 155–156
   as modifier of noun, 26
   as subject, 210
   omitting, 29n, 103n
   preceding descriptive adjective, 28
   refers both to persons and things, 213
   relative pronoun:
     as object of clause, 29
     subject of clause modifying noun, 29
the, 26, 28
   and **that,** 155–156
   before a non-countable noun, 158
   some specific uses of, 163
   with plural countable nouns, 157
their, 26
then, conjunctive adverb, 229n
the number of, 211
there:
   agreement in sentences introduced by, 212
   appearing in subject position, 3
   uses of, 212
therefore, 229n
these, 28
   as modifier of noun, 26
   as subject, 210
they'll, 6
they're, 6
they've, 6
think over, 185
this:
   as modifier of noun, 26
   as subject, 210
   preceding descriptive adjective, 28
those, 28
   and **the,** 157
   as modifier of noun, 26
   as subject, 210
through, 172
thus, 229n
to, 172
to-phrase used instead of indirect object, 2
today, 37

tomorrow, 37
   with present progressive, 76
   with simple present, 74
tonight, 37
too:
   in connected affirmative statements, 51
   indicates more of quantity than needed, 40
   modifying adjective, 2
     indefinite adjectives, 27
too much, 41
toward, 173
trousers, 199
try followed by infinitive or gerund, 146
try on, 185

UNABLE, 111
under, 172
underneath, 172
until, 42, 174
up, 172
usually, 73
   position of, 36
used to + simple form of verb, 82, 83

VERY, 2
   indicates large amount or high degree, 41
   modifying adjective, 3
     descriptive adjective, 28, 40
     indefinite adjective, 27
   modifying adverb, 3
very little, 41
very much, 41

WAS in negative statement, 3
wasn't, 3
waste money on, 188
well, 36
we'll, 6
were:
   in clauses involving wishes, 121n
   in clauses of condition, 124
   in negative statement, 3
we're, 6
weren't, 3
we've, 6
what, introducing question:
   as object of verb or preposition or modifier of object, 13
   as subject or modifier of subject, 13
when:
   as conjunction introducing clauses modifying verbs, 42
   in clauses of condition, 124
   introducing question, 13
whenever, 42

where:
   as conjunction introducing clauses modifying verbs, 41
   introducing question, 13
wherever, 41
which:
   introducing question, 13
   omitting, 29n
   refers only to things, 213
   relative pronoun:
     object of clause, 29
     subject of clause modifying noun, 29
while, 42
who:
   as subject of question, 13
   refers only to persons, 213
   subject of clause modifying noun, 29
whom:
   introducing question, 13
   object of clause, 29
   omitting, 29n
   refers only to persons, 213
whose:
   introducing question:
     as object or modifier of object, 13
     as subject or modifier of subject, 13
   relative pronoun, 213
   in clauses modifying nouns, 29
why introducing question, 13
will:
   and **shall,** 62n, 85
   contractions of pronouns and, 84
   in future tense, 62
will be, 64
will have, 63
will have been, 64
will you please, 16
wish (that) + noun clause, 121–122
with:
   accompaniment, 176
   agent or instrument, 176
   indicating manner, 176
women, 198
won't, 4
   in negative questions, 6, 7
won't you please, 16
would:
   and clauses of condition, 124
   and **wish,** 115n
   expressing wants and desires, 115
   softens request, 17n
wouldn't, 4
would rather, 114
would you mind, 16
   in requests for permission, 17
   is followed by gerund, 17n, 145
would you please, 16
woven (weaved), 65
write, 2

YESTERDAY, 37
yet as modifier indicating time, 38
you'll, 6
you're, 6
you've, 6